THE
ABORIGINAL
SOCCER TRIBE

THE ABORIGINAL SOCCER TRIBE

JOHN MAYNARD

FAIRPLAY
PUBLISHING

The Aboriginal Soccer Tribe
by John Maynard

First Edition published in 2011 by Magabala Books.

Second Edition published in 2019 by Fair Play Publishing,
PO Box 4101, Balgowlah Heights NSW 2093 Australia.
www.fairplaypublishing.com.au
sales@fairplaypublishing.com.au

ISBN: 978-1-925914-06-1
ISBN: 978-0-925914-07-8 (ePUB)
© John Maynard 2019

Front cover design and typesetting by Leslie Priestley

Index produced by Mei Yen Chua, Tasmania

Picture Credits
Thanks to the following individuals and organisations for the use of their photos.
*Adelaide Croatia FC, Eileen Perkins, Frank Farina, John Maynard,
Newcastle Regional Library.*

Other photographs sourced from:
*National Archives of Australia; National Library of Australia; NSW State Archives;
Haddon Library of Archaeology and Anthropology, University of Cambridge;
as well as Fairfax Media, Alamy and Getty Images.*

All inquiries should be made to the Publisher via sales@fairplaypublishing.com.au

**NATIONAL
LIBRARY**
OF AUSTRALIA

A catalogue record of this book is available from the National Library of Australia.

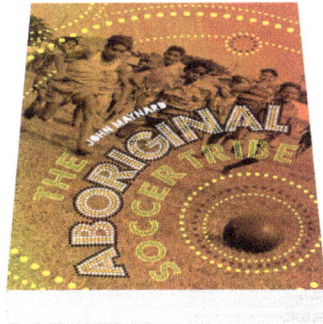

This book is dedicated
to the memory of
two champions on and off
the football pitch,
Charlie Perkins and
Johnny Warren.

Aboriginal Affairs and soccer have been my passions and where
I could work out my problems through both of those two things...
Soccer was where I got my satisfaction, my fulfillment.
Australian Biography VII, Charles Perkins, AO
5 May 1998

'Good luck with your mission – you have my 100% support'.
Johnny Warren MBE, OAM, BEc, ASM, CM
Personal correspondence - 14 July 2004

Contents

Acknowledgements

This book would not have been possible without the wonderful support I have received from many people and organisations. I am indebted for the assistance, guidance and encouragement I have been given over the years from so many. I apologise to any who I neglect to mention. Obviously, the Australian Institute of Aboriginal and Torres Strait Islander Studies (AIATSIS) has always given me great support and played a major role in initially seeing the importance of undertaking this project and awarding the funding to undertake the necessary research. AIATSIS also provided advice for gaining permissions to use images for the original book. I acknowledge former AIATSIS staff member Peter Windsor for his valuable input to the original study. All the people I interviewed deserve my heartfelt thanks for their invaluable input. They include the Perkins family – Eileen, Rachel and Hetti – Vince Copley, John Moriarty, Peter Read, Karen Menzies and Gordon Briscoe. Gordon in particular deserves high praise. He has always proven a source of inspiration to me as an Aboriginal historian. He is someone whose company and intellect I have always valued and found very stimulating.

The University of Newcastle continues as it has for the past twenty-six years to offer outstanding support for my research ventures. Also, to all of my friends and colleagues at the Wollotuka Institute of Aboriginal Studies at the University of Newcastle, who have always provided wonderful support and friendship – particularly Mandy, Cheryl, Joe, Mick and Ray. I acknowledge all those people who have contributed to the Aboriginal soccer story but who are not included within these pages – logistically, it was just not possible that I would be able to find every Aboriginal person in the country who had kicked a soccer ball. I take time to acknowledge the late Steve Doszpot, MLA and Shadow Minister for Sport and Recreation of the Australian Capital Territory, for his valuable insight as a close friend of Charlie Perkins, and for his support of my work. I extend a special thank you to professors Colin Tatz and John Ramsland, who provided invaluable advice on my early manuscript. Both John and Colin are scholars I hold in the highest regard for their expertise, particularly in the area of Aboriginal sporting history. I am also indebted to Colin for his support of the use of photos in this book that are held in the Aboriginal Sports Hall of Fame Collection held at AIATSIS. I thank Harry Williams and Jade North, the two most capped Aboriginal Socceroos, who had the time to meet and speak with me about their wonderful careers.

I extend a big thank you to Magabala Books and all of their wonderful staff who published the first edition of this book back in 2011. This second revised and expanded edition of *The Aboriginal Soccer Tribe* owes a great debt of gratitude to *Fair Play Publishing* for recognizing the book's importance and backing its publication. I take particular time to acknowledge founder and editor of Fair Play Publishing Bonita Mersiades, a true fellow soccer aficionado.

Johnny Warren was an inspiring and passionate football advocate. John was one of the Socceroos greatest players and captains. Although too ill at the time to undertake an interview with me, my discussions with him on the phone and his correspondence delivered inspirational support for the project.

I know Johnny Warren and Charlie Perkins would understand my use of the word 'soccer' as opposed to their preferred term of 'football'. I wanted to clearly distinguish the game – from an Aboriginal perspective – from other football codes in this country, codes which many Aboriginal players have excelled at.

Finally, my own family: Vicky, my wife and history partner, whose support, advice, love and company I adore. Admittedly she is no sports fan, but she has put up with my soccer obsession with understanding, even allowing me to disappear to South Africa (2010), Brazil (2014) and Russia (2018) on my World Cup pilgrimages. My girls, Candice and Courtney, and the boys Ganur, Kaiyu and Kirrin-Yurra, who have all played the World Game and hopefully will retain the love I developed at an early age for this special game.

John Maynard
Newcastle, Australia

Foreword

I was deeply flattered when professor John Maynard asked me to provide the foreword to such an important work on Australian Aboriginal peoples' influence on Australian soccer. I first met John Maynard when he was an undergraduate student at the University of Newcastle – then we discussed political activism and Aboriginal jockeys. A short time later our paths crossed again, when he was working on Aboriginal health, also at the University of Newcastle, and then again in Canberra in 2004 – this time the topic was soccer.

John had started researching his book and had talked to members of Charles Kumantjay Perkins family and John Moriarty. As children Perkins, Moriarty and I were all removed from our families. John Moriarty and I came from the Northern Territory to New South Wales in 1942, because of the War, and all three of us were removed by the Church of England to a boy's home located at Semaphore South, near Port Adelaide. We were raised on Aussie Rules, but our sporting skills were more appreciated by the swarms of 'new Australians' who attracted us more and more to soccer. As very young men we chose to associate with sporting bodies that treated us with respect and that we could afford – gifts of sporting equipment made it possible for us to play soccer whereas, in other codes, we couldn't afford our own equipment. Also, in other codes we were not allowed to change in the same dressing rooms and use the same showers as white Australians. These were some of the disadvantages we faced and are common themes in most of the Aboriginal peoples' lives encountered in John's work.

In *The Aboriginal Soccer Tribe,* John reaches back to the past and demonstrates how Aboriginal social consciousness can propel Aboriginal people into the pursuit of the things they love and the things that give them the opportunity to display their skills. This is evidenced in the success of stars such as John Moriarty and

Charles Kumantjay Perkins. I followed in their footsteps by playing first division in Adelaide, leaving for England in 1961 and finally returning to Canterbury Bankstown, in 1964. However, soccer could not support a wife and family, so the alternative was work by day and study by night. I was drawn into Aboriginal politics in the same way as Perkins and Moriarty.

The Aboriginal Soccer Tribe also looks at the involvement of Aboriginal women in soccer, the women who, in many ways faced double the struggle and who have given so much to the game – names such as Karen Menzies, Felicity Huntington and Bridgette Starr. John also looks into the future and asks: with the looming tsunami of soccer's popularity, is there hope for the many Aboriginal people looking to catch its success? What John is referring to is both the flood of people moving to urban areas for a better life than their parents experienced and the paucity of infrastructure in large rural Aboriginal populations, which are scenes of lingering disadvantage. The question is: do the soccer bodies have a social conscience? And will the rise of Aboriginal women in the game and the popularity of small games like Futsal help bring the human rights for which Aboriginal people are entitled?

Looking into the future, John plants front and centre the fact that soccer has, by definition, forgotten Aboriginal people in its zest for self-development. Individual clubs such as Port Thistle blindly supported us, because without us it would not have existed. Dominated by cricket and Australian Rules, migrants had to beg for playing space and were targeted by Australia's press. What brought us few players to soccer was often that our skills were transferred from Aussie Rules when we were driven away from that code. We chose migrants because they respected us.

When we look to the future of Aboriginal people in soccer it is easy to be optimistic, but as John points out in the final pages of this book, the time is now ripe for Football Federation Australia to provide the support and framework in which the passionate advocates and players of Indigenous soccer can succeed.

Professor Gordon Briscoe AO
Canberra, Australia

CHAPTER 1
Introduction

When I first set out to undertake a study of Aboriginal involvement with the World Game back in 2004, I was filled with pessimism for the future, not just about the hopes and aspirations of Aboriginal people but also for the game's very survival in Australia. Many influential luminaries - including Neville Wran, Nick Greiner, David Hill and George Negus – had tried and failed to shake the game out of years of lethargy, neglect, a negative press and destructive infighting. But as I stated back then none had the clout, firepower, vision or steely will and drive of one of Australia's richest men, Frank Lowy. Following his appointment to lead the destiny of Australian soccer in 2003, this entrepreneur transformed the game almost overnight. There has been a string of staggering achievements: the establishment of Football Federation Australia (FFA), the A-League and the W-League; the exciting qualification and performance of the Socceroos at the 2006 World Cup finals in Germany; subsequent World Cup qualification for the 2010 World Cup in South Africa, 2014 World Cup in Brazil and 2018 World Cup in Russia; the move into the Asian Football confederation culminating with Australia's magnificent victory in the 2015 Asian Cup Final; and the unparalleled success of the Matildas who are deservedly the country's most successful and best supported woman's national team.

But now 16 years later Australian soccer has come full circle and the game is once more a battleground of seeming self-destruction with warring factions vying for control and power. Despite all of the success there was always a simmering of resentment in the background of 'old soccer' with the mantra of 'new football'. There was an enormous vacuum with Frank Lowy's retirement in 2015 and despite son Steven Lowy taking the role as Chairman of the FFA, old wounds had already begun to open. That is not to say that some who were clamouring for faster change did not have some valid points. Certainly, the FFA and the game suffered great embarrassment through the failed and one might say it 'never had a hope' campaign to host the 2018 or 2022 World Cup finals. There has been a constant charge for the A-League clubs to have greater control over the competition, finances and direction of the game. FIFA eventually stepped in to adjudicate an outcome. Former Socceroos and these days football journalists and media commentators have been very influential in forging some of the arguments for change including faster expansion of the A-League and the establishment of an A-League second division competition. However, I would add a word of caution. It is all very well to hold lofty, fanciful ideas and schemes but one must hold a solid financial base to build from. I would also raise the question how would many of the current A-League clubs survive if relegated to a proposed second division? This country is not Europe, South America, Asia or even Africa. Those countries do not have to compete with the AFL, rugby league, rugby union, cricket and the beach to survive. The owners of the current A-League clubs have sunk a fortune into keeping these clubs afloat and I think that if Perth Glory, Adelaide United, Central Coast Mariners, Newcastle Jets, Brisbane Roar or Wellington Phoenix for example were relegated, that would sound the death knell of those teams. The game has entered a difficult time period and one certainly hopes that it is not a return to the dark days of splintered states, groups and individuals tearing the game apart for personal gain and satisfying long held vendettas. The full impact of the departure of the Lowy family and their financial and political clout may not be immediately measurable. Vince Rugari in the *Sydney Morning Herald* indicated that it would certainly be a sizeable hole to fill. It was revealed that Steven Lowy 'frequently footed the bill of the game's previous travel costs. It is understood that Lowy's lush private jet was frequently used by FFA staff to attend overseas events, such as FIFA and AFC meetings that saved the FFA a small fortune in flights each year. Sources suggest that, in one year alone, Lowy's resources saved the FFA close to $1 million in travel costs.[1] A new FFA Board has been elected with Chris Nikou as Chairman and it will be up to them to overcome the current challenges including appeasing those who demand immediate change and balance that with a clear head and less impulsive directives.

....

[1] *The Sydney Morning Herald*, 22 November 2018.

But where has all of this left Aboriginal involvement with the game several years after my first publication? Certainly, an Aboriginal presence in the game was not neglected in the initial projected dramatic overhauls and development by the FFA back in 2008. Just before the kick-off to the 2009 A-League Grand Final between Melbourne Victory and Adelaide United, FFA Chairman Frank Lowy was joined on the pitch by then Prime Minister Kevin Rudd and prominent Aboriginal soccer success stories John Moriarty and Warren Mundine. With Adelaide's Indigenous captain Travis Dodd at centre stage, the FFA announced an exciting and ambitious program of development to foster Aboriginal talent in the 'world game'. The Prime Minister announced: 'This great program is all about providing the best opportunities for our Indigenous players right across Australia to get in, be part of this great game and to make the A-League.' Frank Lowy responded, 'Soccer could help Indigenous Australians improve their life through better health, education and improve skills.' The new program's ambitious target was that Indigenous players will comprise at least five per cent of places in national teams and major competitions by 2019. These were lofty and ambitious targets but now as we look back over the past ten years also totally unrealistic without Aboriginal advice, direction and leadership.

Historically, Aboriginal achievement in the Australian Football League (AFL), rugby league and rugby union is well documented. But in the world game, the Aboriginal presence had been largely missed. Aboriginal players like Charles Perkins, John Moriarty, Gordon Briscoe and Harry Williams attained the highest achievements in Australian soccer - the multicultural environment of post World War II Australia may have offered these players a haven from the prejudice and racism of wider Australian society. Nevertheless, Aboriginal players have been greatly underrepresented in soccer. Over 40 years ago, noted soccer historian, the late Sid Grant was able to state with some authority that Aboriginal players had 'excelled in the junior ranks especially in the Northern Territory, but the instinctively fast reflexes and speed of our native people has been largely unexploited in soccer'.[2]

Why? There is no question that, historically Aboriginal players were largely ignored by the soccer authorities. But before the 1960s they suffered a similar fate

....

[2]   Grant, S, *Jack Pollards Soccer Records*, Jack Pollard Pty Ltd, Sydney, 1974, pp11

in the other codes and sports. Vince Copley has highlighted the absence of Aboriginal players in the AFL arena. In an interview with me in 2004 he said, 'I mean you look at the AFL or VFL at the time. Doug Nicholls may have been one bloke, and another was Norman McDonald – he played for Essendon – and Ted Lovett was playing but apart from that there was nobody.'

Since then, the other football codes have recognised and overcome barriers that stopped Aboriginal players from realising their untapped potential. These codes established connections with and within Aboriginal communities and broke down barriers that had limited and excluded Aboriginal involvement. The AFL, in particular has established training and coaching programs targeting Aboriginal communities, with profitable returns. In the past four decades some of the greatest AFL players of all-time have been Aboriginal.

Michael Lynch, writing in the *Sun Herald* in 2006, noted, 'While virtually all AFL clubs have at least one Aboriginal player on their list – and some, such as Essendon, have made a virtue out of forging relationships with Indigenous communities – few A-League sides, and before them the [National Soccer League] clubs, have had Aboriginal representation.' At the time John Boultbee, head of the FFA's High Performance Unit, recognised that the AFL success with Indigenous players was the model to follow, saying, 'They are certainly an organisation that we can learn from.' Tim Lane wrote in *The Age,* 'Judging by the way they play Aussie Rules, Indigenous footballers might be capable of similar miracles on the soccer pitch.'

Soccer doesn't require expensive training or playing equipment and Aboriginal people have generally opted for 'stadium sports' such as boxing, AFL and rugby league. But soccer seems to have been off the radar for many Aboriginal players until recent decades. I'd suggest this was because soccer was a game that was usually played in the urban area. Aboriginal people were mostly confined to rural or remote localities, so they were living in areas where soccer was largely unknown.

In any discussions about sport and Aboriginal history, the subject of soccer has usually been neglected. In their studies of Aboriginal sporting involvement Colin Tatz with *Obstacle Race* (1995), *Black Gold* (2000), *Aborigines in Sport* (1987), *Black Pearls* (2018) and Brett Harris the *Proud Champions* (1989) have referred briefly to Aboriginal soccer players. Biographical and autobiographical studies like Peter

Read's *Charles Perkins* (2001), John Moriarty's *Saltwater Fella* (2000), Charles Perkins *A Bastard Like Me* (1975) and Gordon Briscoe *Racial Folly* (2010) have delivered short insights into the careers of three of the most significant Aboriginal soccer players. The late, great former Socceroo captain and media personality Johnny Warren's book, *Sheilas, Wogs and Poofters* (2002), presents a biographical overview of Australian soccer, and covers his close friendship with Charles Perkins and his Socceroo and St George team-mate Harry Williams. Similarly, Jack Pollard's *Soccer Records* (1974) delivers a half page summary of Aboriginal involvement in Australian soccer, including a reference to Bondi Neal - a famous (but now forgotten) Aboriginal goalkeeper of the NSW Hunter Valley coalfields and the South Coast between 1903 and 1925.

However, the stark fact remains that none of the publications mentioned have given Aboriginal involvement in soccer the serious consideration or appraisal it deserves. Certainly, the importance of studying and understanding this was recognised by Johnny Warren. In personal correspondence with me in 2004, he had no hesitation in forcefully stating that in the past, 'The authorities, including the Australian Soccer Federation, were negligent in seeing the potential that lies within Aboriginal communities not addressed.' Although very ill at the time, he added, 'Good luck with your mission, you have my 100 per cent support.

Soccer in Australia: A Brief History

From an early age my fascination with soccer was not just confined to the playing field but extended to its history. As a young boy and teenager, I consumed English soccer magazines like *Charles Buchan's Football Monthly, Shoot* and *Goal*. I collected a library of soccer books – histories of the World Cup and top English club teams and players. I pored over these tales of great players, clubs and coaches. My interest in the local game's history was also fuelled along these lines by having the opportunity to speak to old players and look through old newspaper files.

The game's history in Australia is a long one but also one that has been dogged by a bad image, sometimes self-made and at other times cultivated by the media and the other codes. A change in image and final acceptance of the game did not come until towards the close of the twentieth century. This hard-fought acceptance is seen in the changing name of the game in Australia. Before World War I, soccer was known as 'British Association Football'. Immediately after the Second World War, following the influx of European migrants, it gained the derogatory tag of 'wogball'. Finally, during the 1990s, soccer became the 'world game'. This sudden, belated acceptance is tied to the acceptance of post-World War II migrants into the fabric of Australian society in the latter stages of the century. [3]

The game is largely held to have been introduced to Australia by JW Fletcher in 1880, although there are earlier records of its existence, and the first organised soccer match known to have been played was between the Wanderers and King's School at Parramatta Common in 1880. Interstate matches between Victoria and New South Wales were played as early as 1883. But soccer could not gain a foothold against Australian football in Victoria and after 1907 rugby league in NSW, which quickly established themselves as the dominant codes in those influential states. Subsequently soccer found itself fighting for support, participation and media attention in every state and territory. Even in coalmining areas around Newcastle, Ipswich and later in the La Trobe Valley, where the heavy concentration of British miners was high, soccer was very strong but not pre-eminent. [4] It was the private-school educated, rugby-loving cohort that established their game, and the hybrid game of Australian football that dominated the scene. Australia, as with the other colonial outposts of the British Empire, tried to create its own distinct national identity, declaring independence from the mother country in many subtle and at times bizarre forms. One area where a strong, independent national identity has been promoted is sport.

It is ironic that soccer, a truly grassroots and working-class game in Britain, conquered every corner of the globe and became the game of the world except in the former British colonies of Canada, United States, New Zealand, Australia and South Africa. There, either the class-conscious code of rugby or hybrid games such as gridiron or AFL held sway. Until recently in South Africa, cricket and rugby

3   Hay, R, 'British Football, Wogball or the World Game? Towards a Social History of Victoria Soccer', in O'Hara, J (ed.), *Ethnicity and Soccer in Australia,* Australian Society for Sports History, No. 10, Campbelltown, 1994, pp46; Goldblatt, D, *The Ball is Round – A Global History of Football,* Viking Press, London, 2006, pp95

4   Hay, 1994, pp50

union dominated. They were sports tied to the apartheid regimes of the past. The football codes in particular were very much a part of the racial divide there. Soccer became the game of the majority black population, and 'the more popular soccer became with the non-whites the more the whites looked down on it.'[5]

Canada and the United States, for their different reasons, chose to make their own way with games such as gridiron, basketball, baseball and ice-hockey. New Zealand fell under the spell of rugby union from the late nineteenth century. In 1905, a touring New Zealand All Blacks side won thirty-two out of thirty-three matches on a tour of Britain. Beating the mother country at anything was a moment of special significance and this played a major part in establishing rugby union as New Zealand's national game. By this time, British soccer players were already full-time professionals and there was a marked difference between them and the purely amateur teams that colonial countries could put on the field.

With Federation and the creation of the Commonwealth of Australia in 1901, the country began at last to cut the umbilical cord with Great Britain. The Australasian Football Council chose this time to give a nationalistic tone and direction to its code, Australian football. In 1906 it started promoting the game with the slogan 'One flag, one destiny, one football game.' They made the call that only balls manufactured in Australia could be used in games, and every stadium had to fly an Australian flag.

From the late nineteenth century, soccer in Australia did have strongholds in areas such as Newcastle and the coalfields of the Hunter Valley in New South Wales. Many famous teams in this region have records as long as some of England's greatest clubs. But soccer's traditional connection with the working class ensured that the game was viewed with suspicion and disdain by many in the wider privileged Australian community. According to historian Bill Murray, in the 1880s, 'It gained an unfortunate connotation with [British] migrants seeking social advancement and national identity in another country.'[6] This was evident in Australia in the first instance between 1890 and 1910, with the large intake of predominately poor English and Scottish immigrants. The new arrivals quickly

5 Murray, B, *The World Game,* University of Illinois Press, Urbana and Chicago, 1998, pp18
6 Murray, 1998, pp20

formed soccer clubs and set up competitions, but the game had trouble gaining widespread support. 'It was to remain a working-class migrants' game very much associated with the English and the Scots, rather than with those who identified themselves as inhabitants of newly independent and nationalistic Australia… the game was fostered and nurtured as an ethnic sport.'[7] In its early days, soccer confronted a fierce and rising sense of Australian nationalism. Interestingly, and with a startling sense of déjà vu, the opposition the early British soccer pioneers encountered in their new country was to be unleashed ten-fold in the wake of World War II and the onset of large scale southern European immigration. It is quite clear that opposition to the game, right up until the last decade of the twentieth century was grounded in ignorance and fear.

This fear of difference and hostility directed at immigrants remains to this day in the psyche of the wider Australian community. It may well be embedded in the past with deep seated insecurity and resentment over the country starting life as a convict colony. Of even greater significance is the fact that the country's beginning is tied to the invasion, occupation, dispossession and cultural destruction of Aboriginal Australia. The guilt and historical masking of that event and its aftermath has never been adequately dealt with or a healing process even begun.

Soccer was a casualty of the Depression of the 1890s, like all the sporting codes, but increased immigration numbers in the years before World War I saw a revival. The outbreak of the Great War again stalled the game's progress as immigration slowed to a trickle. But at the war's end, a massive increase in immigration from Britain occurred once again. From 1921 to 1925, 36,700 immigrants landed, and many had packed their love of soccer in the shape of a ball in their baggage.

This huge influx of soccer lovers had an immediate impact. In 1923 a visiting Chinese team attracted large crowds of up to 45,000 in Sydney, and an English representative team toured in 1925, playing to sell-out crowds in Sydney (50,000) and Brisbane (25,000). Then, just when the game appeared to be taking off, with large crowds attending matches, a petty rupture over control in both New South Wales and Victoria seriously derailed its progress. This early split in soccer's

---

[7] Jones, R & Moore, P, He Only has Eyes for Poms: Soccer, Ethnicity and Locality in Perth, WA, *Ethnicity and Soccer in Australia,* ASSH Studies in Sports History No.10

direction would be repeated regularly in the decades that followed.

During the 1930s and 1940s the New South Wales State Cup was dominated by clubs from the northern coalfields, led by legendary goal scorers such as Alf Quill and Reg Date. Then, in the wake of World War II, the game had a surge as the large European immigration program brought another wave of soccer-mad followers to Australian shores. However, even as this influx of European migrants swelled the crowds and playing ranks, it caused an immediate racist backlash among the xenophobic wider white Australian public, who not only targeted the new arrivals but also the game that the new arrivals loved.

As early as 1950 the tone was set in stone. A reporter, JO Wilshaw, writing in the *Sporting Globe,* stated:

The whole question of these new Australians being allowed to form national clubs should be the subject of special investigation and although one does not advocate a boycott of these recent arrivals from the playing fields it certainly would be much better if they were assimilated into the ranks of teams mainly of British stock and thus became better 'mixers' instead of keeping to themselves and in some cases endeavouring to settle political differences on the football field.

In answering this attack soccer columnists Andrew Dettre and Laurie Schwab were adamant that: 'Many immigrants were refused access to Anglo clubs and so were forced to form their own organisations and then were damned for doing so.' [8]

The new arrivals and the clubs they formed began to dominate the game. The leading European community-backed clubs broke away from existing organisations to set up their own organisation, culminating in the formal establishment of the Australian Soccer Federation (ASF) in 1961. Their interest in the game meant that visiting overseas teams such as Chelsea, Everton, AS Roma and Manchester United toured during the 1960s and played before very large crowds. But there was another backlash when, Croatian, Serbian, Greek and Macedonian supporters clashed. These incidents played into the hands of the media and opponents of the game,

[8]   Quoted in Hay, 1994, pp70

who used every opportunity to play up violent episodes of 'ethnic soccer rampage.'

Finally, in the early years of the twenty-first century, the then Prime Minister, John Howard, was enlisted to end decades of self-destruction and save Australian soccer. Howard was not the first Australian politician to recognise the untapped global power of soccer. None of the other codes had any hope of making the massive offshore impact and advertising potential of soccer. This was particularly true in Asia, where soccer had the potential to leverage major economic connections and assist Australia in taking advantage of its geographic location. In 2002 Howard was persuaded to instigate the Crawford Report into soccer administration, which made damning findings of power struggles, rorts and infighting. In its aftermath Howard asked Frank Lowy to get involved in plotting a new course for Australian soccer. Initially, Lowy was very reluctant to consider the request. Having been an Australian soccer administrator in the past, he had had more than his share of run-ins with people intent on stalling the game's progress for self-gain or because they opposed it outright. Eventually, after much discussion, Lowy was persuaded to take the reins and the rest, as they say, is history.

Former Victorian Premier Jeff Kennett recognised the changing landscape and the unprecedented opportunities for the future. He believed soccer was the only truly international code of football and that it was on the verge of a shift in Australia of seismic proportions:

> It's a story of wasted opportunity, of political and personal intrigue, of mismanagement and corruption. It depicts the total failure of so many individuals to put their duty to the sport they served above their self-interest.
> The history of Australian soccer since the Second World War, with a few exceptions, is of tragic proportions, greater than you will witness in any opera.
> But it's just that – history.
> Tomorrow is about hope. With the appointment of Frank Lowy as the Chairman of Soccer in Australia in 2003, and the establishment of a new board of management, Australian soccer has a fresh opportunity – perhaps the best it has ever had – to deliver its potential as a sport both at home and overseas.[9]

---

9 Quoted in Solly, R, *Shoot Out – The Passion and the Politics of Soccer's Fight for Survival in Australia,* John Wiley & Sons, Queensland, 2004, ppvii

While this book is ultimately about Indigenous involvement in the world game, it also presents a snap shot of the social and historical experience of Indigenous people in this country since 1788. This history includes invasion, occupation, dispossession, cultural destruction, incarceration on government-controlled reserves, children being separated from their families, as well as the opportunities that sport provided and denied them, the barriers it put in their way. Despite the obstacles, there have been some outstanding Indigenous soccer players and this book seeks to place their story and achievements in its rightful place.

CHAPTER 2
A Personal Connection

Growing up in the Newcastle suburb of Adamstown during the 1950s and 1960s was the catalyst for my lifetime interest and passion in soccer. Newcastle, with its long British immigrant mining history, understandably developed a love for association football and has been long regarded as the nursery for many of the greatest soccer players ever produced in Australia, including the late, great Reg Date and Liverpool champion Craig Johnston.

My family home faced onto the Adamstown Rosebuds junior soccer grounds, comprising several soccer pitches, and in the winter months they were packed with kids. At the bottom of the street was Adamstown 'Oval', home of the famous Adamstown Rosebuds Soccer Club. The Rosebuds hold a history as illustrious as many famous international clubs. They formed in 1889 as a result of British miners coming to the area in 1888. Over the years they have produced a host of Australian international players. Herbert Middleton, my grandfather on my mother's side of the family, was a member of a 1922 Adamstown Rosebuds under 18 team that won the Mick Simmons Cup and Medals. My uncle, Eric Middleton, played in a representative junior team that boasted future internationals Allan Johns and Frank 'Snip' Parsons.

My own junior and school career as a soccer player was far from illustrious. In plain terms, I couldn't kick a cow in the guts. That did not halt my enthusiasm for practice and watching games. There was a mob of kids in the street and area in those days, and Saturday and Sunday were big days on the weekly calendar. I would play in a Rosebuds junior team on Saturday morning - not the best team of my age group either. On most occasions we were annihilated by the opposition. After the soccer it would be off to Broadmeadow racecourse, where our mob of kids had a hole burrowed under the fence, and we would cart around chaff bags, filling them with empty drink bottles. You got sixpence for each bottle handed in and we did some roaring business in those days. My father was a top-class local Koori jockey, but my mother and other relatives would feign not knowing us and hurriedly turn in the opposite direction and disappear into the crowded betting ring if they saw our dirty street urchin appearance and activities.

Sunday was the big match at Adamstown Oval and we would trek down there. The bigger kids in the group would pull a paling off the fence or burrow a hole into the ground so we could get in to watch the Rosebuds do battle. What I remember most of those days were the fabulous meat pies covered in rich tomato sauce and, of course, collecting bottles. Filling that chaff bag at the racecourse and Adamstown Oval added a sizeable return for effort. I would be encouraged by the older boys to stand in front of people with a forlorn look on my face, watching them drink. My downcast eyes would get the better of them, and eventually, more often than not, the person would say, 'Here son, you take it.' Our mob included my cousin Gary 'Bulldog' Middleton and Dennis 'Gungha' Taylor.

Gungha had come down to Newcastle to follow in the footsteps of his older brother Gordon in a career as a jockey. Gordon himself had followed the path of other Koori jockeys like Stan Johnson, Merv Maynard (my father) and Normie Rose, all of whom had begun racing careers in the stable of Newcastle trainer Keith Tinson. Years later, Gordon recalled his arrival in Newcastle, getting off the train at Broadmeadow aged only fifteen and being picked up by my parents. Gordon laughed that we shared the backseat of my father's FJ Holden - I was at the time lying in a bassinet, aged one. Gordon Taylor looked to have a bright future on the track, but weight ultimately went against him. Weight also stalled the jockey dreams of his younger brother Gungha. Gungha remained a track work rider, stable hand and character of the Newcastle track scene for decades. He was always like an older brother to me and only ever had a kind word. Many years later, in the early 1990s, Gungha was tragically killed in a house fire.

I remember so many great matches and players in those years. I recall going to Newcastle Sports ground to watch visiting international teams, like the Italian side AS Roma in 1966 with their giant, spider-like goalkeeper Fabio Cudicini, and the great Manchester United side of 1967, which contained players such as Bobby Charlton, Denis Law, Nobby Stiles and of course the incomparable Georgie Best.

But our passion in those far off-days was for the 'Town', the name by which the Adamstown Rosebuds were affectionately known, and it never waned. Adamstown had great seasons and great players, including Bobby Cameron, Ray Baartz, Colin 'Bunny' Curran, John Doyle and Ron Giles. One special year was 1968. Adamstown had a fabulous season, winning the minor and major premierships as well as the Daniels Pre-season Cup competition. The arrival of Ken Whitmore at the club from Wallsend during the off-season was the high point of Adamstown's year. Whitmore was a goal-scoring freak, immediately becoming a crowd favourite. I recall one of his first games playing for Adamstown against Lake Macquarie; it was the one of the first televised *Match of the Day* recordings from Adamstown Oval, with Tas Taylor and Noel Harrison on the microphone. I can still remember Whitmore receiving the ball some 35 yards out from goal and sending in a screamer to score in a 1-1 draw. Adamstown went on to meet Lake Macquarie again in the Northern New South Wales Grand Final played at Macquarie Field Speers Point. The Rosebuds won the match 4 – 2. Gungha, Bulldog and I were seated on the grass directly behind the Lake Macquarie goals. Kenny Whitmore took a free kick with such force that when it hit the back of the net, it sent all the steel pins holding the goal nets into the air and raining down on our jubilant and celebrating heads.

I also began to take an avid interest in the fortunes of the Australian national team, particularly their 1970 World Cup qualification quest, and listened to all their matches broadcast on ABC radio, hosted by Martin Royal. What an incredible performance they put up, traveling around the globe to beat Japan, South Korea and Rhodesia, before falling at the final hurdle against a very good Israel side, after enduring a FIFA-orchestrated marathon of travel to get there. The Socceroos lost the first match in Tel Aviv 1-0 and could only manage a 1-1 draw in Sydney. I was a fourteen-year old spectator at that match, my parents having driven me down to the old Sydney Sports Ground to witness this disappointing finale to a heroic qualification effort. Johnny Watkins scored our late equaliser after Mordechai Spiegler had given Israel the lead against the run of play. This was a very special Australian team, coached by the legendary 'Uncle' Joe Vlasits; it included players like Atti Abonyi, Ray Baartz, Johnny Warren and goalkeeper Ron Corry who excelled at saving penalties. Years later I told Johnny Warren I'd been present on that day and discovered that he still carried deep disappointment, especially about a penalty that he felt should have been awarded to Australia.

By the time I had reached the age of fifteen, my own skills with continual practice, had improved dramatically. I left the Rosebuds and had a season with Hamilton Azzurri, primarily through my high school friendship with Geoff Lingard. He convinced me that opportunities would be better with the 'wogs' - as Azzurri was called by the majority of the local bigoted soccer public. George Strong, a former Adamstown player and then-Azzurri favourite, coached us during that last season of junior soccer.

The following year, the under 16s were made part of senior soccer for the first time. The competition comprised the seniors, reserve grade, under 21s and under 16s, and it all came down to whether you were good enough to gain a contract with these senior clubs. The coach of the Azzurri under 16 team that year was Max Luchessi, an Italian who had been a former top class South Australian representative player and was later a great senior coach with Weston Bears.

I made the final cut and was now a player under contract to a senior soccer club. Our home ground that year was Newcastle Showground. We had a good side and just missed a semi-final berth. I thought about so many of the kids in the school teams and Rosebuds' junior teams who had been top class players but had gone by the wayside and now either did not play or were playing for second or third division teams. I played in one first grade game for Azzurri in a pre-season trial match under lights against New Lambton at the famous Wallsend ground, Crystal Palace, when I was just sixteen. This Azzurri first team included quality players, but despite such talent, we were no match for New Lambton that night and were walloped 5-1, with me scoring the only goal.

Max Luchessi left Azzurri to take charge of Weston Bears the following season and that had some influence on me leaving Azzurri and moving on to West Wallsend, or 'Westy' as the club were known. Alongside Adamstown Rosebuds and Wallsend, Westy could lay claim to being one of the most famous clubs in Northern New South Wales. West Wallsend was a mining centre close to Newcastle and the local team attracted a great following and great players. During the halcyon period of soccer between the 1920s, 1940s, Westy was arguably the greatest club side in Australia. They won a host of trophies and provided a continual line of Australian representative players.

I made my first-grade debut in 1972, at the age of seventeen, in a 3-3 draw in an Ampol Cup match against third division club Muswellbrook under lights at Weston Park. I played several seasons with Westy but never really made it to the top. I came on as a substitute in a few games but didn't break through to the first-grade side. In retrospect, I realise that taking a few seasons out to travel to Europe and not playing curtailed my career. Instead of going to Westy, I would probably have made a better choice if I'd followed my former coach Max Luchessi (who had a high opinion of my potential) from Azzurri to Weston Bears, where he achieved phenomenal success. I have no doubt he would have ensured that my dedication remained focused on the action on the field rather than off it. Nevertheless, I had a great time with Westy, and played over 150 games with the reserve team and made some great friends.

Were there many Aboriginal soccer players in the local competition at that time? I am sure there were some, but they were mostly not identified. Adamstown Rosebuds were always a very far-thinking soccer club and I recall that they brought down an Aboriginal kid from a remote community, who played in their under 16 team at the same time I was with Azzurri. He did not get many games. I don't remember his name, but I do remember him being led around by his team-mates like some sort of exotic curiosity, a captured 'real blackfella'!

There was one outstanding source of Aboriginal inspiration on the soccer field at the time - the incredible Harry Williams. Harry was a lightning-fast and extremely skilful fullback with a St George Budapest side that bristled with international players. St George was without doubt the glamour side of Australian soccer at the time and was coached by the tempestuous and brilliant Frank Arok. I recall Harry playing for St George against Adamstown Rosebuds in a State Cup match at Adamstown Oval around 1970 or 1971. He was someone a young Aboriginal player could immediately identify with and be inspired by. In that match against Adamstown I can still recall his electric overlapping runs down the line. I speak about Harry in much greater detail later in this book. He was a brilliant player, and the fact that he made more than forty appearances for the Socceroos over a long career is a testament to his skill.

CHAPTER 3
Soccer Dreaming

The bulk of the story of Aboriginal involvement in soccer comes in the aftermath of World War II, but the story begins with the British invasion in the late eighteenth century. In the wake of 1788, Aboriginal people and their culture suffered destruction of catastrophic proportions. Some social commentators with a conscience noted the terror inflicted. 'We have not only taken possession of the lands of the [A]boriginal tribes of this colony, and driven them from their territories, but we have also kept up unrelenting hostility towards them, as if they were not worthy of being classed with human beings, but simply regarded as inferior to some of the lower animals of creation.[10] The injustice of these actions prompted some to recommend action to absolve guilt, as in the *Newcastle Morning Chronicle* in 1869 'Their doom is sealed, and all that the civilised man can do … is to take care that the closing hour shall not be hurried on by want, caused by culpable neglect on his part.[11]

The avenue of sport would offer Aboriginal people some hope of acceptance, understanding and survival. In the current century Aboriginal people are regarded as having extraordinary gifts as sportsmen and sportswomen across a wide range of endeavours, particularly in the football codes, boxing and athletics. It certainly took Aboriginal Australians some time to gain not only acceptance on the sporting arena but even the right to take part.

Aboriginal Australia had developed a sporting culture long before Europeans arrived on the Australian continent. Arguments have raged that in fact an Aboriginal

....

10 Chase, A & Von Sturmer, J, '"Mental Man" and Social Evolutionary Theory', in Kearney, GD, De Lacey, PR & Davidosn, GR (eds), *The Psychology of Aboriginal Australians,* John Wiley and Sons Australasia, Sydney, 1973, pp7

11 *Newcastle Chronicle*, 13 November 1869

game was the original source of Australian Football. Writer Jim Poulter noted, 'The Gunditjmara tribe played a game called *marn gook*, or 'game ball'. A ball was made of possum skin and filled with pounded charcoal and bound with kangaroo sinews. Between 50 and 100 men a side played for possession for hours on end.'[12] Early settler accounts of the 1840s testify that this game was predominately a kicking game. The Aboriginal players apparently kicked 'the ball with the instep of the bare foot, and they made strong leaps – sometimes reaching five feet [1.5 metres] above the ground.'[13]

William Blandowski, an early pioneer scientist who explored the Murray River region near Mildura in Victoria's northwest corner, also saw an Aboriginal ball game being played by the Nyeri Nyeri, in 1857. It was at Mondellimin, near present day Merbein and it was a kicking game. Blandowski wrote, 'a group of children is playing with a ball. The ball is made out of Typha roots; it is not thrown or hit with a bat, but it is kicked up in the air with the foot. Aim of the game never let the ball touch the ground.'[14] Blandowski's notes were later used as the basis for an etching by artist Gustav Mützel. What is startling about this engraving is that it depicts an early Aboriginal footballer in a Ronaldinho like pose balancing the ball on his foot.

This keepy-uppy game of football played in Victoria appears to have been a widely spread phenomenon amongst Indigenous groups. In a 1957 book *The Boomerang Book of Legendary Tales* a story is recalled from the Marshall Islands in the Pacific of a ball game called anirep. It was noted that this game consisted of kicking the ball sideways frontwards and backwards. The players had to keep a ball made of soft but tightly tied pandanus fibres in the air without letting it hit the ground. It was:

played in different kinds of rhythm-two-rhythm or three-rhythm, or four-rhythm. The players clap their hands and keep time for the kicking. With two-rhythm clapping, the playing is slow, one, two-one, two-one, two. Everybody starts the

[12] Quoted in Booth, D & Tatz, C, *One Eyed – A View of Australian Sport,* Allen & Unwin, Sydney, 2000, pp10

[13] Blainey, G, *A Game of Our Own: The Origins of Australian football,* Information Australia, Melbourne, 1990, pp95-6

[14] Quoted in Rintoul, S, 'Aussie Rules Originally Aboriginal, Etching Show', in *The Age,* 22-23 September, 2007, pp3

game with that slow rhythm. Then the clapping becomes faster. Soon the players are kicking fast-one-two-three, one-two-three, and then one-two-three-four, one-two-three-four. Those who miss are out of the game. The players laugh and shout when someone drops the ball. [15]

Aboriginal traditional games were all about teaching skills, particularly agility and athleticism, which were integral to the hunting and gathering lifestyle that Indigenous people had adapted to so well. All games were taught and encouraged from a very young age. As social behaviourist Desmond Morris reflected, 'our early hunting ancestors became gradually more athletic' and used 'these advantages and working together as a team – a hunting pack - they were able to plan strategies, devise tactics, take risks, set traps and, finally, aim to kill. Already, you will admit, they are beginning to sound like the perfect prototype for a soccer team'. [16]

The Brazilian Cultural Connection

All Indigenous groups throughout the world have suffered similar experiences historically, encompassing invasion, occupation, dispossession, genocide, cultural destruction and brutal subjugation. Incredibly, the rich traditional culture and lifestyle of Aboriginal Australia, and the suffering in the wake of colonisation, ties this country to the greatest soccer country on the planet – Brazil.

This is the magical Brazil of world soccer, the nation that has won soccer's greatest prize, the World Cup, five times and produced generations of immortal players, such as Leonidas, Didi, Garrincha, Santos, Zico, Romario, Ronaldo, Ronaldinho, Neymar and of course Pelé. Brazil, like Australia, has a history of Indigenous tragedy. As with the British onslaught in Australia, the Portuguese conquest of Brazil was disastrous for the native peoples. They were shot down by the gun, died in their thousands from the introduction of unfamiliar diseases, and were driven into poverty and enslavement working on sugar plantations.

[15] Moodie Heddle, E, *The Boomerang Book of Legendary Tales,* Longmans, Green and Co Ltd, London, 1957, pp91
[16] Morris, D, *The Soccer Tribe,* Jonathon Cape, London, 1981, pp10

Despite the savage genocidal collision of colonisation, Indigenous culture in Brazil has tenaciously survived into the twenty-first century. Just like Aboriginal Australia, the Indigenous peoples there maintain their cultural beliefs and rich traditional stories.

In Brazil great soccer players are 'crafty, agile and impossible to catch' and are likened to a jungle protector, the Curupira, a creature from an Indigenous traditional story. The Amazon jungle forests of Brazil are said to be the haven of this protector of the animals and guardian of the trees. 'It is on everyone's tongues that there are certain demons that the Brazilians call 'Curupira', which often attack Indians in the bush, whipping them, hurting them and killing them,' wrote a nervous-sounding scribe in 1560, only sixty years after the Portuguese first landed on South American soil.[17] The Curupira would lie in ambush on some jungle trail and attack anyone who mistreated the animals or land. He would often take on disguises and ask passers-by for advice, assistance or some simple service, such as tobacco for his pipe. Once distracted, the poor unfortunate would be set upon by the Curupira. To this day, 'the Curupira is a much-cherished story, especially in the Amazon region. He looks boyish, has red hair and is distinguished by one peculiar physical trait: his feet are back-to-front... [when] the Curupira runs in one direction, his footprints run in the opposite way. The Curupira is fast and mischievous. If you try to follow him, you will go the wrong way and be lost in the jungle for ever'.[18]

The Aboriginal people around the Newcastle area of New South Wales, as with all Aboriginal groups across the continent, had sacred ancestors who either descended from the sky or ascended from the depths of the earth. These ancestral heroes were responsible for creating the world and everything in it. Before the ancestors put their creative efforts to play, the earth was a flat, dark lifeless plain. The ancestors moved across this empty plain living, loving and caressing it into form. On completion the ancestors either rose back to the sky or descended back into the depths of the inner earth.

The local Indigenous people retained the stories of creation and also of many other important spirit or deities that had an important role to play in life and place.

---

[17] Hemming, J, *Red Gold – The Conquest of the Brazilian Indians,* Papermac, London, 1987, Preface.
[18] Bellos, A, *Futebol – The Brazilian Way of Life,* Bloomsbury, London, 2003, pp95

Many of these stories were recorded by the missionary Reverend Lancelot Threlkeld when he was based in the area between 1822 and 1841. One such story revolved around social discipline and involved a monster called Puttikan. He lived in the Sugarloaf (Keemba Keemba) Mountains but was known to roam the bushland as far as Lake Macquarie and Newcastle in search of victims. Puttikan's main task, it seemed centred on the clan's most important requirement for the male - the obligation of initiation. Thus, Puttikan's usual victims were uninitiated young men. He would hold up young men in the bush and demand that they open their mouths. If they displayed a missing tooth, which meant they had been initiated, he would let them pass. If they showed that they had not passed through initiation, they were beaten to death. His name translated literally means 'biter'.

Puttikan was described as being a very tall man, covered in hair, with a mane like a horse and a tail like a cutlass. He had long arms and he always kept his head erect. Eerily, the similarities with the Brazilian story of the Curupira and its Aboriginal counterpart are striking. Puttikan had a remarkable physical deformity: his feet and toes pointed backwards. This was a ploy so those following his footprints could not trace him. Puttikan jumped like a kangaroo instead of walking and when his feet hit the ground the sound was like gunshots. The stories relate that his flesh was so strong that neither the fleetest nor hardest of spears nor the most explosive of bullets could penetrate his hide. He howled a cry, 'Pirrolong, Pirrolong' as he advanced on his prey. These two stories link the two cultures.

No Brazilian player epitomised the story of the Curupira more than the magical Garrincha, or 'Little Bird', as he was known. Garrincha is unquestionably Brazil's most famous Indigenous player. He was a member of the great Brazilian World-Cup winning teams of 1958 and 1962. His performances at the World Cup in 1962 were extraordinary; with Pelé injured early in the tournament and unable to play, he almost single-handedly delivered the World Cup to Brazil.

Today, Brazilians connect with the story of the Curupira through the deft skill and fleet-footedness of the soccer player and the samba dancer. Both are trademarks of a national style, flair and obsession. The fluid, electric motion and gyrating hips of the samba dancer reflect the athleticism that Brazilians possess. The samba dancer is imagined as literally connected through movement and beat to the earth itself. This connectedness to the earth through dance is another link between

Brazil and Aboriginal Australia.

The American choreographer Beth Dean made the following observations of Aboriginal dancers. 'From the Dreaming Times, the creation period of the world the [A]borigine has danced on the soft bulldust of his dancing grounds with his powerful thrusting stamp and high knee action, so typical of the men's dance style, as with arms stretched straight, fingers spread wide, following the throbbing music he seems in a single moment to encompass the breadth of the earth.[19] The incredible speed, passion and fury of an Aboriginal dancer held Dean spellbound:

Every now and again a single man would come out from the line and start a few tentative steps, then warm up to a frenzy of excitement with legs pounding into the soil, faster and faster, faster than we had ever seen legs move before, until it seemed that the two legs must in the next instant, blend into one, like the optical illusion of the spokes of a spinning wheel.[20]

Indigenous Brazil and Aboriginal Australia are culturally connected through story, dance and sheer athletic ability.

A Sporting Introduction

Before the 1850s Aboriginal people had little connection with organised sport. However, Christian humanitarians and those with a benevolent aim encouraged Aboriginal people to participate in sport as a paternalistic way of civilising them. In these early years, horse racing, professional athletics and cricket were the main arenas of sporting outlet. There were a number of prominent Aboriginal jockeys, and by the mid-nineteenth century many Aboriginal people were playing cricket on missions, reserves and country stock stations. Missionaries believed that such games – cricket in particular – made them more industrious and loyal.

Cricket was widespread in Aboriginal communities of the time, with successful players and teams at missions including Poonindie in South Australia; Coranderrk in Victoria in the 1870s and 1880s; Cummeragunja in New South Wales in the

....

[19] Dean, B, *The Many Worlds of Dance,* Murray Publishers, Sydney, 1966, pp39

[20] Dean, B, *Dust for Dancers,* Ure Smith, Sydney, 1956, pp78

1880s; New Norcia in Western Australia between 1880 and 1905; and Deebing Creek in Queensland from 1894 to 1906. One of the most significant (and famous) sporting moments of this period was the highly successful Aboriginal cricket team's tour of England in 1868. Without question, the stars of this very good team were Johnny Mullagh and Johnny Cuzens. Mullagh was afforded the tag of the 'Black WG' (after 'WG', the renowned English cricketer WG Grace), and his statistics were impressive: In England he played 43 matches, scoring 1,679 runs at an average of 22.5.

Sadly, by the turn of the century, Aboriginal opportunities to play cricket and many other sports had declined. According to the historian Richard Cashman, this was related to 'the replacement of a benign paternalism by a more pessimistic institutionalised racism by the turn of the century. With greater segregation and less contact between Aborigines and Europeans at work, there were fewer opportunities and incentives for Aborigines to continue playing cricket.' [21]

Placed under the strict control of government protection Boards and similar agencies, Aboriginal people were largely cut off from the wider community. The authorities of the day felt the 'need to protect Aborigines from the depredations of white society was overwhelming, and the ensuing legislation produced both legislative fences and the administrative decisions to physically locate Aborigines as far away as possible from whites. The exclusion of Aborigines from Australian society had begun in earnest... with the general acceptance of Social Darwinism, which popularised racist views that Aborigines were an inferior race doomed to wither and disappear.' [22]

As a result of this process, many Aboriginal sportsmen and women, despite outstanding talent in cricket and other sports, such as running, were denied the greater recognition and representative opportunities they richly deserved. Sporting opportunities of any type during this period were extremely limited because of the restrictive government policy of segregation, which confined Aboriginal people to mission stations and reserves, usually located in rural or remote settings. Despite these tightly enforced barriers to Aboriginal sporting participation the archival

[21] Cashman, R, *Paradise of Sport - The Rise of Organised Sport in Australia,* Oxford University Press, Melbourne, 2002, pp44
[22] Booth, D & Tatz, C, 2000, pp44

record provides evidence of some early Aboriginal soccer stars whose skill demanded that they gained a spot on the field.

Quilp - The Ebony Dinmore Bush Rat

I am indebted to the forensic archival work of Dr Ian Syson in uncovering the story of Quilp recognised as one of the earliest recorded Aboriginal soccer players. The discovery of Quilp was facilitated by the recently digitized archives and wonderful Trove newspaper resource of the National Library of Australia. Syson uncovered a photograph of the Dinmore Bush Rats a Queensland football club when searching the Trove pictorial archive. He was amazed to find 'bang' in the middle of this image an Aboriginal player named simply as 'Quilp'.

The Dinmore Bush Rats were listed as the second premiers in Ipswich in 1910. Syson was puzzled with intrigue who was this Quilp? Where was he from? How was he playing British Association Football at that point in time? And what was he doing prominently placed in the very middle section of this photograph. Further searching of Trove unearthed greater details of a remarkable sportsman and character for so long forgotten in memory and history. Quilp's, real name was John Baramba (Jackie) Lynch, and he was born in the Gulf Country of North Queensland. The earliest uncovered reference to him is under the name Quilp and he was charged for drunkenness and disorderly conduct in the Ipswich Police Court in 1901. The article goes on to say he was a second offender and he would be similarly arraigned in 1902. The first reference to his football career reveals that he was a player for the Reliance team from Dinmore in 1904. In a match played at the Pineapple Ground (great name for a football ground) close by the Roma Street markets. The press coverage is somewhat confusing because it states that Quilp was sent from the field for back chatting the referee but then is noted as scoring the winning goal. Whatever transpired it appears that Quilp's goal was responsible for some severe protests from the opposing team and some bitter feelings erupted. Quilp was later seen to be arguing with the referee and was sent off.

The coverage of the game revealed that the Reliance team were off to a solid start in the match and Quilp had a shot on target that appeared to the spectators as not to have gone in but the referee awarded a goal. Syson has stated the significance of the moment as Quilp's goal is most likely the first ever scored by an Aboriginal senior soccer player. It is possible that Quilp had scored goals prior to this match but this one was recorded in the press. He is noted as playing for the Dinmore Bush Rats against a combined Brisbane selection in 1908 and also took the field for the Rats against Blackstone Rovers. In the press reports he was frequently referred to as the 'ebony Quilp'. Like other early Aboriginal sportsmen, he was versatile in his sporting endeavours including being noted as playing competitive quoits and boxing as a featherweight in 1909.

Ten years later Quilp was noted as being employed as a shooter and tracker for the noted buffalo hunter, Patrick Cahill. One incident of Quilp in his hunting capacity was reported in *The Queenslander*. Apparently when faced with a charging buffalo Quilp's horse fell and he rolled clear of the animal, but the buffalo was bearing down headlong with 'its nostril distended, and its eyes full of murder'. Quilp miraculously remained calm and still until the animal was but a foot from him before rolling to one side and avoiding the charging and enraged animal. The newspaper went on to state that Quilp had avoided death by a hair's breadth as if the animal had gored him it would have been certain death. Newspaper coverage later has Quilp recorded acting as a referee for a soccer match. This would surely represent a first for an Aboriginal officiating as a referee in any senior football code.

Further coverage in the *Queensland Times* in 1919 records a correspondent raising the question where the former buffalo hunter and famed soccer star Quilp had ended up? He went on to state that he had in front of him a photo of Quilp buffalo hunting in the Northern Territory in the employ of Mr Patrick Cahill of Toowoomba. The *Queensland Times* suggests he was an all-round gifted sportsman across all physical activities. He was described as playing as a winger on the soccer field. There was even a suggestion that he gained the nickname Quilp in reference to a racehorse with the same name and because of his speed, decisive and intelligent running on the wing.

Quilp or Jackie Lynch is recorded as dying in Murwillumbah in 1930. He was described in the press as 'a celebrated local character' but sadly additionally held up for ridicule and noted for his 'comic banter, foolishness and propensity for harmless mischief.' Apparently, there were only four others beside the

Church of England reverend to pay their respects to a remarkable individual. Quilp's story as best as we are able to ascertain from the fragmented newspaper coverage provides us with but a glimpse in to the life and times of this early Aboriginal soccer star.

Bondi Neal – The Star Goalkeeper

A sudden and unexpected economic downturn in New South Wales in the early years of the twentieth century saw work opportunities decline and out of work miners moving from the Newcastle area to Pelaw Main in the Hunter Valley. Hundreds of men got jobs at new mines in the coalfields there. The Pelaw Main and Stanford Merthyr collieries both enjoyed rapid development and success. The miners brought their love of soccer to the area and quickly formed several teams. Pelaw Main Soccer club was established in March 1903 after an inaugural meeting being held on a vacant block of land near Gillon's General Store.[23]

Playing members were signed for two shillings and non-players at one shilling – there was no shortage of people willing to join. The formation of the club resulted in a hive of activity. A ladies Committee was formed, and plans were made to secure a playing strip. Working bees prepared the ground, which was close to the new public school that had opened only a few months earlier. Before the 1904 season started, major work was carried out on the pitch.[24]

One young miner who had trekked to Pelaw Main was an Aboriginal man named Bondi Neal. Neal would achieve instant local fame as a talented sportsman and the first Aboriginal representative soccer player. Sid Grant recorded that the 'part Aboriginal Bondi Neal was a keen, versatile sportsman. He played senior cricket with Kurri, senior soccer with Kurri, Weston and Pelaw Main, and Rugby Union and Rugby League with Kurri ... He once threw a cricket ball 66 yards [60 metres] with both hands.[25]

---

23 Grant, 1979: pp62-63; Hetherington, H, original unpublished manuscript compiled in Northern New South Wales Soccer Council, *History of Soccer in Northern NSW 1884 to 2000 and Sydney & South Coast 1880 – 1957*, New South Wales State Library, Sydney, 2003
24 Ibid.
25 Grant, 1979: pp137

Today, Bondi Neal remains still something of a mystery man. We have written evidence that he was an Aboriginal man from the South Coast of New South Wales who made his way to the Coalfields to gain work as a miner. We know that he was an extraordinarily gifted sportsman. But we don't know where on the south coast his family and tribal connections lay. So many aspects of his life remain unknown. There is little in the numerous newspaper sources about the man himself, only the match reports describing his wonderful goalkeeping ability. Recently uncovered material on Trove has provided some missing pieces of the puzzle and provided additional archival material about the man and his background.

In some respects, the fractured picture we hold of the life of Bondi Neal mirrors the national experiences of Aboriginal people during this period – a time of monumental and catastrophic change. At the start of the twentieth century, Aborigines in New South Wales had far greater freedom of movement and working opportunities than they would have within one to two decades. By that time, most Aboriginal people still confined to the bush were facing a more vigorous and oppressive level of government control over their lives. This harsh and confronting regime was a response to the so-called 'Aboriginal problem', a phrase frequently used in newspapers and official documents of the time.

In 1883, the New South Wales government formally established the Aborigines Protection Board. It was to eventually take complete control over every aspect of Aboriginal life in New South Wales in a most systematic way. The Board did not make decisions with long-term goals in mind for the Aboriginal population. This was clearly identified by the New South Wales Parliament, which said that there would be no need to increase the funding for Aboriginal people as they were dying out. The non-inclusion of 'full-bloods' in the census under section 127 of the Commonwealth Constitution of 1900, reflected the 'unstated consensus that their exclusion would before too long be made a reality by the eventual demise of the 'dying race'. [26]

The expansion of Board power and control over Aboriginal people had not yet occurred when, in 1903, Bondi Neal made his trek from the South Coast of New

[26] Smith, L, *The Aboriginal Population of Australia,* ANU Press, Canberra, 1980, pp23

South Wales to the coalfields of the Hunter Valley, near the city of Newcastle, for work opportunities in the mines. Despite his sporting versatility, it was as an outstanding goalkeeper on the soccer pitch that Neal is best remembered. He was a member of the newly formed Pelaw Main team that was beaten by Broadmeadow in the 1904 Newcastle grand final 1-0. Three years later, Pelaw Main and their richly talented goalkeeper overcame the disappointment of losing in 1904 when they won the 1907 grand final. At the conclusion of the season, Pelaw Main had finished on top of the ladder of ten teams, with the Wallsend Royals in second place. The two leading teams fought out a thrilling final at Newcastle Showground. The score was 2-2 after ninety minutes. But Pellaw Main won 4-2 in extra time and took a major soccer trophy home to the coalfields for the first time.

During that 1904 season a large crowd of 400 people watched a fiercely fought local derby match between Pelaw Main and Heddon Greta. The match, which ended in a 2-2 draw, had some exciting incidents on and off the field: 'Pelaw Main's goalie Bondi Neal stopped two penalties. Thrice the referee, Harry Speers of Dudley, held up play as spectators crowded the visitor's goalmouth while stones were thrown at the keeper. Play became heated in the final 20 minutes and fights broke out among partisan fans. Player Chris Picken, also a first grade Rugby Star, remarked, "I was glad to hear the final whistle." Strange but true, referee Speers was cheered by both teams and many of the crowd. Years later, when living at Kurri Kurri, Harry remarked – "Yes, the strangest game I ever refereed. I gave a penalty to each side but when Neal fisted Picken's drive over the bar pandemonium broke forth." But "at the tasty banquet after the match we were all good friends".[27]

In 1908, Neal left Pelaw Main and signed with the Kurri Kurri club. His departure was timely, because a trade depression and the long coal strike of 1909 sent the Pelaw Main mine and soccer club into recess. Neal would eventually be joined by a number of his former team-mates who either signed with Kurri or Weston. The Kurri club was going through a revival generated in part by the enthusiastic efforts of former Minmi star player 'Jockey' Stevenson. It was during the 1908 season that the first Cessnock v Kurri clashes occurred, and the two teams would establish a fierce rivalry. The first match ended in a hard fought 2-2 draw, but in the return

....

[27] Hetherington, H, 2003

clash in front of more than five hundred supporters at Kurri, the locals were victorious, 3-2. These close encounters came to typify Cessnock v Kurri clashes in all codes over the years. In another game that season at Newcastle Showground, the *Newcastle Morning Herald* reported that Neal was the goalkeeper for Kurri against Adamstown Rosebuds. The Rosebuds won the match 3-1, but Neal obviously had a good game: 'the Kurri goalkeeper had a hot time defending, which he managed to do successfully.'[28]

Neal continued with the Kurri club during the 1909 season. His form was so good that he was selected as the representative goalkeeper for a combined Coalfields team that played against the visiting Western Australian team at Maitland Showground in May 1909. There was much anticipation in the local press with the visit of the Western Australian team. The *Maitland Mercury* reported, 'The Albion Ground has been engaged for the match. The local team comprises a fairly strong combination and a good game of soccer is sure to result. "Soccer" is the predominant game of Great Britain and is very fascinating. Those who have the opportunity should not fail to see this match'.

The day of the match was beautiful, with a light westerly wind blowing across the ground, the conditions undoubtedly responsible for attracting a crowd of more than 1,000 supporters. Match reports in both the *Newcastle Morning Herald* and the *Maitland Mercury* reveal that the Western Australian team had by far the better of the first half scoring two goals to nil. If it had not been for the brilliance of Neal between the sticks, the visitors would have had a much greater lead at halftime. The commentary was quite glowing of his performance. In the first five minutes he was 'called upon on two occasions to save, which he did brilliantly.' The visitors went ahead after fifteen minutes, when a player named Robertson scored a brilliant goal. As reported by the *Maitland Mercury*, the visitors continued to attack relentlessly: 'Robertson broke away with the ball at toe, and supported by Bogle, another score for the visitors appeared imminent but Neal saved well, at a critical moment and was applauded for his efforts. In another smart move from the West Australian team, a passing movement resulted in their second goal of the match. The halftime score remained at 2-0 to the visitors. The second half followed the

28 *Newcastle Morning Herald,* May 25 1908

script of the first, with Neal continuing to frustrate all attempts to beat him. 'Allen and McCreery then took the ball at toe, and Roskam had a shot at goal but Neal again proved himself thoroughly safe and reliable'. The final whistle blew, leaving the visitors with the spoils, but Neal's performance the highlight of the match.

Neal left Kurri and moved to Weston for the 1910 season, at the same time that this famous club adopted their black and white striped shirts with black shorts for the first time. Neal played two seasons with the Weston club. In about 1912, he left the coalfields for his native South Coast. Neal is most certainly the most famous early Aboriginal soccer player and he was unquestionably an incredible athlete. When I wrote the first edition of this book in 2010, I could find no further evidence of Bondi Neal after his return to the South Coast but through the work of Ian Syson and the age of Trove we now know that his football career continued down south.

As Syson articulates 'the tendency of Aboriginal subjects and soccer moments to recede from view means that researching the history of Aboriginal soccer players is like searching for one needle in two haystacks. Fortunately, the recent developments in digital and searchable archives have shifted the odds a little in favour of finding the needles'.

Walter Ernest 'Bondi' Neal was recorded as passing away in Wollongong in 1953. His obituary notice claimed he was 89 years old at the time of death.[29] Syson felt this was 'unlikely given that he was still playing senior football in the 1920s'. Then again Neal was an incredibly gifted athlete and we know that Stanley Matthews played up until he was 50 years of age. Goalkeepers have proven longevity in the game. Only recently the Egyptian World Cup goalkeeper Essam El-Hadary became the oldest player to ever appear in World Cup finals history when he played against Saudi Arabia aged 45 years old. It appears that Neal was born on the south coast in the late nineteenth century. Records indicate that his mother was an Aboriginal woman (described as 'half-caste') and his father was Scottish. Syson reveals that a 1925 newspaper account hints that the name Bondi was a 'corruption of the nickname, Bunda (kangaroo), given to him by Aboriginal friends as a youngster in acknowledgement of his athletic abilities'.[30] The name

29 *Illawarra Daily Mercury (Wollongong)*, 1 August 1953: pp4
30 *Bundaberg Mail (Qld)*, 14 September 1923: pp2

might derive from several potential sources including Bundhi (club, nulla-nulla – used for both fighting and throwing) a word from the Gathang Aboriginal group in close proximity to his time on the coalfields around Newcastle. On his return to the South Coast he came with a star player's reputation. He went on to play for several clubs in the Wollongong area, receiving plenty of media attention for his performances. He was involved in another game on the South Coast between Woonona and Corrimal that witnessed crowd disturbances. The game ended abruptly when the crowd stormed onto the field challenging the referee's decision and 'some miserable coward struck the referee, Mr. T. Westwood in the mouth then took good care to make himself safe by mixing with the crowd; unfortunately, he got clear away.'[31] Bondi Neal had an outstanding game for Corrimal: 'Bondi in Corrimal goal, certainly saved Corrimal from defeat, he was the most reliable player they had' and his superb performance may have riled rival supporters.[32] After another match between Balgownie and Woonoona in 1921 there was even a poem cited in the *South Coast Times* and *Wollongong Argus* describing both Bondi Neal in goal and another legendary player Australian captain Judy Masters:

Judy played a rattling game,
And into Bondi flew;
Before the game was half way o'er
Bondi was black and blue
… Balgownie finds their stride,
For Hilly scores a beauty;
Old Bondi almost cried. [33]

In 1923 he was playing for the South Coast champions Woonoona against northern NSW top side Wallsend in a Gardiner Cup tie. He finally hung up his boots in the mid 1920s and focused his attention on acting as a goalkeeping coach. During the 1942 season Corrimal's young goalkeeper Jennings was reported to be 'a pupil of Bondi Neal who electrified the crowds as a keeper in the days gone by'. In 1944 it

31 *South Coast Times and Wollongong Argus,* 25 June 1920: pp13
32 Ibid.
33 *South Coast Times and Wollongong Argus,* 15 July 1921: pp8

was noted in the press that the 'veteran keeper "Bondi" Neal was interesting himself in Woonoona's play… with particular emphasis on the goalie's work, and some fans are asking whether Bondi's services are being retained by the Woonoona club for the forthcoming season.'[34] He was no mean cricketer either and his lightning scoring with the bat included hitting 96 runs in just 35 minutes hitting nine sixes. He was once recorded as throwing a cricket ball 101 yards. It appears that he was badly injured in a mine accident during the 1930s. A community fund raiser was held for the former 'star goalkeeper' by the Balgownie club to assist him after the accident.[35] Bondi Neal certainly deserves his place as one of the truly great Aboriginal players.

Willie Allen
- World War I Hero and Sports Star

Willie Allen, a Larrakia Aboriginal man from the top end was unquestionably one of the Northern Territory's greatest athletes in the early years of the twentieth century. Much like Bondi Neal he was a versatile and talented sportsman across a number of games He was a top-class cricketer, AFL player and also a representative soccer player. Allen's sporting success evidently opened doors of acceptance rarely experienced by Aboriginal men of that region and time period. He was even allowed access into the Palmerston Rifle Club. This was no easy feat seeing that the Rifle Club was 'a bastion of White society' and overcame and challenged the elevated racial politics of the period. The year 1911 was a standout year. He competed in two major athletic carnivals including running in the 'blackboys race' as well as open events. The accolades flowed freely on his cricketing exploits and he was acknowledged by the Darwin cricket club 'as the best all round player in the club'. In December that year the British warship HMS *Prometheus* visited Darwin. Coinciding with this visit a number of sporting and social events were held including Darwin's first British Association Football match. The British warship had its own football team and a match was arranged giving the locals an opportunity

[34]   *South Coast Times and Wollongong Argus,* 31 March 1944: pp12
[35]   *Illawarra Mercury (Wollongong),* 26 May 1949: pp2

to play against some of the British navy's best. Willie Allen's selection in the Northern Territory representative team made him one of the first Aboriginal players selected to represent his state or region. It is an amazing fact that despite Allen's physical and athletic ability that during the First World War he 'attempted to enlist in the Australian Imperial force but was rejected on medical grounds'. [36] Allen, like his sporting record suggests, was not a man to take rejection lightly. He would spend three years as a volunteer cable guard, a role that saw him alongside a group of men who were given the task of protecting Australia's communication cable that was a potential target during the war.

In 1917 he travelled across the country to Brisbane and another attempt to enlist. Following horrific casualties on the Western Front the military authorities had relaxed the previous barriers that had excluded Aboriginal enlistment in May 1917. [37]

This time Allen was warmly accepted into the 11th Regiment of the Australian Light Horse. At this late stage of the war the need for horses was abandoned and Allen was required as a rifleman. He initially disembarked at the Suez Canal four months before the end of hostilities. He saw action at Semakh in Palestine, Cairo in Egypt and Tripoli before the war ended. While waiting to embark for home Allen's regiment was called back in to action to put down an Egyptian revolt in March 1919. Initially he arrived back in Darwin where he stayed for several months. During this period, he resumed playing AFL for the new Vesteys team coached by his legendary former Aboriginal teammate Reuben Cooper. On his discharge from military service Allen relocated with his wife and family to Brisbane where he lived and worked for decades. He passed away in 1959. [38] Like Bondi Neal, Willie Allen deserves to be remembered as a great sportsman and an early representative soccer player.

The stories of Quilp, Bondi Neal and Willie Allen reveal that we did have some exciting early Aboriginal star players that graced the game in this country.

---

[36] Stephen, M *Colour Bar: Remembering and Forgetting Northern Territory Football 1916-1955,* pp31-32
[37] Maynard, J, The First World War, in *Serving Our Country* Ed. Beaumont, J & Cadzow, A, New South, Sydney, 2018, pp76
[38] *NTNews,* April 25, 2015

A 30-Year Hiatus

Back in 2010 I assumed that it would be another 30 years before another group of Aboriginal soccer players made an impact on the round-ball game. But further research has uncovered dozens of interesting and exciting Aboriginal intersections with the game that I will shortly reveal. Certainly, during the time period between the wars, the Aboriginal population was largely confined and controlled on heavily restricted state government reserves. This confinement certainly restricted the opportunities to play sport of any kind. Many lived in deplorable conditions, with serious health problems and little hope of a future. By the 1950s, soccer had become a game connected with the urban cities, British descendants in the mining centres or, in the wake of World War II, European migrant communities. Aboriginal people, primarily isolated in remote or rural settlements, had little chance of seeing or playing soccer. The containment of soccer in the Australian cities and its lack of growth in rural areas was recognised back in the early 1960s. It made front page news in *Soccer World* in 1963:

> *Every country's soccer strength lies in the provinces even though the leading sides of the world come usually from the large cities and capitals.*
>
> *In Australia, however, this depth of country talent simply does not exist.*
>
> *Soccer in Australia is largely confined to the coastal areas with the code flourishing in Sydney, Newcastle, Wollongong, Melbourne, Adelaide, Perth, Brisbane and Hobart...*
>
> *However big soccer becomes in the large coastal cities the sport will never rest on solid, durable foundations if there is no large supply of country talent.*

This absence of soccer from the critically important rural and remote parts of Australia was belatedly recognised more than 40 years later when, in 2010, Football Federation Australia (FFA) published its new *National Curriculum*. In the section titled 'Omission of Talent from Regional Australia', the FFA clearly targeted a move to rectify this large gap in the talent pool:

For most Australian sports rural locations are much better (per capita) than big cities at generating athletes. Unlike other football codes in Australia, football has been predominantly a city game (75% of all Australian A-League players develop in large cities).

This is consistent with football (soccer) in Australia having been fostered by 20th century European immigrants and their children, who tended to cluster in the capital and industrial cities. The historical immigration dynamic that has underpinned football in Australia appears to be weakening. This poses a major threat to Australia's future talent pool unless offset by a much greater share of young athletes from rural areas. Since players need to be included into the game at an early age, this would require initiatives that make football much more accessible in rural Australia and at the same time, would also draw many more Indigenous Australians into the game.

Now nine years on from the release of the *National Curriculum* one would be left to question the continued lack of development and progress of the game away from the urban space including that of targeting Indigenous players.

Missing History

Incredibly as far back as 1886 there was a strong push to include several Aboriginal players in an Australian representative soccer team to tour Great Britain! The selection committee had been chosen to pick the Australian squad and 'if possible, to include several Aboriginal players'.[39] This decision was most likely following upon the success of the all-Aboriginal cricket team tour of Great Britain in 1868. Sadly, the soccer tour fell through and a great early opportunity was lost.

What if an Australian national team had toured Great Britain in 1886? What would it have done to promoting the position of the game in this country? It would have been 21 years before rugby league was ever played in Australia. The Australian team would not have been so disadvantaged in playing full time soccer professionals

[39] *The Morning Bulletin (Brisbane)* 10 July 1925: 11, *The Truth (Brisbane),* 21 June 1925: pp8, *The Daily Standard (Brisbane),* 18 June 1925: pp8

35

as they would later. What impact may such a tour have had on the AFL at this early stage? What if as requested several Aboriginal players were a part of this first ever Australian side? Certainly, ponders thinking about.

In June 1924 the Chief Protector of Aborigines in Queensland Mr. JM Bleakley presented four beautifully carved boomerangs to the visiting Canadian international soccer team on their tour of the country. The boomerangs were made 'by the natives at Barambah settlement. One boomerang was awarded to the manager, captain, trainer and goalkeeper of the visiting team. The Canadians expressed deep gratitude and appreciation of the gifts. Aboriginal people from Barambah were well known for their boomerang, null-nulla and spear throwing performances prior to major football events'. [40]

In 1925 for the first time England toured Australia and the powerful professionals were too strong for the Australian opposition remaining unbeaten on the tour. They played against a Queensland selection as part of the tour. Like the Canadian tour the year before the Chief Protector of Aborigines Mr. Bleakley was asked to provide some Aboriginal cultural connection to the match. This time Bleakley gave the Australian team an Aboriginal war cry that they were to sing out against the visitors prior to kick-off. It appears the war cry was much like a performance of the Maori Haka. The war cry was meant to demoralise the English players who later described it 'as a weird blood curdling abo war cry'. [41] The song and its meaning was printed widely in the press prior to the game:

Kaial gumm

Jenung

Balai-balieir

Yana!

The words were repeated twice with heightened ferocity. In translation the words were said to state:

Led by the chief

In fighting we kick with the feet

Go thee O Chief and present the challenge.

---

[40] *The Daily Standard (Brisbane),* 10 June 1924: pp2
[41] *The Morning Bulletin (Brisbane),* 10 July 1925: pp11, *The Truth (Brisbane),* 21 June 1925: pp8, *The Daily Standard (Brisbane),* 18 June 1925: pp8

The song was further described as a welcome and a challenge and literally meant – begin the fight, fight hard and may the best tribe win. The English were presented before the game with a beautifully carved Aboriginal message stick with the war cry inscribed as a challenge of war. The war cry apparently did not intimidate the English who won the match 11-0. The practice of awarding Aboriginal cultural gifts to visiting overseas players and teams clearly remained into the future. In 1967 the Australian F.A presented a gift to George Best during Manchester United's 1967 Australian tour. The gift featured a magnificent ornately decorated boomerang mounted in a frame sitting above a badge of the Australian Football Association.

In June 1933 the Queensland soccer council had been approached to support a tour of Queensland by a soccer team from the Torres Strait. A Mr. S. Gillard from Thursday Island informed the soccer authorities that he was keen to bring his 'native' team south as soon as possible. The proposed tour intended to play games in Brisbane, Rockhampton, Bundaberg, Mackay, Townsville and Cairns. It was intended that the tour would coincide with Exhibition Week in Brisbane. It was suggested that the Islander soccer tour would provide a carnival attraction. As well as playing soccer the Islanders 'would give demonstrations of spear throwing and other native performances which would be a valued attraction as a public spectacle'. It was interesting to note that the Islanders could not undertake the visit 'until a deposit has been paid to the Chief Protector of Aborigines against their return'.[42] The tentacles of government control over Aboriginal lives was well and truly in place by 1933.

In 1952 a newspaper article highlighted that a young 19-year-old Aboriginal soccer player James Musgrave from Queensland had been brought down to Sydney to play for Bankstown. The article mysteriously announced that prior to Musgrave only two or three Aboriginal players had played major soccer during the previous 20 years. Who were these players? The president of the Bankstown club, Mr Jack McFarlane had been in Queensland and saw James Musgrave playing first grade for Blair Athol against Ipswich. McFarlane was instantly impressed by Musgraves' play at centre back and offered him the chance to play in Sydney. Musgrave travelled down and trialled with the Bankstown second grade team and showed

---

[42] *The Telegraph (Brisbane)*, 9 June 1933: pp3

promise. He initially stayed with McFarlane but was reported as looking for permanent accommodation. No further evidence survives on his soccer career.

Another article with a picture highlighted an Aboriginal Boys' Brigade Company at the Ooldea, United Aborigines Mission receiving a soccer ball sent from the West Bromwich Boys' Brigade in England.

Photos and film provide further evidence of more widespread Aboriginal soccer involvement.

A picture held in the New South Wales state archives shows a group of Aboriginal boys at Cubawee Aboriginal School in the late 1920s or early 1930s. The front boy is holding his soccer ball as he stares at the camera. Another image shows a large mob of Aboriginal kids in mad pursuit of a soccer ball at La Perouse in the early 1950s. Another image displays a group of young Aboriginal men involved in a game on the streets of Sydney during the 1960s. Old film footage from Mapoon in 1950 and Mona Mona in 1955 shows Aboriginal mission residents or inmates playing soccer. One of these short films shows Aboriginal girls playing soccer on the beach. Another film reveals Aboriginal children and adults playing soccer on the beach amongst palm trees.

CHAPTER 4
Against the Grain – Charlie Perkins, John Moriarty and Gordon Briscoe

The global impact of the world game on Australia and the subsequent – if little known – transnational movement of Aboriginal soccer players started during the 1950s. It pre-dated the mass movement of Australian soccer players to Europe which began in the 1990s. It is not widely known that Charles Perkins, commonly known as Charlie and arguably the most charismatic and recognised Aboriginal political leader of the twentieth century, was an outstanding soccer player. He was one of three great Aboriginal soccer players of the 1950s and 1960s, along with John Moriarty and Gordon Briscoe. These men followed near identical and entwined paths to the top.

Charlie Perkins was adamant that 'Aboriginal Affairs and soccer have been my passions and... I could work out my problems through both of those two things... Soccer was where I got my satisfaction, my fulfillment.' He was born at the Aboriginal reserve near Alice Springs in the Northern Territory. His parents were Arrente and Kalkadoon people. Perkins was separated from his mother at the age of 10 and placed in St Francis, an Anglican Home for Aboriginal boys in Adelaide, established in 1945 by Father Percy Smith. Here he joined many other Aboriginal boys who had either been placed in the home by their parents to give them better educational opportunities, or who had been separated or taken from their families. Some of his peers included his cousin Gordon Briscoe, John Moriarty, Vince Copley and Wally McArthur, all of whom would go on to have successful sporting careers.

The tragedy of John Moriarty's early life is self-evident. Moriarty was born at

Borroloola on the Gulf of Carpentaria in the Northern Territory. In an interview with me in 2004, he said:

> *I was one of those taken away when I was four years old from the Roper River Mission. Mum took me to Roper, to start school, and that's where I started school, but I was there, just a few days and then I was whisked on the back of an old army truck and sent through to Alice Springs and then on the train from there to Sydney to Ashfield, that's only a staging camp. And then on to St Thomas' in Mulgoa, then we were moved on to Adelaide and to St Francis Home.*

Gordon Briscoe, for his part, was just four years old when he was taken from his Marduntjara mother and institutionalised.

At St Francis House, Perkins, Moriarty and Briscoe – and all the boys in the home – were introduced to soccer. The game would be responsible for these three young men being accepted not just onto the soccer field but also into the wider cosmopolitan soccer community and the world of international travel. These experiences played some part in moulding all three men into inspiring Aboriginal political leaders in the decades that followed. This intersection between the St Francis Home and playing soccer was a pivotal point for Perkins, Moriarty and Briscoe, and it provides a fascinating insight into the connection between sport and political awareness.

Some people point to the later success of Aboriginal people such as Perkins, Moriarty and Briscoe as evidence that the assimilation policy – and removing Aboriginal children from their families – was beneficial and a success. But this analysis does not take into account the fact that success was not the norm, and many Aboriginal children who were taken away would suffer greatly as adults from alcohol, drug addiction and depression.

As Gordon Briscoe highlighted in an interview, they lost their culture and connection with family and community: 'You know there was never any thought of preserving anything, the assimilation process of socialising people who were not European, we were brought into these institutions so young … we were always encouraged to think that we were *part* Aborigines.' There were barriers and enforced process of forgetting Aboriginal ways: 'There was a divide, almost the impossibility of retracing and reconstructing our traditional past that was idealised in our minds.'

The imprint of their experiences in the home would remain with the boys for a long time. The process of assimilation and its impact on their self-esteem was clear to all of them. Briscoe remembered: 'In Adelaide, the prejudice was ripe, we were inhibited to do all the kinds of things we wanted to do, we could see the prejudice of white society.'

They all felt the full brunt of that racism and prejudice, which was an everyday part of wider Australian society during their early lives. They were denied access to so much. Perkins' reflections clearly showed the pain he felt as a young man:

It really hurts you; it slices right to your heart. You can't handle it. I thought to myself, what have I done? How can I rectify this? Can I scrub myself white? Can I do something to myself? Nothing. They really make you feel ashamed of yourself and you feel less of a person as a consequence. It undermines your confidence above all else, and your dignity and your self-respect. Then it develops a reaction within yourself of hatred. It pierced me right to the core of my heart. I've never forgotten those things and I never will. You carry them to your grave. They're scars on your mind. [43]

Johnny Warren, a long-time friend and old team-mate of Charlie Perkins, recognised that acceptance 'as an equal was a powerful panacea for Dr Perkins. To achieve that sense of equality, on an individual level as well as on behalf of his people, was the summation of his life's mission.' [44]

Acceptance Among the 'New Australians'

Perkins would find that acceptance playing soccer opened doors and delivered a glimpse of a level playing field for a young man. The post-World War II influx of

43   Read, P, *Charles Perkins,* Allen & Unwin, Sydney, 2001, pp48
44   Warren, J, *Sheilas, Wogs and Poofters,* Random House, Sydney, 2002, ppxix-xx

soccer-loving European migrants had a major impact not only on Australian soccer but also on the futures of Perkins, Moriarty and Briscoe. Perkins was adamant that soccer 'brought me into the migrant community where I found great satisfaction, no prejudice, no history of bad relations, no embarrassing comments or derogatory remarks, they welcomed me into the fold and I've been there ever since.'

Vince Copley, a lifetime friend of all three men through their shared experiences at the St Francis Home – he later became chairman of Tandanya Aboriginal Cultural Centre in Adelaide – holds invaluable insights into that time. He recognised the different experience with the migrant communities. The new arrivals offered something that these young Aboriginal boys had not previously encountered – acceptance. He recalled in an interview with me in 2004:

Charlie seemed to get on a lot better with the people [in the migrant communities], over the old Aussie Rules group of people. Probably the different crowds, having been to Aussie Rules matches and crowds, despite that there were a few Aboriginal players at the time. I think that Charlie found that within the new group that he mixed with at the time, there was none of the racism. We sort of struggled with the Aussie Rules, not saying it was completely racist but there was a fair bit of it at that time going round. Charlie seemed to be accepted into that particular group [of soccer-playing migrants]. There was a little group, from all around the soccer world. I suppose we all felt accepted into that group. Charlie was the most courageous man in the face of racism and prejudice even at that early stage, he was much more alert in things going on.

During the late 1940s and early 1950s, new soccer clubs were formed which reflected the diverse ethnic backgrounds of the new European migrants. Now there were Polish, Italian, Greek, Hungarian, Croatian, Serbian and Jewish soccer clubs. Australians, in their xenophobic way, quickly targeted the new arrivals and the game they loved. The Aboriginal players recognised this, as John Moriarty explains: 'The so-called new Australians that came through the Italians, and they used to call the people from the Baltic states "Balts" and the derogatory terms like "wogs", "dagos" and all of these things, but they soon put all of that stuff to rest because they started having a lot of impact in the society life, they owned businesses, they owned restaurants and they became a part of the economic structure.'

Gordon Briscoe also reflected on his experience with the European migrants:

When these 'New Australians' came onto the scene, they didn't question our background, because they were people who'd had difficulties, they'd suffered from war damage, they'd suffered from [not] having the freedom to move wherever they wanted to, they were probably being employed for the first time, struggling, but yet still wanting to practise their culture, which was soccer... So when they saw us, they didn't question our background and our racial heritage... and they respected us, because we could do the things that entertained them.

The migrants' interest in soccer meant that the game attracted the wrong kind of attention from the wider Australian community. The game became a target for feelings of unease and fear about migrants. There were attacks against the sport, some of which were extreme. Phillip Mosley described soccer as:

An exceptional forum in which immigrants felt they stood equal with, if not superior to, host Australians; European-style football had already surpassed the British style [of soccer] and immigrants knew they were good... Anglo-Australians generally dismissed the game as a 'wog's' game, but the major codes considered it a threat. In 1952 the VFL [later to be known as AFL] directed suburban affiliates to 'secure all available sporting space in Melbourne in order to stifle the burgeoning threat posed by soccer's migrant inspired growth'. In 1965 Melbourne youths daubed anti-soccer slogans over Middle Park [home ground of South Melbourne club], chopped down the goalposts and tried to set fire to the grandstand. [45]

Amid this animosity, the game was branded – as Johnny Warren was to put it so aptly in the title of his autobiography – as only fit for 'sheilas, wogs and poofters.' The mass media played a major role in this. They had a vested interest in promoting

....

[45] Quoted in Booth, D & Tatz, C, *One Eyed – A View of Australian Sport,* Allen & Unwin, Sydney, 2000, pp141-2

the other codes. As a consequence, soccer was given little press coverage unless it could be portrayed in a negative light, or as 'un-Australian'. 'The game's challenge to the hegemony of the dominant football codes alienated many who had long held these codes to be symbols of what it was to be Australian. Soccer's strong immigrant element drew adverse reactions and ensured that the game received similar treatment from the Australian establishment as was meted out to immigrants in general.'[46]

Despite all this, the vibrant migrant communities continued to worship the game, and to embrace their new homeland. 'Football connected them to their homelands rather than to Britain. They created a football revival which, in the context of the narrow and provincial racism of mid-[twentieth]-century Australia, only served to reinforce the minority status of football or, as it was derisively known, "wogball".[47] Aboriginal people and the migrant community were partners against, and victims of, the entrenched anglophone White Australia policy. As Johnny Warren put it, the 'axiom of "the enemy of my enemy is my friend" rang true and as such, both Charlie Perkins and non-English speaking migrants shared a common bond through the common enemy of racism.

A Legendary Game

The launch of the soccer careers of Perkins, Moriarty and Briscoe could all be tied to a now-legendary minor soccer game that they played while at the St Francis Home in around 1951. The boys at the home were mad on sport and any football code. In his memoir, *Saltwater Fella,* John Moriarty recalled that they would 'play during the holidays from eight o'clock in the morning, from after breakfast, right through till dark. Sometimes we'd even play in the moonlight; we were so full of energy. All we had to play soccer with was a tennis ball, but we'd play six, seven, eight, ten a side often in quite confined spaces in the courtyard at the home. That was good fun, learning to control the ball and so on.'[48] Thanks to those endless

---

[46] Mosley, P, Cashman, R, O'Hara, J & Weatherburn, H, *Sporting Immigrants,* Walla Walla Press, Sydney, 1997, pp168

[47] Goldblatt, D, *The Ball Is Round – A Global History of Football,* Viking Press, London, 2006, pp95

[48] Moriarty, J, *Saltwater Fella,* Viking Books, Melbourne, 2000, pp105

hours of impromptu games with a tennis ball in a small space, the boys developed incredible skills. Moriarty said, 'Usually in bare feet, you'd have to control it, as well as have good eye [coordination] for the bounce of the ball.'

One day, a state under 18 representative team was practising on a soccer pitch next to the home. All the boys from the home were sitting on the fence watching, when an official asked if they wanted to form a team and play a practice match against the state team. The Aboriginal boys jumped at the chance, and on the field, they annihilated the state representative team 12-0. There was Moriarty, Perkins and Briscoe, and also Vince Copley in this impromptu team. He told me in a 2004 interview, 'We had kids starting in that team aged only ten, but we could run a couple of yards faster... The finesse of a couple of our blokes was there to see, they had picked up the game very quickly, and we had Wally McArthur in our team. Wally would in time be recognised as one of the fastest sprinters in Australia and went on to become a great rugby league winger. We just knocked the ball through and Wally outsprinted them.'

A few officials from the Adelaide Port Thistle Soccer Club were present and they immediately signed up a number of these budding stars. Moriarty recalled the invitations to play for Port Thistle Soccer Club: 'I sort of gracefully declined, and they kept talking to us, and in the end, they offered us boots and other equipment, so I put up my hand and said, "Yes thank you," so that's where we got started.'

Charlie Perkins was a first grade soccer player at the age of fifteen, playing with Port Thistle. By 21, he had moved to International United, affectionately known as the 'Redskins'. This new club had no specific ethnic base but was made up of players from all over the world, and Perkins was the star standout player. In the 1956–57 season he moved on to the most powerful club in South Australia at the time, the Hungarian community backed Budapest. During this time, Budapest won a host of trophies and Perkins was voted the South Australian Player of the Year.

John Moriarty, Gordon Briscoe and Vince Copley also initially joined Port Thistle. This was a golden period of Australian soccer and Perkins was known as one of the better wing halves in the country. As a player he was recognised as 'tough, self-confident, stoical and uncompromising. He liked to talk about the game for days afterwards. He was ambitious to be better than anyone else. Off the field he remained, according to the Secretary of the South Australian Soccer

Federation, anxious and shy.'[49]

Perkins had completed an apprenticeship as a fitter and turner after leaving the home, and he worked in a variety of jobs to make ends meet. During this period, his younger cousin, Gordon Briscoe, followed him everywhere and looked up to him. Briscoe watched him play soccer and cleaned his boots for threepence and listened to him theorise. He was fascinated by the chasm between the acceptance and rejection that his cousin experienced over the course of a Saturday afternoon: 'Early Saturday morning Perkins was an unwanted Aborigine, but by lunchtime he was a soccer star. In the evening he was a party-goer and dancer,' even if, as in Briscoe's recollection, the celebration was in 'some dingy little hotel down Rundle Mall. By bedtime he was just another blackfella who could be stopped by a policeman, liable to be asked for his pass and possibly be deported from the city.'[50] Perkins was quick to realise that soccer was a gift and also an opportunity to confront these entrenched racist disadvantages. In an interview at the time he said, 'Soccer, to me, is one way of breaking down the barriers between national, racial and language difficulties.'

Representing the State of South Australia

The successful participation of the Aboriginal boys from St Francis House on the soccer fields of South Australia was now in full swing. Like Perkins, Moriarty made the first team before the age of eighteen. He said in an interview with me in 2004, 'I sort of grew up as a ball player and playing up forward I was able to control the ball and I knew where the goals were.' A number of the Aboriginal boys made the South Australian State Intermediate team. Copley was one, Briscoe another. 'Charlie's brother, Ernie Perkins was a junior, he played in a team higher than us younger people, and he was quite a good soccer player too, but he went back to the Territory and never continued; he would have been a good player.' Moriarty later played for a number of clubs, including International United, Birkalla and Port Adelaide. Both Perkins and Moriarty made such an impact that they became

----

[49] Read, P, 2001, pp53
[50] Read, P, 2001, pp53

regulars in the South Australian state representative team. Moriarty told me, 'In particular it's those games ... competitive matches that brought out your skills as well as your spirit and your desire to play in a team and your desire to win, they were good productive times.' Copley observed in a 2004 interview, 'Moriarty and Perkins were just that good. When South Australian teams were picked, they'd be the first names on the team sheet. Gordon [Briscoe] was also a decent player, and Jerry Hill was another, whose main claim to fame is that he coached John Kosmina.'

Perkins was first selected to represent the state at senior level in 1959 against Victoria. South Australia won the match 3-2 on a waterlogged Olympic Park in Melbourne, with the South Australians adapting to the conditions far better than their opponents. 'Charlie Perkins was the outstanding player afield, and was instrumental in scoring the winning goal, when, after an amazing 60-yard [55-metre] run (challenged all the way), he was brought down eight yards [7 metre] from goal – Bruno Esca scored from the penalty spot.'[51] The second match was won by the Victorians 5-1. On a pitch described as a 'sea of sticky mud' the South Australians were outplayed, yet press commentators noted, 'Perkins again played well, but had little support.'

The following year, in a ground-breaking moment, both Perkins and Moriarty were selected in the South Australian team to visit Western Australia and played two matches against the West Australian State team. Being selected together for the state team was something special. Moriarty remembered, 'We flew over [to Perth] on our first plane trip... and that plane trip took six and a quarter hours from Adelaide to Perth in a DC-6B.' It was all so exciting for these two young men. They played in both matches against the West Australian team, drawing the first game 2-2 and losing the second 2-0. Moriarty reflected on the moment in an interview in 2004, and in particular the great understanding between him and Charlie Perkins on the pitch:

I was playing on the right wing and Charlie was right half... I scored one goal, he had a great understanding of where I'd be, and if I passed back, I'd be on the run to

51 Barkham, LF (ed), *South Australian Soccer Year Book 1960,* Webb & Son, Adelaide, 1960, pp57

get a ball right at my feet. We did that a few times. I was starting to learn that I liked the firm grounds, it was better for my control. I found the Perth ground was so good for my game, that often, I could bounce the ball and lift it over and around just bounce it over the person's head, kick it back over, and volley it... I was whisked off to the ABC studios for a radio interview [after the game] I wouldn't say boo to a goose in those days, and so shy. Those two games were memorable because it lifted your sights, you knew what the standards were in the country and you felt you could match it with anyone.

During one interstate trip in 1960, Moriarty became aware that because he was an Aboriginal, the soccer authorities had to gain permission from the Protector of Aborigines for him to travel with the team. 'This is an insult, having to seek permission from someone I've never met. Who is this person who has control over my life? Being an independent minded person, and having just turned 22, I thought I was representing the State in soccer in my own right, which was as an Australian. I thought, "this is an indignity that no-one should suffer." [52]

Charlie Perkins' International Adventure

In 1957 Charlie Perkins received an invitation from the English first division club Everton, in the city of Liverpool in northern England to go over for a trial. Everton agreed to pay sixty pounds or half of Perkins' fare to England and advised him to gain a clearance from the Australian Football Association before he left. Perkins was encouraged by friends to take the chance as it would only broaden his knowledge of the world and benefit him when he returned to Australia.

Perkins faced enormous disadvantages when traveling to Europe, setting sail on an Italian liner in the cheapest class, with little money and few clothes. The trip to Europe was a nightmare. He suffered severe seasickness and ate little. Disembarking in Genoa, he took a train to Paris, where his bag was stolen. Perkins arrived in London unshaven, with only the clothes on his back and must have resembled a tramp to the Everton officials who were there to meet him. He was given only two weeks to get himself into shape for his trial and received no encouragement from

[52] Moriarty, 2000, pp105

48

either the players or officials. Everton placed him in humble shared accommodation with an Irish player, and despite a great desire to do well Perkins understood he was at a serious disadvantage. All alone and in a totally foreign environment, it would have taken a full six months to get himself up to the level of these full-time professionals. Understandably, the trial did not go well. The standard was unimaginably high.

Perkins played one match for the Everton B team against Manchester United. The Everton players, for their part, gave him no support or encouragement and did their best to derail his chances of success. He was made to look ordinary by the players, who could place a ball on a dime at 50 metres or more, and continually played balls just out of his reach. He had a few dust-ups with them over their undermining tactics. The pitches were also completely different to those in Australia, and this would prove difficult to overcome. Perkins recalled playing in one match where the ground was so wet and heavy, 'plodding through heavy mud six inches [10 centimetres] thick and trying to kick a ball.'[53] His legs felt like lead and he locked up in a cramp. As he hobbled to the sideline, the coach screamed at him to 'get back out there in that field and keep playing.' Perkins was enraged and felt like ironing out the coach. Obviously, this venture was not going to work out, and he quit Everton.

Disheartened and homesick, Perkins often walked the Liverpool streets at night. He gained employment as a fitter at the Mersey shipyards, but racism there forced him to look elsewhere. He gained a job as a coalminer in Wigan and lived with his old friend from the St Francis Home, Wally McArthur, who was at the time regarded by many as the greatest rugby league winger in the world. The mining community had no problem accepting Perkins as one of their own.

Perkins was given a soccer opportunity with Bishop Auckland, then regarded as the best amateur team in Britain. He was an outstanding success. Now fully fit and acclimatised, his performances drew high praise. Perkins recalled later that the best match he ever played was in a game against Crook Town, who had a top-class Irish player Seamus O'Connell, in the side. Perkins was hard, tough and ruthless and O'Connell was played out of the match. Interestingly enough – for the future

53 Perkins, C, *A Bastard Like Me,* Ure Smith, Sydney, 1975, pp44

– Perkins played in a game against Oxford University, won by Bishop Auckland 1-0. During the game he thought, 'How odd it was that I, an Aborigine was playing soccer against all these university characters … it started to go through my mind that I would like to go to university one day. There on that Oxford soccer field I began to think, "Geez, it's lovely around here. These blokes are going to university. I wonder if I could go to university?" [54]

Perkins' performances with Bishop Auckland were of such high calibre that he earned the attention of some first division clubs, including one offer of a trial with Manchester United from their legendary manager, Matt Busby (Perkins' wife, Eileen, still has the letter – a wonderful piece of memorabilia with the Manchester United letterhead, signed by Busby's chief scout, Joe Armstrong). This was the Manchester team that had gained worldwide fame as the 'Busby Babes.' The team had been destroyed horrifically in an air crash in Munich the year before, and Busby was in the process of rebuilding his side. Unfortunately – because we will never know if he would have made it with Manchester United or not – Perkins, suffering acute homesickness, turned down the offer and, in 1959, accepted a paid return ticket to Australia from the Adelaide Croatia club back home. One disappointment during his final season with Bishop Auckland was when they were beaten 2-1 in the semi-final of the English Amateur Cup, and so just missed out on the opportunity to play in a final at Wembley Stadium.

Despite the initial negative experiences and disappointments in Britain, Perkins could at the conclusion of his stay, reflect, 'I've had a good time here. I've seen a lot of things, met a lot of people and found a lot of happiness. The English people in Wigan and Bishop Auckland or England generally, I suppose, are wonderful. They are decent people and give you a fair go. They treated me better than I was ever treated in Australia… [Now] I was on my way back to my country, my people and problems.' [55]

The chairman of Adelaide Croatia, Brenko Filipi, was the driving force in bringing Perkins back to captain-coach the Croatia team. Moriarty remembered Filipi as being 'rich and he drove around in a huge brand new Chevrolet.' He treated

---

[54] Perkins, 1975, pp50
[55] Perkins, 1975, pp50

Perkins like a son and took great delight in his accomplishments on the pitch. And with Perkins on the team, Croatia, who were in the South Australian second division, romped away with the title, losing only one match, winning sixteen and drawing one. They gained promotion to the first division. In addition, they won the Advertiser Cup (now the Federation Cup), beating Cumberland United 4-0 in the final, and also made the Ampol Cup Final, losing to first division giants Adelaide Juventus 1-0.

The 1959–60 season, by any measure, was a stellar one. Press coverage at the time described Perkins as 'the master tactician [who] did all the damage with his hard to combat manoeuvres... what a complete player Perkins is – recognised as one of the leading wing halves in Australia, he can move to centre forward, inside-forward or centre half and operate in a most effective manner.' [56]

The following season Perkins encouraged his cousin, Gordon Briscoe, to join him at Croatia. Initially Briscoe had played with Adelaide clubs Beograd and Polonia after leaving Port Adelaide but had moved to the country for work and was playing in Port Lincoln, representing that district in both soccer and Australian football. Reflecting on that time during an interview with me in 2004, Briscoe commented, 'All the stereotypes, well the migrants knew fuck all about that ... they didn't have those ingrained social prejudices. The new arrivals had no qualms in paying for our services on the field, they moneyed up ... because Aussie Rules didn't pay us, they gave me money in Port Lincoln to play and they paid me for scoring goals and things like that. Aussie Rules didn't pay us.'

Perkins and Briscoe had a great season with Croatia in 1961, winning the Ampol Cup Final and running third in the first division championship. Perkins was a fixture in the South Australian representative side, playing as vice-captain. If Perkins was the general on and off the field, Briscoe was his sergeant major, always at his shoulder in any stink – both on the field and off it. There were of course, family ties and connections between these two men, but it was also a bond of mutual respect, trust and admiration.

Charlie Perkins had benefited from his European adventure, As Vince Copley noted:

Going to Europe at that time and being Aboriginal was a big thing. All of those things and being homesick, Charlie said it was a very tough time, but it made him a very good soccer player. I mean he was a good one when he left, but when he got back, he was better. You could just see the difference in his style. When he came home and coached Croatia and took them to the premiership, he was just unbelievably strong. I have always said that Johnny Moriarty was such a skilled player and Charlie was a hard player. But if you wanted to pick a team Charlie would go in first.

John Moriarty - The Crowd Pleaser

There was a wealth of soccer talent at this time, and both John Moriarty and Charlie Perkins were mixing it with the very best in their representative games for South Australia. The Australian State Championships were held in Melbourne in 1960 and Moriarty and Perkins played in all three games for South Australia, including a draw with Queensland and narrow defeats to New South Wales and Victoria. In a 2004 interview with me, Moriarty reflected that the New South Wales team:

… had the Austrians Leo Baumgartner, Erwin and Herbert Ninaus, Karl Jaros, Walter Tamandl. I got on very well with Walter, Baumgartner was a dignified man, the Ninaus brothers were a lot more introverted and they were pretty tough players. Karl Jaros was a very elegant player, he played in the halves and they had other stars as well like Johnny Barr that played for Australia. We held our own in quite a number of the bigger games… Those state games that we played, were just so different, so exhilarating… different atmosphere, different standard of play, people are much sharper, you know, match your skills and your wits with the best and that really held you up. I can still smell the grass and the freshness of the turf of the training grounds.

Moriarty had an outstanding game against New South Wales. He was lightning quick, could play the ball with either foot and was very difficult to mark. South Australia won a host of free kicks, as Moriarty beat player after player. He continually frustrated the New South Wales defence, who resorted to foul play to try to stop him. Years later, he remembered, 'If this is the way professional players play, I won't have a bar of it. I'll just show them how to play real soccer.' [57] He came off the ground covered in bruises but well satisfied with his display.

Moriarty achieved a wonderful milestone at the conclusion of the 1960 State Championships in Melbourne, when he gained selection in the Australian side to tour Southeast Asia. He was the first Aboriginal selected to play soccer for his country. But sadly, he was denied the opportunity to actually play. Australia was expelled by the world governing body, FIFA, for poaching players from European clubs without paying for them. The ban lasted nearly two years and Moriarty would not be given the opportunity again. 'None of this changed the fact that I'd been picked to represent my country. I was on top of the world. I really felt I'd earned my place and I was walking on air. Of course, not getting to play was upsetting, but I was also still seething about needing permission to play soccer interstate. In fact, that was one of the things that brought me to the Aboriginal rights issues. And it did so at the beginning of a time of great activity.' [58]

Vince Copley said of Moriarty's missed opportunity: 'Had they not been thrown out by FIFA, Johnny Moriarty may have had as many caps as Johnny Warren.' Moriarty's form in the State Championship was also instrumental in him receiving an approach from Sydney club Prague. He accepted the offer and moved to Sydney. But he played only a handful of games before he found himself demoted to the reserves. Politics was at work. He gained a release back to South Australia, where his soccer skills were appreciated by the clubs and fans.

Moriarty had a father figure and guiding influence in coach and friend Mick O'Malley. O'Malley had coached him at Port Adelaide early in his career, and they worked together at Osborne Power Station. O'Malley had played as a left-back for Australia. As Moriarty recalled, 'After work he'd take me on a one to one coaching, I just loved it, he'd make me work, he'd take me for hours and hours. It didn't just develop my skills but my stamina as well, so he had me running, I'd be dead tired, and he'd kick the ball and say, "Put some pace in it and then get it," and I had to get it under control in under a second... and there were strenuous competitive things,

57 Moriarty, 2000, pp116
58 Moriarty, 2000, pp118

gymnasium work, boxing, the lot, you had to be tough to survive.'

Mick O'Malley was Irish. His family had moved from Northern Ireland to Glasgow and he'd done his national service in Malaysia. From there, he'd visited Australia and ended up settling in South Australia. He was from a family that had known struggle and his travels gave him a worldly perspective. He had escaped an Ireland riddled with narrow sectarian violence. That background encouraged him to view the world and all within it with compassion and understanding.

John Moriarty enjoyed those years of the late 1950s playing under O'Malley's guidance at Port Adelaide. He recalled when speaking with me, 'I used to confide in him a lot, particularly with my soccer... and I said, "Look I've been offered to play with Adelaide Juventus." And he said, "Listen son," with his broad accent, "Grab it with both hands, it's the best club here, the best players are there and if you want to get on with soccer, that's where you've gotta be."' So, on his mentor's advice, in 1961 Moriarty joined the Italian-supported Adelaide Juventus team. The perks were obvious - eating at fine Italian restaurants and wearing tailor-made Italian suits. 'I remember some of those competitions, I'd kick a goal and the tailor down the road would make me a tailor-made pair of trousers and the support was just phenomenal.' Moriarty proved a great favourite with the Juventus fans. 'It was the best move I've ever made, the Italian people just accepted me as if I was theirs.'

Despite the incredible acceptance Aboriginal players gained with these clubs, racism and prejudice were not entirely absent from the round-ball game. During his interview with me, Moriarty said, 'prejudice is always there, there was less of it, significantly with soccer, although I did strike it in one game and I got abused, called a black so-and-so for the whole game. I threw the ball at this bloke and hit him in the face and I was sent off, that bloke used it, and they ended up winning the game.

Charlie Perkins felt he was better equipped to deal with racism on the soccer pitch. 'Someone can call you nigger out on the football field and who cares, everybody calls everybody else names. You might have a bit of a punch-up, but you enjoy it in the push and heaving sweat, a bit of blood and slush that goes with the football.' [59]

---

[59] Read, 2001, pp64

After a couple of seasons with Juventus, John Moriarty finally decided to join the European caravan, setting sail for Europe with a group of friends in 1963. He had been previously approached about possible opportunities with English clubs Tottenham Hotspur, Arsenal and Everton, but a lack of funds had stopped him until now. When he finally took the plunge, he made an error in timing. He had planned to play in Europe, but he arrived in October. It was midseason, and it was impossible to break into it.' He went on a European sojourn with his friends instead, visiting more than thirty countries. However, he still carries disappointment over not pushing harder with soccer opportunities:

> *One of my big regrets of that time is that I didn't settle with a soccer club. I just trained in Sweden. The truth is I was really enjoying myself. I was twenty six and what really stuck out for me was meeting and mixing with people. I had always been told I was very narrow in outlook; that trip overseas broadened my outlook considerably... Even so I regretted not playing in England, or not giving it a go there. I lived with that for the rest of my life. I'll never know if I'd have made it.* [60]

Moriarty was also forthright on the difference in attitudes between people in England and those in Australia at that time. '[The English] enjoyed life; they enjoyed people for what they were. If you were a likeable person, they didn't discriminate on colour – at least the people I met didn't. In Australia discrimination was enshrined in law.'

Despite his regrets about missing a crack at top-flight European soccer, the travel broadened Moriarty's horizons immeasurably and things would never be the same. He told me, 'I was accepted in the society in Europe readily... I travelled through thirty two countries and principalities and I was never discriminated against on colour. I felt you know, why isn't Australia like this?'

After nine months of travel and wonderful times. Moriarty was called back to Australia to play for Adelaide Juventus again in the Australian soccer championships. The club paid for his flight home. He arrived back in Australia on 11 June 1964 and

---

[60] Moriarty, 2000, pp136-7

'went straight from the airport to a Juventus home game, at Hanson Reserve. When I walked onto the ground the crowd forgot the game for a moment and turned to greet me. I'll never forget that welcome. People still mention that moment to me.'[61]

In 1965 Moriarty's soccer career was prematurely brought to an end by a savage collision with a goalkeeper. The force of the impact ripped one knee cartilage completely off; the cartilage on the other side was half off. He underwent surgery in an attempt to reconstruct his knee. After months of rehabilitation, Moriarty made a comeback but lasted just two games before his knee gave out once more, ending what had been a great soccer career.

Speaking with me in 2004, Moriarty was adamant that 'soccer was a blessing for me, on the social side as well, being able to achieve my self-esteem, the culture of soccer enabled me to move out of that system that we were brought up in, you know, that totally racist system, being a second class citizen and Aboriginal under differing laws and we had to live with it. But soccer lifted me out of that because of the soccer fraternity encouraged me to do it.'

Importantly, it was during this period of the early 1960s that Moriarty, along with Perkins, came into contact with a number of influential non-Indigenous Aboriginal rights campaigners, such as Dr Charles Duguid and Don Dunstan, who encouraged them to become involved in Aboriginal affairs. Moriarty recalled, 'I started taking petitions around. Dunstan spurred us on, and we gained a lot of support, in the form of signatures and petitions, that were presented in the State Parliament.'[62] A newspaper report of the time noted that soccer players including South Australian vice-captain Charlie Perkins, John Moriarty, Gordon Briscoe and AFL players Ben Johnson and Wilf Huddleston were seeking 20,000 signatures to present to the South Australian Parliament. As Perkins declared at the time, 'All we ask is freedom – and not to be subjected to the insults that so often come our way.'

So as a stellar soccer career ended for Moriarty, another began. He was a foundation member of the local Aborigines Progressive Association and the South Australian branch of the Federal Council for the Advancement of Aborigines and Torres Strait Islanders (FCAATSI). In 1967 he completed a Bachelor of Arts in

----

61 Moriarty, 2000, pp138
62 Moriarty, 2000, pp118

history and geography at Flinders University and in 1971 was awarded a Churchill Fellowship. He moved to Canberra in 1973 to take up a position with the Department of Aboriginal Affairs (DAA) and rose rapidly. In 1974 he served with several advisory groups and subsequently moved to Melbourne as Director of the DAA for Victoria and Tasmania. The following year he was appointed national chairperson of the National Aboriginal and Islander Day Observance Committee (NAIDOC). Moriarty left the DAA in 1988 to work as a private consultant in Aboriginal affairs to public and business agencies. He and his wife, Ros, also run the design firms Jumbunna (Moriarty's Aboriginal name) and Balarinji, producing high-quality fashion goods inspired by Aboriginal arts and crafts, most famously the designs worn at one time by Qantas staff and carried by a number of Qantas elaborately decorated aircraft.

Gordon Briscoe - 'The Big O'

Gordon Briscoe decided to follow the example of Charlie Perkins and in 1959 travelled to England to further his soccer career. He was offered a trial with Hemel Hempstead Rovers, an English amateur team just outside London. The trial went well; he made the first team and enjoyed his soccer. He obviously impressed some scouts because he was offered a trial with first division club Preston North End. Preston had a proud past and also an Australian connection. Joe Marston the renowned player from Sydney who in the 1950s pioneered the international career path followed by so many Australian players - spent five seasons with Preston North End in the early 1950s and played in a losing FA Cup Final with them in 1954.

During his time with Preston, Briscoe played matches for the B, C and reserve teams. Famous international Tom Finney was assistant coach at the time. It was tough playing matches in heavy snow, ice, mud and rain, and just when Briscoe appeared to be settling in, he injured his ankle badly and it took months to heal. The injury curtailed his hopes of breaking through with a soccer career. The game was not paying the bills and he got work at a steel fabrication factory. Briscoe met his wife, Norma, in the United Kingdom, and they married and lived there happily. In an interview with me in 2004, he agreed with Moriarty and Perkins' comments about England, saying that he found great acceptance there:

Well, they didn't know what an Aboriginal person was, and because of our background, we'd say, "I'm an Aboriginal" ... and they'd say, "Well what's that?", and then we'd have to explain our background. But they treated you in the same European way, they were very self-interested. And that's how we were able to get past some of the problems. If you could play soccer, amongst people who knew something about soccer, you were put on a pedestal... if the coach said, "You do this, and you do that", and you did that, and then you did that well, you were given an opportunity to go further up the slippery pole.[63]

It is probably fortunate that Perkins, Moriarty and Briscoe were in England during the late 1950s and early 1960s. At that time, it was a place of near full employment, with a strong economy. The large intake of migrants in the aftermath of World War II, particularly from the West Indies, Pakistan and India, had not yet become the subject of concern and vocal opposition from the wider population. But by the mid to late 1960s with the British economy in decline and competition for jobs and housing high, racism and prejudice would become rampant.

Gordon Briscoe was not in the same class of soccer player as Charlie Perkins or John Moriarty. This is supported by those who saw all three play and also by the fact that there is little archival evidence available about his playing career. Perkins and Moriarty, in contrast, gained a lot of press coverage and accolades. But this oversimplifies the situation. One cannot escape the fact that Gordon Briscoe played with an English first division club – no mean feat, and one that obviously stamps him as a very good player in his own right. Briscoe was not a crowd pleaser with dazzling ball skills, nor a general who dominated the pitch. He was, however, an outstanding athlete and a 90-minute team player who gave his all on the field.

After returning to Australia in 1964, Briscoe's soccer career scaled down. He relocated to Sydney and studied at night during his early years there, matriculating to the Australian National University in 1969. In 1971 he accepted a position as a field officer with the recently established Aboriginal Legal Service in Sydney. In the same year he and Shirley Smith (Mum Shirl) established the Aboriginal Medical Service in Redfern and persuaded Fred Hollows to become its first Medical

---

[63] Authors interview with Gordon Briscoe, 7th October 2004, Canberra

Director. With Hollows as director and Briscoe as assistant director, the two men later cooperated in running the national trachoma and eye health program. This program had screened 110,000 people by 1981, when Hollows and Briscoe resigned from it in protest against Commonwealth government proposals to pass Aboriginal health funding to the states.

In 1972 Briscoe attempted to enter federal parliament. As an Australia Party candidate, he unsuccessfully contested the sole Northern Territory seat in the House of Representatives against the sitting Country Party member, Sam Calder. Briscoe moved to Canberra in 1974, where he worked in ensuing years for the Commonwealth Department of Health, Aboriginal Hostels Ltd, the Central Australian Aboriginal Congress and at the Australian Institute of Aboriginal and Torres Strait Islander Studies (AIATSIS). He studied at university throughout the 1980s and 1990s, gaining a Bachelor of Arts, Master of Arts and PhD from the Australian National University. In 2004, in recognition of decades of work on behalf of his people, Gordon Briscoe was awarded an Order of Australia.

The Push for Change

Charles Perkins had returned from England not just a much better soccer player but also more worldly wise. He was anxious to force change but quickly learned that 'Adelaide society was as racist as it had always been.' Despite success on the soccer pitch and the acceptance and reverence that he, Moriarty and Briscoe, were afforded by the migrant communities, the racism, prejudice and oppression of wider white Australia were always present in their daily lives. At dances Perkins would still catch the loud whisper, 'Who told that boong to come in here?' John Moriarty recalled, 'That rejection seemed to hurt Perkins the most: Charlie was bitter toward white women.' The sense of stigma, and the impact of such shocking racism on a person's self-confidence, are clearly evident in Perkin's memories:

> I used to go to the dances at Port Adelaide Town Hall. And the room would be
> full. Now you imagine this scenario, how you'd feel. You're an Aboriginal.
> Everybody knows you walked in the room, no other Aborigines there. All the
> girls'd be round the side. Remember how they used to do it in the old days.

And all the blokes'd be up the other end, right? The music'd start and you go to one, asking. I used to make a point of going and asking each one. They'd all knock you back.' Oh, we don't dance with Aborigines.' 'I don't dance with blacks.' Everyone. I'd go right down the whole lot. Then I'd do it again, and with the lights on as well. It's hard going you know. I had a couple of dances, but not many, mainly more by accident. Everyone's watching as well, and they're all your age. Then I'd go to the next one. You wanta try that... I was not going to back down for no bastard. No one was not going to let me be where I wanted to be. You're torn apart – but what do you do? It's awkward, it's embarrassing, terribly embarrassing, it's very difficult, but you go and do it anyhow. You gotta do it. [64]

One thing incidents like this emphasised was the strength, conviction and courage of Charles Perkins.

But this enforced social isolation changed dramatically when he met his future wife, Eileen, at a dance – at a soccer function, she later recalled. 'I'd just come back from [holidays] in New Zealand, an old friend invited us to go to a soccer function, and I noticed him come in with his friend Gordon Briscoe... he just seemed to float across the room, and looked very distinguished... so the friend introduced us. And that's how I met Charlie... Two weeks later I knew I was going to get married to him.' Charlie Perkins was immediately accepted by Eileen's parents – being Aboriginal was no issue for them. Although as Eileen pointed out, her parents had no time for a previous boy she had brought home – he was a Catholic!

Eileen recognised the impact soccer had on Charlie and its importance to him. In an interview with me in 2004 she said:

It was something that he just adored. He loved the sophistication of the game, the brainwork that went into it, and the natural ability that he had, it just clicked for him, and also that he was accepted by the people who were playing soccer in those days, which were the New Australians, and he was totally accepted, being so good at the game and so handsome, they just all adored him, and so it just meant so much to him, opened many doors to him. I only met him

----

[64] Read, 2001, pp48

after he'd been to England, so he'd been playing soccer a fair while and was very well established by that time… that season I met him, they won the Cup, he was captain coach of Croatia, and to win the Cup, well, I couldn't help but be impressed, could I?

There was also an unmistakable bond between Perkins, Briscoe and Moriarty. Eileen recalled, 'I don't know how close they were as children, but certainly as teenagers and young men, they were very close, and I wonder if it just was soccer that bonded them, I think with soccer, it's such an intelligent game.' John Moriarty expressed similar sentiments, saying that Perkins and Briscoe 'played [together], they boarded together, they stuck together, very close with their game and social life… But we were all close, in a sense that we were together, you know?' There was an unquestionable bond of lived experience between the three young men.

Midway through the 1961 season with Croatia, Charlie Perkins became restless for new challenges. The thought of university study, which had first been sparked on a soccer pitch in Oxford, was now a high priority. He discussed his plan with his new wife and his mentor, Branko Filipi. Both encouraged his dream. This was obviously a difficult decision for the Croatia club chairman because he was supporting the loss of a player regarded at the time as 'the most experienced and accomplished player in South Australia', as well as the young man who he had virtually adopted. But Perkins had decided that Sydney was the best place for him now, and a university degree was his main aim. 'When I came to Sydney my deep interest in sport was transferred more to Aboriginal affairs. I realised that Sydney was the centre of the mass media and this was where I could get an opinion across to people in Australia.' [65]

Charlie and Eileen Perkins moved to Sydney in 1961 and he enrolled at the University of Sydney, studying arts. He had in his mind that soccer would pay his way through university. He trained with the Bankstown soccer club for a week but was told he would not make the team. He had a discussion over coffee with officials from the Sydney Prague club, but they also declined his service A lucky meeting with an old soccer chum, Hungarian Les Suchanek, put him in touch with the wealthy Greek-backed club, Pan Hellenic. He had a training run with them and was given a run against arch rivals Sydney Prague in a trial match. Perkins was never one to let an opportunity go begging. He had an outstanding debut, scoring a second-half hat-trick that sent the Greek fans mad with delight. He was an instant celebrity with the Greek community, and he and Eileen were guests at every Greek restaurant, café and deli in inner Sydney. Within three months he was captain of the club, and in six months, captain-coach.

Vince Copley highlighted this acceptance, and he noted the sacrifices that Perkins and his wife made when they moved from South Australia:

His success with Pan Hellenic in Sydney ... The Greeks loved him, and he did do it hard. When he and his wife finally left South Australia, they'd just got married, the money wasn't there. He called himself an electrical fitter but that was not going to be his calling, he had an urge for the betterment of Aboriginal affairs around the country. He and Eileen had to battle through some tough times, but they came out on top and that just shows the courage that they both had, you know what I mean. For him to get over anything, any racism that was occurring in his life at the time off the field, was not easy. But to the Greek community he was revered.

Eileen Perkins confirmed Copley's view in an interview with me in 2004. She recalled that after moving to Sydney, they were in struggle town. 'The Greeks would always give us free food, and you know, another kilo of bananas if we bought one, they were very generous, but we didn't partake of that too much, because we were always home, he was studying. It's a little bit incorrect to say that soccer financed his university. It was five pounds if you lost, ten for a draw and fifteen for a win.'

At the start of the 1962 Sydney soccer season, Perkins was front-page news in *Soccer World*. An article headlined 'Australian Star Parade' showcased both his soccer ability and his future direction:

Pan Hellenic's only Australian born player is also Sydney's most 'dinky-di' soccer star. Charlie Perkins is part Aboriginal born in Alice Springs 26 years ago... Toward the end of last year, Charlie Perkins a qualified fitter and turner, settled in Sydney and progressive Pan Hellenic signed him. He proved an immediate success and he should be a real crowd pleaser in the coming competition. A clever, scientific forward with a well-placed shot, Perkins has already made his mark on Pan Hellenic's forward line, which is playing with much more finesse. One of this fine players' aims in life is to fight for equal status for [A]boriginals. He is very active in social work and truly a tremendous personality on and off the field.

Perkins' three-year career with Pan Hellenic was an exciting period in his soccer life. The young Pan Hellenic club had only won promotion to the Sydney first division in 1961. Perkins began scoring regularly. In a match against South Coast United, Pan Hellenic won 2-0, with Perkins scoring and receiving five-star notices. As reported in *Soccer World,* both teams thrilled the crowd of more than 3,600 'with fast vigorous play, which switched from end to end. South Coast had more of the play in the first half, but it was all Pan Hellenic in the second half when Perkins gave a superb display of skill and general ship to lead his side to a convincing win.' He scored again against Bankstown in a hard fought 2-0 victory in front of 3800 people. Again, in *Soccer World:* 'Pan Hellenic completely outplayed Bankstown... The Bankstown half-back line was off form and proved unable to cope with Perkins' men.'

The reason the Greek supporters loved Perkins was undoubtedly his passion and commitment to the game:

I used to play my guts out. I'd play the game till I could play no more. I gave it everything. I'd just about bleed on the field. That's what I always told the players. I said, 'Look I want your blood outta you when you are playing, I want blood. I don't want no half measures, you've gotta give everything, 120 per cent. You gotta die to win.' And I used to do the same. I remember one time I fell over in a tackle and the ball was running past and the bloke came in to kick it – and I put my head on it! I think back how crazy that was, but I was determined to win. [66]

---

[66] Read, 2001, pp74

Perkins was Pan Hellenic's leading scorer in 1962, and his sparkling form during the season saw him selected in the New South Wales state squad to play Queensland. The following year Pan Hellenic made the minor semi-final, losing to South Coast United. The pre-game program described the Pan Hellenic team as one 'characterised by boundless enthusiasm, incredible determination and moderate polish. On a given day, when the ball runs for them, Pan Hellenic are just about the hardest team to beat.' Perkins himself was described in the press in glowing terms: 'In Charlie Perkins, skipper and right half, they have at once an intelligent, hard solid player who tries to put 100 minutes into 90.'

In February 1964 Perkins decided that despite three great seasons with Pan Hellenic and incredible fan support, it was time to move on. His new club was Bankstown. After a flying start to the season, Bankstown sat on top of the premiership table and Perkins' contribution was considerable according to the press: 'Perkins' brilliant attacking performances at left half have put Bankstown on the road to premiership success.' In one important match, Perkins was at the centre of a brilliant victory and post-match fist fight, which made the papers: 'In the biggest upset in years Bankstown had outplayed Prague to win 3-1. After the referee had blown full-time Prague centre forward Norbert Boradaracco went "looking" for Bankstown halfback Charlie Perkins. Both players came to blows and Perkins had his mouth split. The players were separated by club officials and other players.'

But the successful start was not sustained, and Bankstown fell away in the title race. Throughout the season, Perkins struggled with injuries, university studies and frequent suspensions after being sent off. Perkins' love for the game was being tempered by his now-frequent appearances before the New South Wales Disciplinary Committee. He was quoted in the press at the time:

What I've copped this year is unbelievable... soccer referees appear to pick on me all the time. I think it is a question of giving a dog a bad name... I've really been given the run-around this season and my enthusiasm is disappearing fast. This latest incident was typical, I was 30 yards away from the free kick and then I find I'm being sent off... I thought it was for swearing and now I find out it was for a rude gesture... But my confidence is sapped. I'm scared stiff to play my natural game.

I play the game hard, the way I was taught with Bishop Auckland in England. After all soccer is a man's game. But I played it fair and don't go in for the dirty, niggling tactics of some players. I love the game but if I get picked on again then I shall give it away for good.

Perkins was also suffering from serious ongoing kidney problems. He had first felt the impact of kidney trouble while living in ramshackle shared accommodation in Adelaide with Gordon Briscoe and some other young men. He woke one morning freezing cold and too sick to go to work. After three days in bed with severe chills, he drove himself to hospital. He thought he was dying. He was diagnosed with nephritis, a serious inflammation of the kidneys – what people once referred to as 'a cold in the kidney.'

From Perkins' perspective, this was the start of years of problems with his kidneys. And it would persist. In his last season with Bankstown he couldn't understand why, despite training relentlessly, he tired badly at the end of each game. Eileen Perkins reflected on the impact that the illness was having on her husband. 'When I first met him [in Adelaide], in that nine months, he was hospitalised, with kidney problems... And it's just amazing that he was able to play soccer professionally in Sydney.'

After Professional Soccer

In the press Charlie Perkins the soccer player was described as 'an Aborigine and mighty proud of it.' He understood the importance of promoting his achievements, but more meaningful to him personally was that he had to be seen as an Aboriginal achiever. For Perkins, it was not just about taking on opponents on the soccer field but tackling head on all of the ingrained and unfounded stereotypes that wider Australian society held about Aboriginal people. By 1964, his goals and objectives had become fixed in his sights. 'With my new status and the financial rewards, it brought, I was now in a position to pursue my immediate objective of a university career, and beyond that, I hoped a revolution in race relations in Australia. [67]

....

[67] Read, 2001, pp66

Perkins graduated from the University of Sydney in 1965. He was only the second Aboriginal person to graduate from an Australian university, and as Eileen Perkins told me in a 2004 interview, he was adamant that he was 'the first to identify [himself as an Aboriginal] … you know it took courage to identify in those days, that was half the struggle.'

He then embarked with a group of non-Indigenous university students on the Freedom Ride - and eventual Aboriginal political immortality. This trip across rural New South Wales emulated the Freedom Rides of Martin Luther King and the United States Civil Rights Movement. They visited outback towns in New South Wales and brought the shocking living and health conditions of Aboriginal people to the attention of the media and wider general public. Through the media, they revealed the deep racism, prejudice and segregation imposed over Aboriginal people by the rural communities. Aboriginal people were denied access to theatres, swimming pools, hotels and, in some cases, even the streets of the towns.

The Australian Freedom Ride will forever remain one of the pivotal moments in Aboriginal history, and it provided the perfect political and public launching pad for Perkins. From that point and for the remainder of his life, he was at the forefront of Aboriginal political activism. He would play a role through the Foundation of Aboriginal Affairs in the campaign that led to the overwhelming 'Yes' vote in the 1967 Referendum, which gave the federal government joint power with the states over Aboriginal affairs in the Australian states. He would contribute decades of his working life to tirelessly battling to improve Aboriginal living conditions, as a public servant with the Department of Aboriginal Affairs (DAA) and later with the Aboriginal and Torres Strait Islander Commission (ATSIC).

After so many years, soccer now took a back seat in Perkins' life. But his love of the game would stay with him for the rest of his life. He and his family moved to Canberra. There, in 1970, his kidneys collapsed. He received a transplant and, as Eileen Perkins said in an interview in 2004, 'It kicked him along again… he met a lot of friends in soccer, in Canberra, and he helped establish clubs and his love of soccer just kept him involved.' Perkins continued to play recreational soccer with the Canberra Old Boys, alongside old mate Johnny Warren. Eileen Perkins recalled, 'Johnny Warren was such a fanatic. Charlie injured his knee, Johnny wouldn't let him go off the field and after that injury there was no more dancing.

I used to curse Johnny Warren for that'.

The Australian Capital Territory Shadow Minister for Sport and Recreation of that time, the late Steve Doszpot, a long-time close friend of Perkins and a team-mate in the Canberra Old Boys, recalled those days in correspondence with me. 'As the name suggests, we weren't exactly novices, but we did play against mostly younger teams in the Canberra League 6th Division, like the [Royal Military College] Duntroon Cadets, who would do umpteen laps of the oval before the match, while we got puffed out by simply doing up our bootlaces.' Dozspot reflected that Perkins was having trouble with his knees, ankles or feet, but that rarely stopped him from playing. 'He mostly ignored the pain and was an incredible sight as he beat players half his age. Sometimes when the pain became too much, and he just couldn't run, he would end up in goals and even there he showed the class of his football pedigree as he pulled off saves that Mark Schwarzer would be proud of today.

Dozspot remembered one very funny incident when former world bantamweight boxing champion Lionel Rose came along with Perkins to watch a game. After the match they dropped Lionel off at Tuggeranong, in southern Canberra, where he was staying with friends. But the friends weren't at home and Lionel had forgotten his keys. Dozspot said, 'So there we were on all fours, with Lionel climbing on our backs – and he was no featherweight by this stage – to try and get in through a window, when Charlie asked Lionel, "You sure this is the right house?" Lionel admitted he wasn't totally sure. We just all collapsed laughing, with Charlie looking at the possible headlines the next day: "Perkins and Rose Arrested in Tuggeranong House Break-in."

During the 1990s, back in Sydney, as Eileen tells it, 'even, like, up until probably three years before he passed away, he'd go Sundays and play soccer. He'd stand in the goals if his knee was too bad… they'd meet at the pub after the game on Sundays, and it was such therapy for him, just to, you know be with the boys, and all that sort of stuff, so it served him all his life, his love of soccer. He went overseas, he saw two World Cups, he just got a lot of satisfaction out of soccer.'

Both Charlie Perkins and John Moriarty would give back to the game through serving on the boards of several prominent soccer bodies. Perkins was president of National Soccer League (NSL) team Canberra City, vice-president of the Australian Soccer Federation (ASF) from 1987 to 1989, and president of the Australian Indoor

Soccer Federation for ten years. John Moriarty served as a board member of Adelaide Juventus (later Adelaide City) and acted as an advisor to Football Federation Australia.

Ever the visionary in outlook, Perkins during his time as vice-president of the ASF, envisaged a very different approach and future for the game than some were prepared to support. A report in *Australian Soccer Weekly* soon after his election indicated that he intended to take it to the top, even if that meant challenging for the top position in the future. 'Perkins is known for his vigour in any problem that he tackles. He said: "My aim is to increase the image of the sport. We will have our share of media coverage. I don't know whether I will press ahead for the ASF presidency, but sometimes you have to move ahead with your aspirations."'

Only months later, press reports circulated that Perkins was mounting a campaign to take charge of the ASF and set an exciting new course for Australian soccer, one that would have been decades ahead of its time. *Australian Soccer Weekly* reported:

> *Have no doubt about it – Charlie Perkins is testing the water to see if he has the support to become the next President of the Australian Soccer Federation.*
> *'I will only be prepared to handle the job if I am wanted. It will call for the implementation of a corporate plan to lift the standard and image of the game... There is a deliberate campaign to hold soccer down. We have no image, no base and no authority in the sport. We have to have a product. If so, crowds can be doubled. A media strategy is required. We must pound on doors to see that we get pages towards the back of the afternoon papers. We are a big force in this country We have never used our muscle, but now we have to turn around and insist on what we want.'*

Perkins served as vice-president of the ASF with distinction throughout his two year term, but his dreams of change were thwarted from within. Johnny Warren was forthright about the soccer authorities' failure to take up the opportunity that Charlie Perkins presented to them, as reported in the *National Indigenous Times*: 'The tragedy is that [Perkins] had so much to offer the game, but because he never backed away from his opinions the hierarchy couldn't handle him. [Perkins] wanted change, but those who run the game have never been keen on that.'

Perkins remained at the forefront of the Aboriginal fight for justice until his untimely death in 2000. Throughout his dynamic and often turbulent political career, he was compared to such individuals as Martin Luther King Jr and Nelson Mandela. His death left a void in Aboriginal political affairs that has been impossible to fill. Johnny Warren had no hesitation in stating, 'Perkins was a champion – a real Ben Hur, smashing his way through Australia's race politics, and football was his first chariot'. [68]

Warren himself passed away four years after Perkins. As one correspondent noted at the time, Warren would 'be fondly remembered by our Indigenous community as being a life-long supporter of various campaigns and a proud adherent of the "black armband" view of Australian history. When his old mate Charlie Perkins passed away a few years back, Johnny gave a beautiful speech about the unifying power of sport, that the blackfella and the whitefella are equal as soon as the whistle blows. He said we should all be working towards universalising those parameters.'

Exceptional Men of their Time

Charles Perkins, John Moriarty and Gordon Briscoe, running against the grain, made an indelible imprint on Australian soccer and Australian society. Some fell under the spell of these men and their achievements. Warren Mundine was one who could remember how Perkins and Moriarty inspired him to play soccer in the early 1960s. He told the *Australian* in 2009:

> *I was about six years old and John Moriarty, who was the first Aborigine selected for the national team, came and visited us with Charlie Perkins. I remember it was a big buzz for us around the house. They were the flashest blacks I'd ever seen, they had the cleanest shoes, and those two blokes were also champion footballers. I was very impressed.*

....

[68] Warren, 2002: ppxx

Some say fate has a major role to play in anyone's life, and when you look at the lives of these three individuals, there is little doubt about that sentiment. Certainly, being taken from their families at a young age and placed in a boy's home in Adelaide, close to a soccer playing area, was a major reason for their rise to prominence. Of equal importance was the acceptance they gained from the migrant communities in the wake of post-World War II immigration, and the influence of international travel and experience, which broadened their outlooks. The combination of a successful sporting career and subsequent high-level achievement at university is highly unusual for top sportspeople – in any sport. The time at university ensured that Perkins, Moriarty and Briscoe were articulate and eloquent activists, armed with educational knowledge that was tempered by grassroots experience of pain and hardship.

All three men were high achievers on and off the soccer pitch and were recognised for their services to Aboriginal people and communities. Moriarty was awarded an AM and Perkins and Briscoe were both recognised with an AO. They remain inspiring role models for current and future generations of Aboriginal people.

CHAPTER 5
The Aboriginal Socceroos

In the years after Perkins, Moriarty and Briscoe retired from soccer, there was an explosion of activity in Aboriginal affairs, in which all three men played a major part. Perkins had led the 1965 Freedom Ride across New South Wales. The Gurindji walk-off at Wave Hill over land and working conditions took place in 1966. The 1967 Referendum was intended as a new era for Aboriginal people, with the Commonwealth Government now having the power to make laws for Aboriginal people in the states. The Protection Boards were abolished, and the assimilation directives of decades were swept away with a new policy and catch cry of 'self-determination'. Aboriginal activists took to the streets in mass demonstrations and a revolution in Aboriginal policy was in the air.

Despite the optimism and hope in the wake of the 1967 Referendum, disillusion, frustration and depression quickly followed. A succession of federal governments made little headway in easing the living conditions and inequality experienced by Aboriginal people and communities.

In 1972, the Aboriginal Tent Embassy was established on the lawns of Parliament House in Canberra, to protest the Commonwealth Government's continued lack of action over legitimate Aboriginal claims. This highly innovative action sparked a heavy-handed police response. The Embassy occupants issued a petition outlining a five point plan, which addressed Aboriginal rights to land, including mineral deposits; preservation of all sacred sites; $6 million in compensation; control over the Northern Territory as a state within the Commonwealth; the parliament in the Northern Territory to have an Aboriginal majority, and title and mining rights to all land within the Northern Territory.

The Embassy witnessed the birth of a powerful and sustained movement. Mass demonstrations by Aboriginal people and their supporters coincided with the 1988 Bicentennial celebrations. In the 1990s the High Court ruled in the Mabo case that native title existed over particular sections of land; the Commonwealth Government passed a new law dealing with land rights called the Native Title Act; the report of the Royal Commission into Aboriginal Deaths in Custody was tabled; the Human Rights and Equal Opportunity Commission undertook an inquiry into the separation of Aboriginal and Torres Strait Islander children from their families, and the subsequent findings were published as the *Bringing Them Home* Report. The reconciliation movement began, and in the Corroboree 2000 walk across Sydney Harbour Bridge, half a million people marched in support of Aboriginal people. In 2004 the Commonwealth Government abolished the first and only nationally elected body representing Aboriginal people, the Aboriginal and Torres Strait Islander Commission (ATSIC), established in 1987, which left Aboriginal Australia without a unified national voice. Somewhere along this roller-coaster ride of Aboriginal experiences, Aboriginal involvement in the world game unexpectedly and suddenly, finally took off.

Harry Williams – 'Fancy Nancy'

Coinciding with the start of this tumultuous time was the arrival of the man regarded by many as the greatest ever Aboriginal soccer player, Harry Williams. Many years after his extraordinary career on the pitch, I contacted Harry, then living in Canberra, and rode around with him while he bought some new tyres. When the tyres were being fitted, we had a coffee and discussed his career. He later wrote a note of support: 'I believe your work is vitally important not only to the Koori community but also to the wider community and indeed the [soccer] fraternity.'

Williams was a lightning fast and extremely skillful fullback renowned for his electric overlapping runs down the line. He played in the all-conquering St George Budapest side of the early 1970s. This team bristled with international players like Mike Denton, Adrian Alston, Johnny Warren, Manfred Schaefer, Atti Abonyi, Jim Fraser and Alan Ainslie. St George was without doubt the glamour side of Australian soccer at the time and was coached by Frank Arok. Harry Williams made 43 appearances for the Socceroos, including 20 full caps and will be forever remembered as a member of the Australian side that qualified for the 1974 World Cup finals in West Germany. Interestingly, the exploits of Perkins, Moriarty and Briscoe did not play a part in his choice of sporting career.

For a fullback of those times, Williams was very gifted. I was privileged to see him in action during his peak years. His rise was meteoric, to say the least, as he was selected for the national team after making just six first division appearances for St George. He started his career as a striker and only moved to fullback to cover for an injured player. He recalled in the *Koori Mail* in 2005: 'Because of my attacking flair, I also chimed-in in attack, so I was an overlapping fullback. In a lot of ways, I became like a second winger.'

It was Williams' showboating skills on the training paddock that gained him the nickname 'Fancy Nancy'. He said that you needed to be very disciplined in a match as a defender, but at training, 'There were times I couldn't resist and tried all sorts of tricks. One-night Atti Abonyi started calling me "Fancy Nancy" and that's how I was often known with the players.'[69] Johnny Warren had similar memories of Williams' entertainment value and skill: 'He was a tremendous talent and a terrific bloke to have on tour. He played as an attacking left-sided winger [fullback] and was one of those players who loved to entertain the crowd with fancy tricks and dazzling skills. All the boys used to call him "Fancy Nancy" because he was always trying something out of the ordinary.'[70]

Immensely proud of his Aboriginal background, Williams is adamant that his heritage was never an issue on the field: 'No one went about congratulating me because I was an Aboriginal soccer player.' He was equally forthcoming on his own fortunate introduction to the game and Aboriginal people's limited exposure to it. 'The opportunity for Indigenous Australians to play soccer was probably more limited. Most Aboriginal communities were introduced to league, union, Australian football, boxing and to some degree basketball. I was exposed to soccer by a friend across the street at six years of age. For me, it was just a question of circumstances. It just happened. Maybe, it was fate, or maybe it was chance. In hindsight, maybe it could be called luck.'[71] He was adamant that there was pressure to play other codes.

69 Wallace, N, *Our Socceroos,* Random House, Sydney, 2004, pp71
70 Warren, J, *Sheilas, Wogs and Poofters,* Random House, Sydney, 2002, pp187
71 Wallace, 2004, pp70

Here was an Aboriginal kid growing up in the rugby league heartland of the mighty 1960s St George Dragons, and many thought he would have chosen league. 'Billy Smith [St George half-back of the 1960s and 1970s] was a good family friend and he always said to stop playing that sissy game and come to play rugby league.'

Like the earlier Aboriginal soccer groundbreakers, Williams was also candid about the impact of the migrant communities, and the connection that he experienced with them. In the *Sydney Morning Herald* in 2006 he remembered, 'I actually always felt at home with the migrant communities. We found common ground through the round ball, and the shared interest built up a great understanding. We were all soccer players, and it didn't matter where we were from. Soccer is a great leveler for that all over the world.'

Harry Williams first broke through with the Socceroos on their ambitious 1970 World Tour, which followed their near-miss qualification for the 1970 World Cup finals in Mexico. This was a tour that brought a squad of young players to the fore, who would serve Australian soccer with outstanding success. Under a young coach, Rale Rasic, the squad included players like Peter Wilson, Jack Reilly, Jimmy Rooney, Ray Richards, Jim Mackay, Colin 'Bunny' Curran and Adrian Alston. For Williams, it wasn't just being selected in the Australian squad for the first time that had him prickling with excitement; before then, the furthest he'd ever travelled was the ferry to Manly. As a member of the Socceroos he became an instant international jetsetter, visiting exotic locations like Hong Kong, China, Israel, Iran, Greece, Switzerland, England, Ireland and Mexico. Iran in particular was one of the most challenging places. There were armed guards everywhere, 50,000 men - no women - in the crowd, and thirty-foot high [ten-metre] fences around the ground. 'We were away for eight weeks and, in many ways, it was really the start of the unity and preparation required for the '74 World Cup.' [72]

The tour was an outstanding success and produced several impressive victories, including wins over Greece and Israel. The victory over Israel in Tel Aviv at least provided some comfort and revenge for the loss to Israel at the final hurdle in the World Cup qualifications the year before. Rale Rasic proved himself an astute coach and tactician, with a great capacity to motivate young players. He recalled

....

[72] Wallace, 2004, pp68

74

one light-hearted incident involving Harry Williams on the tour:

'It was in Luton [in England] that some of the players were given an awful fright one night. [Adrian] Alston was showing some of the players a few sights in the area when he pointed to a far paddock where two girls had been murdered years earlier. It was said that when there was a full moon the girls would appear.

'This night the boys saw a shrouded dark figure distinguished by white teeth across the paddock. For once, Alston, the joker of the squad, was speechless. But as the figure drew closer the nerves eased. It was Harry Williams, the only Aborigine in the squad. Harry had a great laugh when told why the players were so quiet and looking very pale.'

Harry is a great guy with a terrific sense of humour. He was always easy going even though he was on the end of light-hearted comments from team-mates such as: 'Come out of the shadows, we can't see you' and 'If you don't watch it, we will give you a white eye'. Rasic reflected they were 'different days I guess, and I suppose things like that would not do in these days of political correctness.'[73] Williams took no notice of the banter and had plenty of comebacks of his own. He later emphasised that being part of that Socceroos squad was being a part of a family:

There were jokes and banter with the other players, just like there was with guys from other backgrounds, but that was it. Things like Noddy [Alston] asking me to smile in the dark so that he could see me ... so I'd remind him that he was only a £10 Pom, then ask him when he last had a bath. No one took offence because this is a big part of Aussie humour, and everyone would take a gentle dig at each other, just to get a laugh. It was a part of the atmosphere of the squad in the early 70s. It was a big family where the players were the kids, and Rale played the father figure. In fact, he still does.[74]

Williams was a regular selection on this tour and would cement his spot in Socceroos squads for nearly a decade to come. He made his debut for the Socceroos in a match against a provincial side from Macau, becoming the first Aboriginal international soccer player: 'It was still a very special feeling to pull on the green

73 Gatt, R, *The Rale Rasic Story,* New Holland Publishers, Sydney, 2006, pp68
74 Wallace, 2004, pp70

and gold shirt. It is a huge honour to play for your country, and I was made to feel very welcome by Rale Rasic and the squad.' Williams was part of what was regarded as a golden era for Australian fullbacks. Several outstanding individuals graced the Australian team during the 1970s and 1980s, including the likes of Doug Utjesenovic, Colin Curran, Bobby Hogg, George Harris and Jim Tansey. The quality of those players competing for spots makes Williams' record of appearances even more impressive.

Undoubtedly, one of his greatest achievements was being selected for the successful Socceroos squad for the 1974 World Cup finals in West Germany. Williams only came on as a replacement for Colin 'Bunny' Curran in the final match, against Chile, which ended in a 0-0 draw, but that was enough to ensure that he would go down as the first Aboriginal player to play in the World Cup finals. The Socceroos had been beaten 2-0 by East Germany and 3-0 by eventual winners West Germany in their earlier matches, but their performances as part-timers up against full-time professionals was inspiring. Years later, in a 2009 interview with the *Weekend Australian,* Warren Mundine could still recall watching Harry Williams come on to the field in his history-making moment on a 'flickering black and white TV ... 'He was the first Aborigine to make the World Cup and he definitely won't be the last. With his big afro hair, he was a great inspiration to us all, because in those days only a handful of us played the game.'

Looking back at the World Cup finals experience, Williams said, 'We were all pretty excited about qualifying. It was a once in a lifetime thing for all of us ... Just to get there [to Germany] and actually play was a bonus ... we were all part-timers who had full-time jobs.

Coach Rale Rasic recalled, 'The 1974 World Cup was like Gallipoli to Australia - a special moment in history ... Our players were heroes, but they were not treated as such by the federation. Yet the Australian media, especially those sections not normally involved in soccer, were absolutely marvellous to us - before, during and after the tournament.'[75]

The 1974 Socceroos embodied the sense of unity and strength that was to be a

....

[75] Micallef, P, *The World Cup Story: An Australian View,* Philip Micallef Publishing, Sydney, 1994, pp112

feature of Socceroos squads in the future. In an interview in the *Sydney Morning Herald* in 2006 Williams said:

> *It was the start of the formation of the new Socceroos - it was an exciting time ... We were a very strong unit - that was our underlying strength in 1974, the key factor that got us through and the reason we are still close today. We were a bunch of part-timers who trained three days a week after work. Our focus was going to work, feeding our families and paying the bills. There was a tremendous camaraderie - we were prepared to go out and die for each other.*

Harry Williams also took part in Australia's unsuccessful 1978 World Cup finals qualification campaign. Rasic, who was highly respected by the players, had been controversially replaced as the Socceroos coach by an inexperienced and virtually unknown Englishman, Jimmy Shoulder. Years of factional infighting, greed and division among the Australian soccer authorities undermined and derailed all hopes of capitalising on the 1974 successes. After early victories over Taiwan and New Zealand, the Australian team finished last in the final group of Iran, South Korea, Kuwait and Hong Kong. Williams reflected on these changed times: 'The atmosphere in later Socceroo camps was different mainly due to the change in player personnel. It's like when you walk into someone's house, and it can feel like a home straight away - but when you walk into another place it has a different feel about it. The chairs, tables, walls and roof are all there, but one feels totally different to the other. The '70 – 74' squad was home; it was family.' [76]

There was also a high personal cost in being a part of the Socceroos teams in those days. The players were not full-time professionals and they had jobs in the real world. Williams lost jobs because of the travel and overseas tours. 'I found work again reasonably easy, but it wasn't the best way to live. I also lost a marriage; so, playing for Australia had some major costs.' [77]

After a great international career and winning every honour available at club level with St George, Williams moved to Canberra City in 1977. He spent several

[76] Wallace, 2004, pp70
[77] Wallace, 2004, pp72

seasons with the Canberra club playing in the National Soccer League (NSL). He had his last game at the age of 39 playing for Monaro in the Australian Capital Territory State League in 1990. Some have lamented that Williams was not afforded the accolades that his feats on the soccer field deserved. In an interview with me in 2004, Vince Copley said, 'You ask Aboriginal people today who Harry Williams was, and nobody would know. When Harry was playing, he was a great player and represented Australia so many times.' The recognition of Williams and the other Aboriginal soccer greats and their extraordinary feats is long overdue. Vince Copley underlined the importance of this, and the role that these individuals can still play in encouraging and inspiring Aboriginal people and communities:

When I look back, Charlie, Johnny, Gordon and Harry they played soccer, and were great players. But in regard to soccer they didn't really leave enough mark on the Aboriginal community and that is sad because they should have been able to do that. But you know, you can ask most people or kids now days what they played, who they played for or what they did and they wouldn't have a clue and that's the saddest part of the story. So what we need to do is I mean rather than just bringing Charlie up as an activist who pushed government, that he was also a very talented soccer player. Johnny Moriarty rather than just being known as a businessman and Harry who was capped as many times as most of our great soccer players ... all of this should be held up and recognised.

On retiring from soccer, Williams immediately began taking a more active role in Aboriginal affairs, working at the Aboriginal and Torres Strait Islander Commission (ATSIC) on social, economic and social justice issues and later as the Director of the Indigenous Services Unit for Australian Capital Territory Corrective Services. Through his work in Aboriginal affairs, Williams had the good fortune to come into contact with Charlie Perkins. 'Charlie loved to talk and was always on the go. He was a very good soccer player as well as politician and did some great things for Indigenous Australians.'[78]

In late 2005 Harry Williams was reunited with the 1974 Socceroos family once

[78] Wallace, 2004, pp72

again when the old players gathered at the Telstra Stadium in Sydney to watch the historic match between the new generation of Socceroos and Uruguay. They saw Australia finally break the thirty-two-year hoodoo, replicating the feat of the 1974 team to qualify for the World Cup finals ironically, again to be hosted in Germany. The stadium erupted when John Aloisi slotted home the final shot in a penalty shoot-out. The old Socceroos connected with the same surge of joy they had tasted all those years before. They were all jumping, shouting and hugging. Williams told the *Koori Mail:* 'I was caught up in the whole atmosphere, too, just like everybody at the ground ... It was an amazing experience. We jumped up and down and hugged each other ... it was a fantastic feeling. It was fantastic to see this side qualify. It's been a long time coming. We've arrived as a football nation. Australian soccer has come of age.'

Williams also foresaw the future when he reviewed Australia's chances at the 2006 World Cup finals in Germany. He was quoted in the *Sydney Morning Herald* in the run-up to the team's departure saying:

The key is getting a result against Japan, and a draw is an achievable result against Brazil. The extra string in our bow is Guus Hiddink. With all due respect to our previous coaches, we've now got a brilliant strategist. He has the confidence of his players, he's able to look at the players available and get the results. We've finally got it all together, and I think we're capable of going into the next round and further.

Harry Williams was one of the speakers at the launch of the 2018/2022 Australian World Cup bid at Parliament House, Canberra in June 2009 because of his status as the first Indigenous Australian to play for his country and to play at a World Cup finals tournament. Other speakers on that day included Prime Minister Kevin Rudd, Opposition Leader Malcolm Turnbull and Socceroos captain Lucas Neill.

The hiatus that followed the retirement of Perkins, Moriarty and Briscoe from professional soccer repeated itself after Harry Williams left the professional game. He was a big act to follow and he left a void. It would be ten years before another Indigenous player would wear the green and gold for the Socceroos when Frank

Farina was selected for Australia as a 19 year old, and more than 20 years before another Aboriginal player, Kasey Wehrman, would do so. You can't help but think of the opportunities lost because the game wasn't encouraged within Indigenous communities during Harry Williams' high-profile era. Then again, the game itself was battling to survive internal self-destruction and a complete lack of direction. The Socceroos qualification for the 1974 World Cup in West Germany should have been the catalyst to launch the game at all levels, but this opportunity was lost. Interest from young Indigenous players began to surface during the 1990s. Maybe this was due to greater television exposure of the Premier League in England and also the 1998 and 2002 World Cup finals being telecast live in Australia, drawing big audiences.

Kasey Wehrman -
Prince of the Acrobatic Goal Celebration

The first Aboriginal international after Harry Williams was Queenslander Kasey Wehrman. He was born in the small mining town of Cloncurry in western Queensland, the second eldest of seven children. He is Aboriginal through his father, Alan. As he told the *Newcastle Morning Herald* in a 2010 interview, 'My father was pretty good with history and was always telling us stories of how it was back then.' His parents separated when he was a young teenager and his mother relocated with the kids to Brisbane. With the move to Brisbane, his soccer career took off.

Wehrman had come through the junior ranks in Mount Isa and spent 1995 and 1996 with the Queensland Academy of Sport. His senior career started with the Brisbane Strikers in 1995. He picked up a National Soccer League Championship in 1996–97 and was named the NSL's Under 21 Player of the Year the same season, as well as Indigenous Sportsman of the Year by the Queensland Indigenous Council. A serious ankle injury at the 1997 World Youth Championships threatened to curtail his progress. While he recovered, ankle problems would prove an ongoing source of frustration throughout his career. He represented the Australian under 23s (the Olyroos) on eleven occasions, including being a member of the 2000 Olympic Games squad in Sydney, where he scored a memorable goal against

Nigeria. He made his Socceroos debut against Fiji in a 3-1 victory in Brisbane during the 1998 Oceania Nations Cup.

Wehrman was regarded as a very skillful, livewire player, and his 100 per cent no-holds-barred approach had some call him temperamental. One interviewer labelled him the 'Weirdman', gifted with sublime skills and the prince of the acrobatic goal celebration. These goal celebrations have been likened to Nadia Comaneci's triple somersaults with a twist. Wehrman has said that the acrobatic celebrations were something he learned at an early age: 'There wasn't much to do up where I come from in North Queensland when I was growing up so my mates and I used to tumble around a lot and put holes in my friends' parents' walls. I suppose this is where I learnt it. It is still part of my routine because it's always good to score goals.'

In 1999 Wehrman played two matches for the Socceroos against a starstudded, triple champion-winning Manchester United team. The matches were not without controversy, firstly because the Australian Soccer Federation had previously announced that the Socceroos would never play matches against touring club teams again. Secondly, Socceroo Simon Colosimo was seriously injured in a bad tackle by United's Andy Cole. The Socceroos were beaten 2-0 and 1-0 in the games but Wehrman gained Man of the Match and rave reviews. He said, 'I was just happy to walk away with a good performance. They were obviously pretty good opposition, so it was satisfying not to get our backsides kicked as everybody expected.'

That same year, Wehrman moved from Brisbane to join the Perth Glory for a season but fell foul of club officialdom. Nevertheless, his performances had attracted international interest and he signed for Moss FK in Norway in 2001. In an interview with the *Newcastle Morning Herald* in 2010 he recalled, 'I spent nine years in Norway and enjoyed every minute of it.' He played two seasons with Moss before joining Lillestrøm SK, where he played 121 matches between 2003 and 2007. 'Lillestrom are one of the traditional clubs and hold the Norwegian record for the most consecutive years without being relegated. We won a cup competition and came second in the Royal League.' He later moved to Fredrikstad FK. The weather in Norway was something to contend with and certainly differed from Cloncurry. 'In the winter it can get tough especially in the pre-season. Sometimes it got down to minus 10 or 12 at training. If it got any worse we would train indoors, but most clubs have their own artificial ground outside. You put the right clothing on, get out there and get into it. If you are smart you put on two pair of gloves and made sure you wore a beanie.'

Wehrman's career probably suffered because of a lack of exposure in the Australian press. Spending just under a decade plying his trade in Europe, he seemed to drop off the radar of both the press and selectors. Nevertheless, during his career he played 12 A-internationals for the Socceroos, including a surprise recall for a friendly international against Ghana in London in November 2006 - after having spent five years on the outer with the international selectors. He told the *Newcastle Morning Herald,* 'I was a little disappointed that I didn't get more of a run [for Australia) when I was in Norway. But that's the way it is.'

There was much speculation that he was the target of A-League interest before the start of the 2009–10 season, including overtures from clubs such as Queensland Roar, Perth Glory, Melbourne Victory, North Queensland Fury and Gold Coast United. But in August 2009 it was announced that he had signed a loan deal with Norwegian club Lyn for the 2009–10 season. In late October reports suggested that he was about to join English club Preston North End on a free transfer. Further reports from the Norwegian media speculated that there was interest in Wehrman from clubs in Denmark. In the end, Wehrman signed with the Newcastle Jets for the 2010–11 A-League season. After nine years playing at a very high level in Europe, he quickly proved a very valuable acquisition for the Jets. His standout performances gained him the captain's armband, and his wealth of international experience could readily be drawn on by the club.

The unexpected departure of coach Branko Culina from the Jets during the turbulent Tinkler years would have an impact on Wehrman's position at the Jets. Despite quickly becoming a fan favourite, Wehrman was sensationally dropped from the Jets squad after publicly questioning then Jets coach Gary van Egmond. He never played for the club again much to the dislike of local Jets fans. Wehrman would take on the role of player coach with the Western Pride in the Queensland National Premier League for two seasons before he returned to Norway, the country where he had spent nine seasons plying his football trade and the home of his wife. Kasey Wehrman deserves to be recognised as one of the very top Aboriginal players to grace the game in this country. One is left to wonder what

Kasey may have achieved but for untimely serious injuries and his own strong-willed clashes with coaches and management.

Jade North - Biripi Pride

Jade North is unquestionably the most accomplished Aboriginal soccer player since Harry Williams. He made his debut in the national league in 1998 with the then Brisbane Strikers. He was just sixteen. A very proud Biripi Aboriginal man born in Taree in 1982, the much-travelled North has compiled an imposing curriculum vitae. He has won national soccer titles with three different clubs, including championships in the old NSL with Perth Glory and Sydney Olympic Sharks, and two A-league championships with the Newcastle Jets and Brisbane Roar. He became the first Indigenous captain of a national championship-winning team when he skippered the Newcastle Jets to victory over the Central Coast Mariners in the 2008 A-League Grand Final. He was a member of the Australian team that was beaten by Brazil on penalties in the Under 17 World Cup Final in 1999, and he was a member of the Olyroo teams that competed at the 2004 Athens and 2008 Beijing Olympic Games. By the close of his career in 2017 North had played 41 times for the Socceroos including becoming its first ever Indigenous captain, when he skippered the team in a match against Singapore in 2008. His career in any measurement has been a stellar one.

North was a soccer player from the age of eight. His family moved to New Zealand and he lived there until he was eleven years old. The family returned to Australia, to the Brisbane suburb of Sunnybank, where he attended high school and where he 'lived and breathed soccer.' He told *Deadly Vibe* in 2004, 'I used to love watching the game on TV when I was a kid and my uncles used to play a bit when I was younger ... They used to take me down the park and kick some balls around and that's what really got me started ... When I hit high school there were camps for this thing and soccer just became part of my school work. I'd do a bit of training, a bit of school work, then more soccer.'

As a kid, the young Jade North had some favourite players and idols, including Argentinean superstar Diego Maradona and Roberto Carlos of Brazil. He thought Maradona 'was the biggest name at the time and was an amazing, skillful player.'

North was recognised very early on as something quite special. He played with Brisbane club Rochedale Rovers, and the senior coach, Kieran Cooper, recalled for the *Koori Mail* his pleasure in coaching North during his early development:

> *We had Jade here for about three seasons when he was 14 or 15... At the time we didn't have a division 1 side in his particular age group, so he played in the division 2 side where he was head and shoulders above the rest. We encouraged him to move on to a better side to help better himself. I think he went to Beenleigh after that. When Jade was with us he was a mid-field player and he was just sensational. He had everything and was lethal with both feet. As a junior he was pretty quiet and kept to himself. He did his talking on the field and let the ball do the work for him.*

North's obvious talent was responsible for him receiving a soccer scholarship to the Australian Institute of Sport (AIS) in Canberra for a year. After leaving the AIS, outstanding performances for the Brisbane Strikers and in the Australian under 17 World Cup team established that he was a player going places. He moved from Brisbane to the Sydney Olympic Sharks in 2001, where he played for two seasons. His performance for the Sharks in defeating Perth in the 2002 grand final drew rave notices and saw him gain selection for the first time with the Socceroos squad. The Socceroos coach at the time, Frank Farina, was reported in the *Koori Mail:* 'Jade has had a fantastic year, culminating in the Socceroos selection. I think that the improvements that Jade has made in the last 12 months show that he has got a very bright future in the game.' North himself was ecstatic: 'It's a dream come true to make the national training squad – it's a real honour.' He described the excitement he felt at gaining selection in the squad. 'It is a great feeling, right from when you first get the letter in the mail ... you open it up and the first thing you see is "Congratulations you have made the team", that is always an excitable feeling. Going to camp and into training - no matter what levels, 17's, 20's, 23's or senior team - I have been involved in every level there is in Australia and every time I have gone out it has been an honour.' [79]

---

[79] Mid North Coast Focus, viewed 18 January 2007. www.focusmag.com.au

Winning his first national soccer grand final in 2001–02 with the Sydney Olympic Sharks against Perth Glory in Perth was another momentous occasion. North described it to *Deadly Vibe* as 'amazing ... the crowd was huge over 43,000 people. The odds were against us and the crowd was against us. But you need to be strong enough to overcome those things and, at the end of the day, it's 11 on 11 on the field, even if a crowd of 43,000 is against you ... At the end of the grand final the crowd left before we could even collect the trophy. But we still did a lap of honour even though there was no one left in the stand!'

Perth had revenge the following season, beating Sydney Olympic 2-0 in the grand final. North felt the season was somewhat disappointing. 'Even though we finished with the minor premiership, we didn't play as well as we could have during the finals. It was disappointing to lose the grand final after winning it the year before. I was still pretty happy with my form through the year, even though it didn't quite match up to the previous season, where I won club player of the year.' After the loss, North decided to get with the strength: he joined Perth Glory and moved west. In a 2003 interview with *Deadly Vibe* he said, 'The Glory has a huge supporter base and it's going to be awesome playing for them, especially when the finals come around and we have 20,000 to 40,000 people cheering us on.' It proved a very successful move as he was a member of the Perth team that won their second successive grand final beating Parramatta Power 1-0.

North was subsequently selected as a member of the 2004 Olympic Games under 23 team. Olyroos coach Frank Farina told the *Koori Mail:* 'Jade is a naturally gifted athlete who brings an extra level of versatility to the Under-23 squad that I have chosen. He is very strong defensively and can quickly join in any attacks when we go forward. He also has a good deal of experience at NSL level.' Being an Olympian and member of Australia's Athens team was an exhilarating experience, especially as the Olyroos performed above all expectations: they drew with Tunisia 1-1, annihilated Serbia and Montenegro 5-1, and lost to a Carlos Tevez inspired Argentina 1-0 in the group stages. They suffered three unjust suspensions for the quarter-final clash with Iraq, and the loss of these key players left them sadly depleted and beaten 1-0. Nevertheless, they proved to be the most successful Australian Olympic team since the 1992 team reached the semi-finals.

During these years, North was easily identifiable on the pitch with his flowing dreadlocks, although he copped plenty of flak from his grandmother over 'that hair.' He, however, believed that 'it's good to have your own image. Certainly, in today's sporting world, dominated by the need for corporate sponsorship, it doesn't hurt to stand out from the rest.' [80]

The victory of Perth Glory in the 2003–04 season signalled the end of the old NSL and the establishment of the Frank Lowy-led Football Federation Australia (FFA) - and the onset of a soccer revolution unparalleled in the history of the game in Australia. The A-League was set up and North signed with the Newcastle Jets for the inaugural season. This was like a homecoming, as North was now back close to his home community of Taree. 'Living only two hours away it is easy to go back there. Whenever I get a bit of time off or in the off season I go back and see my grandparents and family, so I do try to get back as often as I can.' [81]

In the first season the Jets made the minor semi-finals but were beaten by eventual grand final runners-up and fierce local rivals, the Central Coast Mariners. The second year of the competition, the Jets were wallowing in last place after several rounds. Coach Nick Theodorakopoulos was sacked and replaced by the assistant coach, Gary van Egmond. The upheaval had a remarkable effect and the Jets went on an incredible run that saw them once again make the play-offs. They won their minor semi-final but North was red-carded and suspended for the following week's preliminary final, in which Adelaide beat them in a penalty shoot-out. The Jets played scintillating football that season and were far and away the most entertaining team in the competition. Adelaide were beaten in the grand final by Melbourne Victory - a team that the Jets had demolished only weeks before to the tune of 4-0.

The Jets cruel loss to Adelaide was, however, a trigger for better things to come the following year. North was promoted to captain the Jets for the 2007–08 season, replacing the retiring former Socceroos captain Paul Okon. The honour of becoming the first Indigenous captain of an A-League team was not lost on North. He told the *Newcastle Morning Herald* after the announcement:

---

[80] Mid North Coast Focus, viewed 18 January 2007. www.focusmag.com.au
[81] Mid North Coast Focus, viewed 18 January 2007. www.focusmag.com.au

I had not really thought about it until Dutchy [van Egmond] put me on the spot this morning. Apart from a couple of games with the Olympic team, I have never been captain not even in juniors. There will be extra pressure and responsibility, but it is a challenge I am looking forward to. When you look at the two [captains] before me, Paul Okon and Ned Zelic, they are big shoes to fill. They were two of the best players this country has ever produced. I am very proud of my Aboriginal heritage ... This is another milestone.

Coach Gary van Egmond was quick to sing the praises of his new skipper, telling the *National Indigenous Times:* 'He's at an age where the players respect and look up to him both on the training ground and on the pitch. It's a great responsibility and one I think Jade will embrace and really excel at. He has been involved in the Australian team, has had many years in the National Soccer League and is held in high esteem by the boys.' So close the year before, the Jets continued with their exciting brand of free flowing-possession soccer. North recognised the opportunities the season held, saying in an interview with the *Koori Mail:* 'We have a good hardworking squad and there is a strong bond between all the players. This is an important component when it comes to the critical times of the year. We have the capacity to go all the way and take out the championship this year.'

North also recognised that the game was now riding a crest of a wave after the heroics of the Socceroos' performance at the World Cup finals in Germany in 2006. North had played with that team in the early World Cup qualifiers and was a part of the training squad but narrowly missed coach Guus Hiddink's final selection for Germany. The *Koori Mail* reported that he felt the game had 'more focus since the start of the A-League, but since the World Cup, the passion for the game has exploded in Australia. This also has been shown by the respect which has filtered down to the players in the A-League competition. It also brings bigger names to our competition and is putting bums on seats along with giving our game profile.' The Jets finished second on the A-League ladder in the 2007–08 season and would eventually beat arch rivals Central Coast 1-0 in a thrilling grand final at the Sydney Football Stadium in front of 36,354 people.

The Jets had beaten the Queensland Roar in the preliminary final to make the grand final. During the lead-up to this match, newly elected Prime Minister Kevin Rudd had apologised to the Stolen Generations. Jade North was obviously moved by the importance of the occasion. In an interview with the *Newcastle Morning Herald* at the time, he said:

> *It is a proud moment in Australian history for someone to come out and acknowledge the Aboriginal people and say sorry. It is great for the Aboriginal people to get some recognition in Australia. We are the forgotten people. Look at the Maori people in New Zealand. Their culture is so big. Everyone knows about their culture and respects it. Here in Australia, not many people know about the Aboriginal people and their plight.*

North proudly displayed a tattoo with his tribal name, 'Biripi', on his left arm. Pointing to it with pride, he reflected that the message held special significance. 'It shows the respect I have for my family and acknowledges where I came from.' Speaking of his newborn son, he added, 'When Zane is old enough to understand, I will explain to him where he is from and how proud he should be.' The 2008 grand final victory over Central Coast was an exhilarating spectacle, and it could have been the start of a soccer dynasty for the Jets. This was an exciting young team with the potential to dominate the code in Australia for several years to come, but sadly for the coach, players and supporters, it was not to be. Over the next two seasons the team disintegrated. Several players in the grand final-winning team left and joined other clubs, as, eventually, even captain Jade North did.

The season following their grand final victory was a disaster. The Jets finished bottom of the table, a remarkable drop for a team crowned champions the previous year. Mid-season, they lost North when he departed overseas, signing for South Korean club Incheon United.

Initially, North had signed a million-dollar marquee contract for new A-League franchise the North Queensland Fury for the 2009–10 season. Part of the deal gave North a role as the new club's Indigenous ambassador. It was a tough decision for a player who had made such an impact in Newcastle. He told the *Newcastle Morning Herald,* 'I love Newcastle and everything about it, the place, the players, the fans. They have been fantastic, but this was an opportunity, which does not come along very often. I had to take it. I have a family and have to do what is right for them... My heart will always be at Newcastle. I was born at Taree and consider this home, but players come and go. That is football.'

Part of North's deal with the Fury included an exit clause that if he secured an overseas contract, the Fury would release him from his contract. Only a month after signing with the Fury for the 2009–10 season, it was announced that North was signing with Incheon United in South Korea instead of North Queensland. The deal was reputedly worth nearly $2 million over three years. Still under contract to the Jets until the end of the 2008–09 season, North played his last game for them against arch rivals the Central Coast Mariners on Boxing Day 2008. He was adamant that a move overseas had been a long-term goal and that he had done everything he could possibly do in Australia for now. Coach Gary van Egmond delivered a fitting tribute to his departing captain, telling the *Newcastle Morning Herald* that North 'managed to get himself in the Australian team while playing at Newcastle, one of the few players involved in World Cup qualifications when the socalled big boys from Europe came back. So, you can see how good a player he has been, and he's represented the club with real distinction and real leadership in that captaincy role.'

It was obvious that North had the 2010 World Cup finals on his mind when he decided to move to Korea. He had no illusions, as was reported in *Australian Football Weekly:* 'I'll continue to say that unless you're playing overseas, it's much harder to gain a regular place in the Socceroos and as my greatest ambition is to play in the next World Cup, my next move must be overseas. And the financial rewards of playing overseas would also be a bonus.'

There would be problems in the move to South Korea that North could never have envisaged. Simple things. For example, he was not allowed to have 'North' emblazoned on the back of his shirt because of the political tensions between South Korea and North Korea, and 'Jade' had to suffice. He was initially buoyed by the experience of playing for Incheon, telling SBS *The World Game,* 'The football is of a high standard and I haven't felt as fit as I have now in my whole career. Every training session is like playing a game. It took me three or four months to get up to speed but I'm feeling great now.' However, the honeymoon was soon over. North made only eight first team appearances for Incheon and found his Korean adventure extremely frustrating.

Nevertheless, he continued to be selected by Socceroos coach Pim Verbeek in the Australian team - although, ominously, Verbeek pointed out that players would need to be getting game time with their clubs to be considered. North was a part of the team that beat Japan at the MCG in June 2009 and thus tied up Australia's qualification for the 2010 World Cup finals in South Africa. But his position with his Korean club was causing some problems. He told SBS, 'I played three games in a row for Incheon after returning from international duty against Japan and things were going well. But for some reason I haven't been in the squad in the past five weeks and it's now just a matter of keeping fit and trying to get a move. Everybody knows this is a vital time for all of the Australian boys and it's crucial I'm playing regularly. I came here to play regularly at a good level, and that's not happening anymore.'

But again, despite the difficulties and lack of game time for his club, North was chosen to play for the Socceroos against a very strong Republic of Ireland team in Limerick. The Socceroos - depleted because five regulars were missing from the side - produced a stunning performance to crush the Irish 3-0, with two Tim Cahill goals and a spectacular last minute 30-metre screamer from David Carney. North rated the performance of the team as the finest he had ever been involved in. In an interview with SBS he said, 'That was the best Socceroos performance I've seen - and we were without five regular starters. Everything just flowed, the movement and also the finishing. We played with a lot of freedom and desire and drive and we caught them cold.' The victory against Ireland allowed Australia to climb to an unprecedented FIFA rating of fourteenth in the world.

In early September North was part of the Socceroos team that played South Korea in a friendly in Seoul. The Australians battled gamely but were largely outplayed by the slick Koreans, 3-1. North would be the first to admit that the game against Korea was not one of his best. The Australian team was again depleted, with a number of key players being unavailable. North also had to play out of his now more familiar position in central defence, instead playing at fullback. He was one of several players left exposed by the lively Korean attacks. The loss and North's performance meant that he wasn't selected for the Australian teams that played three matches against Holland and Oman. The lack of opportunities with his club in the short term left North out of Verbeek's planning. Unfortunately, the move to Korea had not provided the impetus to cement a permanent spot in the Socceroos squad, as he had hoped.

North remained philosophical and focused about his future, telling the *Weekend Australian*, 'I'm from a mission in Taree, [so] if you just follow your dream and work hard and put everything you have got into it, you can start seeing your dreams come true. I've taken little steps throughout my career to the goals that I have set and hopefully, I will be living my dream next year [at the World Cup in South Africa].' He had also recognised sometime back that the change in Indigenous participation in the game was now well underway. In an interview in the *Sun Herald* in 2006 he said:

> *I've been going around the community for a few years now, and I can definitely see some progress. Football, it's a different game for a lot of them, but more and more kids are getting interested.*
>
> *They know about the Socceroos, they know about the World Cup. The more they get to see and hear about us, the more they will want to get involved. There's a lot of talk about introducing a new [soccer] program into the community, so it's only going to get bigger and better. The potential is incredible.*

As the year turned into 2010, the World Cup year, North's future remained in limbo until he finally gained a move away from Incheon to join Tromso in Denmark. This move also proved frustrating as he battled with injury and had limited game time. Nevertheless, when Pim Verbeek announced his pre-World Cup squad of thirty-one players, North was in the squad. The squad's intensive training program was followed by a final hit-out against New Zealand in Melbourne. North gained no game time and when the squad was cut to 28 players before departing for South Africa, he was one of the players given the news that their World Cup dream was over. Knowing Jade North and how much being part of a World Cup team meant to him, I can imagine the devastation this news caused. The lack of game time over fifteen months and a run of injuries had derailed his hopes.

North signed with Wellington Phoenix in the A-League. His performances brought him back into the Socceroos squad post-South Africa, and he was selected for the Asian Cup in Qatar. He made a couple of appearances in the tournament, which saw the Socceroos finish as runners up to Japan.

North subsequently signed with Japanese club Tokyo FC, and things certainly got off to a more than shaky start! He was undergoing his medical in a Tokyo hospital on 11 March 2011 when the building started shaking violently. The calm soccer club doctors reassured him that everything was okay. But he was witnessing first-hand one of the most catastrophic earthquakes in history, and it was the most frightening experience of his life. As North told Fox Sports, 'I was ... running on the treadmill and all wired up to the machines. The aftershocks keep coming, we're having one now while I'm talking to you. And really, it's chaos, there's roadblocks and hardly any food or water in the shops.' When he finally got back to his accommodation, there was no way to contact home and reassure his family of his safety. Watching the television coverage only added to the terror of the moment because he could not understand Japanese.

The tsunami that followed the earthquake caused horrifying damage and massive loss of life. Then, with fears about radiation from crippled nuclear power plants mounting, North's club sent him back to Australia and safety. He was forthright, however, that although the Japanese J-League had been suspended indefinitely in 2011, he would return to Japan when given the okay and fulfil his commitments to Tokyo FC. The devastation of the earthquake and tsunami may well have derailed Jade's hopes with Tokyo FC he would only play four games for the club before another short term stop with Hokkaido Consadole Sapporo also in the J-League. He made 23 appearances for the club in 2012 before he returned to the A-League and five seasons with the Brisbane Roar. The highlight was unquestionably capturing the A-League championship beating Western Sydney Wanderers 2-1 in the Grand Final: 'I'll never forget our passionate fans and winning that 2013–14 championship at Suncorp Stadium against the Wanderers in front of a sea of orange.' Despite a great season and being a member of a championship winning team, he would for the third time fall short of gaining a spot in the Australian world cup squad for Brazil in 2014.

In 2016 Jade North proudly and deservedly accepted the NAIDOC week Sportsperson of the Year Award. It was acknowledged that besides his outstanding on field achievements he was additionally an 'Ambassador for the Mini Roos, the Leukemia Foundation, the Indigenous Games and the Indigenous Football Championships, Jade is an inspiration beyond the sports field'. [82]

North himself recognised the importance of the award personally to himself:

Out of all the Socceroos games that I played, the A-League Championships I had won, this individual award was my biggest sporting achievement to date. It was one of the proudest moments in my career.

North also could not contain his disappointment and dismay with Football Federation Australia's complete lack of understanding or recognizing the magnitude of him gaining such an award:

But Football Federation Australia had no idea that one of their players won this prestigious award. It had to take one of my friends to contact the FFA to let them know that. If that had been an Adam Goodes in the AFL or Paddy Mills in basketball everybody in that code would have known about it. That is how far behind we are as a code when it comes to Indigenous football, that the governing body didn't even know that I had won. [83]

In a remarkable personal confession and word of warning to others Jade North confessed that he had suffered throughout his career with depression. The scale of the illness he battled vividly described in an interview 'I used to wake up in the morning and I physically felt sick, I had anxiety and depression and it was like a vicious circle.' One of his greatest moments in football lifting the grand final trophy with the Jets was brought into context:

I remember to this day when I held the trophy over my head at Newcastle, it should have been one of the happiest days of my career, but I went back into the change rooms, everyone was celebrating, running and jumping around and I was sitting in the corner with my head down.

....

[82] http://www.naidoc.org.au/awards/winner-profiles/jade-north
[83] http://www.ftbl.com.au/news/jade-north-my-dream-for-indigenous-football 26 Jan 2018

I should have been enjoying that moment, and I wasn't. Not because I didn't want it, I wanted to feel like everyone else. But depression, and being on medication, just wouldn't let me be who I wanted to be.

He had first revealed his battles with depression back in 2014. He had worked tirelessly with Dr. Neil Halpin who had worked with both the Newcastle Knights and Jets. North stated:

I used to sit in the shower every day with the hot water going for about half an hour, just sit in the bottom of the shower because that would make me feel good, and then I'd have this sick feeling coming on and that would help me try and get through the day. [84]

North's condition and the demons he faced make his football achievements and list of honours even more remarkable. In mid 2017 North announced the launch of his "Kickin With A Cuz" football program initially in collaboration with the Wollongong Wolves Football Club and the Illawarra Local Aboriginal Land Council. North revealed that the new program was a 'not-for-profit initiative designed to reach young boys and girls through football, with a vision to create a sustainable pathway and outcomes centered around enabling kids to make better life choices.' [85]

North emphasised the importance and direction of the program:

There will be a strong focus on Indigenous and disadvantaged communities in an effort to open up new football pathways as I firmly believe utilising sport and community are the perfect avenues to reinforce education, health and responsibility to our next generation and this is exactly what 'Kickin With A Cuz' is all about... The program sessions expand to include the importance of regular school attendance and education, community engagement, health culture, future pathways and where applicable closing the gap. [86]

....

[84] Radbourne, L, *North on Depression: 'I Wanted to Be in A Dark Room, Away from Everyone,* Feb 14, 2018
[85] http://footballnsw.com.au/2017/07/14/jade-north-launches-kickin-with-a-cuz-football-program
[86] http://footballnsw.com.au/2017/07/14/jade-north-launches-kickin-with-a-cuz-football-program

At the age of 36 Jade North retired at the conclusion of the 2017–18 season. Whatever transpires in the future, he has made an incredible impact as a gifted and proud Aboriginal soccer player, who is more than worthy of following the Soccer Dreaming tracks of people like Perkins, Moriarty, Briscoe and Williams. Football Federation Australia should not hesitate in finding a role for him in its future directives of engaging and encouraging Indigenous participation in the game. A more respected role model would be hard to find. In a worthy closing address to his career he is looking to the future:

I'm not sitting around wondering what I'm going to do when I retire from playing football. I already know. There's a hole in the game in this country that needs to be filled and I'm going to help fill it. I've come to realise that's my life's calling. There should be way more Indigenous players like me in our game, from the kids right through to the professionals in the A-League, playing overseas and representing the Socceroos.

There are a number of reasons there aren't, some that are difficult to deal with and others that could have been overcome, but I'm not going to make this a blame game and harp on about opportunities lost. That would be a waste of time and energy. I'm about getting the future right.

I'm proof you can come from a small town – Taree, in my case – and go on to play professionally, both here and overseas, represent the Socceroos and even captain my country. I played alongside some of the greatest players this country has produced, from the Golden Generation. So, I know there is hope, and diamonds in the rough, in these Indigenous communities. They've just got to be identified, encouraged and given the incentive to do well. [87]

Travis Dodd - The Flying Wing Warrior

A powerful, fast and determined winger, midfielder or striker, Travis Dodd was born in Adelaide and played junior soccer in Elizabeth. He was subsequently

[87] https:www.playersvoice.com.au – *'The Big Hole in football by Jade North'*

invited to join the South Australian Sports Institute before signing with Adelaide City in the old NSL. He became Adelaide City's youngest player of all time when he made his debut in 1996 at the age of 16 years and 281 days. He moved to Newcastle in 1999 and became a crowd favourite with his incisive running and ball control. He spent four seasons making more than a hundred appearances for the Newcastle Breakers and Newcastle United. In 2003 he moved to Parramatta Power and played in the team beaten in the grand final by Perth Glory. While with Parramatta Power, he became only the fifth player in NSL history to come on as a substitute and score a hat-trick.

Dodd gained international club experience at the end of the 2003–04 season, when he played first with Malaysian club Johor FC and then with the Greek first division side Panionios. Playing with the Greek club gave him a taste of top-flight European soccer, as he played and scored in their UEFA Cup first-round victory over high-profile Italian side Udinese. Unfortunately for Dodd, his career with Panionios was short-lived. He played only nine games for the club before a change of manager saw him lose his spot in the senior squad. He returned to Australia in 2005 and joined Adelaide United.

Dodd and Adelaide United got off to a flying start in the new A-League, winning the inaugural Premiers Plate by a seven-point margin. They could not reproduce this form in the play-offs, unfortunately, and missed a grand final place. His coach at the time, former Socceroo great John Kosmina, told the Koori Mail: 'Travis is an important player in our group, as he can score goals as well as create. He is a constant threat to opposition teams with his pace. On top of that he is a good character to have around the club, a good bloke and is happy to be involved in the odd practical joke which is great in a team environment.' Dodd had an additional highlight during the season: making his 200th national soccer appearance.

Winning the premiership by such a margin surprised some, but not Dodd. In an interview with the *Koori Mail* he said, 'Most of the media on the east coast didn't rate us. We were supposed to be contenders for the wooden spoon. So, it has been great to silence our critics.' Dodd spoke in reverent tones of his coach, John Kosmina. 'He has been great for me. Although I've had 10 years in the Australian National League competitions, Kosi is the first to have given me a shot and believed in me as a player.' Kosmina said, 'Travis is a unique athlete who could have had a career in track and field. There is no doubt he is a great natural athlete and we needed to work hard to combine his football and athletic skills. He needed to play the games - in the past he has been an impact player coming off the bench - and we are turning him into a ninety-minute footballer.'

In the wake of the Socceroos exciting performances at the 2006 World Cup, a sense of euphoria continued to follow the team, despite Dutch master coach Guus Hiddink departing for Russia. The Australian team's first major assignment post-World Cup was to qualify for the Asian Cup finals. They did so with a clinical performance against Kuwait at Aussie Stadium in Sydney in front of over 32,000 fans in August 2006. The match was significant on a number of levels. For one, the Australian press finally acknowledged that the soccer juggernaut was well and truly on the move with the *Daily Telegraph* editorialising:

When around 32,000 people turn out to watch a Socceroos team devoid of a single World Cup participant, Australian football knows it must be on to something. That something, at the moment, is the rollon effect of Australia's heady and heroic performance in Germany two months ago.

The sport is riding the crest of a wave so powerful that tens of thousands of fans in the tough Sydney sports market jumped on for the ride, even if that meant watching an all A-League outfit tackle an amateur Kuwait side ranked 100th in the world on a chilly winter evening.

The night held special significance for two Socceroos, Travis Dodd and teammate Jade North. Two Aboriginal Socceroos on the paddock at the same time was indeed a groundbreaking moment and both players had excellent games. North was very solid in the heart of the defence and later told the *Newcastle Morning Herald,* 'It was the biggest game of my career. I had a heap of family and friends in the crowd.'

But it was Dodd who drew the real accolades. The *Telegraph* reported:

Socceroos' new boy Travis Dodd provided the antidote to a nagging World Cup hangover for Australia last night as they sealed their place at next year's Asian Cup Finals. Dodd the Adelaide wide man scored one and made one for substitute Sasho Petrovski, as he announced his arrival at the relatively late age of 26. After clinically converting his strike in the 76th minute, Dodd used his lacerating pace to weave past two challenges to free up the Sydney FC man for Australia's 86th minute sealer.

Dodd's goal forever etched his name in history as the first Indigenous goal scorer in the green and gold of the Socceroos. Speaking with the *Koori Mail,* he said:

Looking at the replay a couple of times after, the ball came off my boot perfectly, and went directly between two defenders, it's nice to be a part of history that no one else can rewrite. To be able to tell my son when he's old enough and hopefully the grandkids that I was the first Aboriginal player to kick a goal at international level is naturally pretty special. To have my family there and to score in a debut match playing at home was a highlight of my career so far.

Dodd was hopeful for the future when speaking with the *National Indigenous Times:* 'I know Arnie [Socceroos coach Graham Arnold] has spoken about using the European-based players for the match in Kuwait and against Bahrain at home he'll have everyone available. So, it's just a matter of keeping up some good form in the A-League and hopefully getting another chance.

Former Socceroo Aurelio Vidmar - at the time Adelaide United's assistant coach - felt that Dodd had taken his game to another level. He told the *National Indigenous Times:* 'The way he set up that second goal with his speed, there's not too many players around the world with that sort of speed.' Graham Arnold was ecstatic about Dodd's performance, telling *Deadly Vibe:* 'You rely on that type of person. Travis is the type of player that can really step up ... And when you've got pace like that and you can play like that, you can easily adapt to the international stage.'

The historic moment of two Indigenous Socceroos playing in the same international game was not lost on former great John Moriarty, who was certainly uplifted and saw the potential for the future, hailing it as 'the great breakthrough' in the *Sydney Morning Herald:*

They're both fantastic footballers and they're great role models. I mean what more can you ask for? Playing for the Socceroos and putting on performances like they have. We can get many more Jade Norths and Travis Dodds into the national team. It's an old dream. If you can get an Australian team peppered with Aboriginal players, think of how well we could do ... it's the ideal sport for Aboriginal people. Their bone structure. Their coordination, hands, feet, eye. They've got speed and dexterity. They're naturals, but we haven't tapped into it all.

Dodd wasted no time in dishing out some advice of his own to Football Federation Australia (FFA) over the opportunity of encouraging Indigenous kids to take up the game: 'I hope [it encourages others to see] there's not enough Aboriginal kids playing the game. The AFL does so well to get out into the communities with their kick-start programs and I think the FFA really need to look at that and embrace something like that in the communities. There's so much talent out there and a great potential for the game.' Dodd's form after his Socceroos heroics fluctuated, but he had started to improve again by the end of the season. He admitted that his performance playing for Australia had affected his game. 'I kept trying to play out of my skin - worrying about my form and the results of it.'

As premiers in the 2005–06 season, Adelaide, with grand final winners Sydney FC, became the first A-League clubs to qualify for the Asian Champions League. The Asian campaign was one of new and exciting experiences. Adelaide failed to progress from the group stage but gained invaluable experience for the future. Their group consisted of Chinese champions Shandong Luneng Taishan, Korean champions Seongnam Ilhwa Chunma and Vietnamese League and Super Cup winners Gach Dong Tam Long An. Adelaide finished a credible third in the group, which included a 3-0 victory over Long An thanks to a Travis Dodd hat-trick. Dodd scored four goals in the campaign and said in the *Koori Mail* that this league was 'a tough competition on an international stage. Our position on the table doesn't reflect how well we have played ... We lost to the Korean national champions because of an own goal in the away fixture and were 2-0 up against [Seongnam Ilhwa] with 40 minutes to go, before drawing 2-2.'

Dodd hinted at the time that he had thoughts of chasing an overseas contract. Uppermost in his mind was a way of improving his chances of Socceroos selection. 'I have a year on my contract with Adelaide United left and will consider overseas offers after that. Playing in the Asian Champions League is a great chance to be in the shop window so to speak. At this stage, I believe I have a year or two left to take the opportunity to go overseas. An important part of this process would be making the Australian squad.'

Months later, after long negotiations, Dodd re-signed with Adelaide United - a long-term contract for three years that would see him remain with the Reds until the age of 31. As coach Aurelio Vidmar noted: 'It is good that we have been able to secure a local lad like Travis ... [who] has been here since the start of the ... A-League.' In the absence of regular captains Michael Valkanis and Paul Agostino during the season, Dodd captained the side with distinction. He told the *Koori Mail* that this responsibility 'really helped my game ... I have been really grateful to the club for the opportunity ... While captaincy is a huge honour and one day I'd love to be the outright captain of the club, I need to continue to work hard and gain the respect of my team-mates and the coaching staff.'

The following year, in the 2006–07 season, Adelaide United finished second in the Premiers Plate and made their first grand final appearance against Melbourne Victory but were annihilated 6-0. Adelaide had a man sent off early in the match and never really recovered. Dodd told the *Koori Mail,* 'Playing at Telstra Dome [in Melbourne], the pitch was enormous, and Melbourne suited that ground really well. Being something like 3-0 down with ten men at half-time, the mindset was for it not to get any worse. It became embarrassing and, in the end, we were defenceless.' Even so, as runners up in the grand final, they were guaranteed a spot in the Asian Champions League for 2008.

The 2007–08 season was a frustrating time for both Dodd and Adelaide. The Reds suffered greatly because of player injuries and, for the first time, failed to make the play-offs. Travis Dodd was awarded the captaincy of Adelaide United in 2008, replacing Michael Valkanis. After the disappointment of the previous season, 2008–09 was to prove a memorable one, both for him and for Adelaide United. In a game against Perth Glory, he became the first Adelaide United player to play one hundred competitive games for the club; he scored the only goal of the match for a 1-0 win. Then Adelaide finished the season as runners up in the premiership, although they were again beaten in the grand final. Dodd scored eleven goals from midfield during the season.

Adelaide's performances in the Asian Champions League of 2008 against Vietnamese champions Binh Duong, Chinese champions Changchun Yatai and Korean club Pohang Steelers were extraordinary, and set the benchmark for future A-league clubs to follow. An away 0-0 draw with Changchun in the final group-stage match made Adelaide the group winners and the first Australian team to progress to the knockout stage of the tournament. Dodd's performances throughout this campaign were inspirational. His powerful runs from midfield were a constant threat to opposing sides.

In the quarter-final Adelaide faced Japanese champions and Emperor's Cup winners Kashima Antlers. Adelaide drew 1-1 with Kashima at home with a goal from Dodd but faced an enormous task to get a result in Japan. A goal by Robert Cornthwaite midway through the first half more than made up for his own goal in the first leg. Adelaide defended magnificently, and their win saw them through to the semi-final stage. Adelaide faced Uzbekistan club FC Bunyodkor. In the first leg, before a large home crowd of 16,998 (498 over capacity), they put in a standing-ovation performance to beat the Uzbeks 3-0. They defended like men possessed in the return leg, losing 1-0, but progressed to the Asian Champions League final 3-1 on aggregate. Adelaide lost 5-0 to Japanese club Gamba Osaka over two legs in the final, but this does not detract from the merit of their performance throughout the competition.

Adelaide United's run in the Asian Champions League brought a number of the players under the glare of interest from Asian clubs, and Dodd was at the centre of that attention. Rumours circulated wildly that he was linked to a big money move to Japanese champions Kashima Antlers, and he himself was caught up in the excitement. In an interview with *The Age* in early 2009, he said:

I am contracted for two more season in Adelaide, but I am 29 years old and unfortunately the game here doesn't allow you to set yourself up financially. The A-League is a great League to play in, the lifestyle is great, and my family is here in Adelaide, but the opportunities financially are there in Asia. They are a lot greater. You need to make the most of it when you can, as you're not in the game a long time. There has been a lot of talk of Kashima, but I am not sure if they are in a position to put a bid in at the moment. It's a bit frustrating.

Unfortunately, the interest from Kashima did not result in a move to Japan and Dodd remained with Adelaide. But coming second in the 2008 Asian Champions League meant Adelaide gained a place in the FIFA Club World Cup. In their first game in the Club World Cup, against New Zealand team Waitakere United, Dodd scored a captain's goal for a win that saw Adelaide United progress to the quarter-finals. This meant the Reds secured another rematch with Asian Champions League rivals Gamba Osaka - their third meeting in three weeks. Adelaide played valiantly and had enough opportunities to win the match but went down 1-0. However, they then won 1-0 against Egyptian club Al Ahly to place fifth overall in the Club World Cup and were rewarded with the fifth-place winnings of US$1.5 million.

Many commentators felt that Adelaide had suffered during the season because of their tight schedule, which saw them in the running for an unthinkable treble of trophies: the Asian Champions League, the A-League premiership and grand final. Sadly, they would finish the bridesmaid in all three events. Dodd was philosophical about the jampacked schedule: 'It had its pros and cons ... the benefit of it was that we were playing quite regularly, getting a lot of time with each other. Considering there were a lot of new faces in the squad, it was good to keep playing those games. On the other hand, it was a lot of travel and to come through it as we did was fantastic. We had to go to Tashkent and China, for example and it took us 30 hours to get there.' The travel and time difference were difficult to deal with. Adelaide had again qualified for the Asian Champions League for 2010. But getting so desperately close in *three* competitions - Dodd felt the disappointment keenly. He told *The Age:*

After the final game of the season I was gutted. To have had the season that we have had, with all the midweek games, to play as well as we did at Gosford and for it to end that way ... I think we deserved to score a couple of goals more. To lose a championship on goals scored, I was very disappointed. I dwelled on things after in the hotel room. You can't help it. All I could think about was games we lost by the odd goal - the Melbourne one where we lost 3-2 late in the

match - or the game where we were 3-0 up against the Central Coast and let
them get back.

You think, if we could have held on there, if only we could have conceded
one less goal in a match, or scored one more ... I'm sure it's possible. But it's
something we can't bring back. It's true the coaches tell you, that you have to
stay focused throughout the season, because it all could come down to goals
scored or goal difference.

Despite standout performances while leading his club side to an Asian Champions
League final and as runners up in the A-League premiership and grand final, Dodd
found himself banished from national selections. Commentators raised questions
about Dodd's absence from the Socceroos side. It seemed particularly odd given a
long-term injury to regular wide right flanker and Blackburn Rovers player Brett
Emerton and especially so when Australian teams were being chosen from
A-League based players. Dodd 's absence remained somewhat puzzling.

An article in *The Age* in 2009 delivered timely and valuable advice to soccer
authorities about the value of Travis Dodd as a liaison, with and link to,
Indigenous communities:

If Football Federation Australia [FFA) wants to challenge the AFL's domination
of Australia's Indigenous communities, it could do a lot worse than make
Adelaide captain Travis Dodd its travelling ambassador.

With Newcastle's' title-winning skipper Jade North moving to South Korea, Dodd
was the only Indigenous captain in the A-League ... Dodd who had turned 29,
believed soccer could make major inroads into the nation's Aboriginal communities
- a vein of rich sporting talent mined so proficiently by the AFL and Rugby codes
- but it will not be easy given the resources and time those sporting bodies have
invested in luring the best Indigenous talent. Asked if he gets fed up that his
Indigenous status often gets mentioned in articles and features, Dodd is forthright:

I am a footballer, yes, but I am also Indigenous, and I do think it's important to
mention it, especially when there are a lot of other Indigenous players going

around. The AFL has got a bucket load [of players] and if we want to promote the game and get the game to their communities, I am happy to be seen as a role model. I think, previously, soccer has missed a big opportunity, but the AFL has been around a lot longer, they have a lot more funding and organisations backing them. But I am sure the FFA will get behind it and start to promote the game in communities and we will, in a few years start to see Indigenous players coming into the game. If Indigenous boys can succeed in Australian Rules and Rugby, they can also do it in soccer.

The FFA named Travis Dodd and Kyah Simon their Indigenous Ambassador to coincide with the launch of their new Indigenous program. Dodd was enthusiastic about the potential of the program, telling the *Koori Mail:*

The FFA have started a great new initiative where they are looking for 5 per cent of the A-League playing personnel being from Indigenous heritage by 2018. Last month there was an Indigenous football festival in Townsville for boys and girls between the age of 12 and 16. The kids had a lot of fun and players from that event have been identified for elite junior programs in their home states. I want to see more Indigenous kids playing our game and would be keen to help the next generation of Aboriginal soccer players reach their potential.

Adelaide had another stirring Asian Champions League campaign in 2010. They beat the 2009 Asian Champions, South Korean side Pohang Steelers, as well as Chinese club Shandong Luneng and Japanese team Sanfrecce Hiroshima. They finished top of their group to progress to the last sixteen stage. They lost a nail-biting match against their South Korean opponents Jeonbuk Motors 3-2 in extra time.

Dodd carried niggling injuries into the 2010–11 A-League season but eventually regained his place in the side. The Reds finished third on the ladder and went on to beat Wellington Phoenix in the first week of the Finals Series. They were subsequently beaten by the Gold Coast and knocked out. At the end of the season, Dodd announced that he had signed with the Perth Glory for the 2011–12 season. In the second year of his contract with Perth Dodd tore his anterior cruciate ligament (ACL) in a match against Melbourne Victory. He would be sidelined for twelve months and was still unable to take the field after more than a year of rehabilitation. The Glory eventually announced that his contract would not be renewed. He returned home to Adelaide and signed with the North Eastern MetroStars in the South Australian Premier League. Sadly, he again tore his ACL in the last game of the 2016 season. It would bring an end to another great Aboriginal soccer career. He signed with Adelaide United as an assistant coach for the reds W-league team in 2017. He was also a sought after commentator for Foxtel Sports A-League coverage. Whatever happens in the future, Travis Dodd has been an outstanding player and has had a wonderful career. He will undoubtedly play a prominent role in the future, inspiring young Indigenous players to take up the game.

David Williams – Explosive Fire Power

David Williams was regarded by many as one of the most exciting Australian prospects to arrive on the soccer scene since Harry Kewell first burst to prominence with Leeds United. Williams, a dynamic forward, possessed explosive, electric pace and exquisite ball control. He has a terrific shot with either foot and was packed with drive and enthusiasm for the game. He has represented Australia at every level - Under 17s, Under 20s, Under 23s and the Socceroos.

Williams was born in Brisbane, went to the Northside Christian College and was a member of the Queensland Academy of Sport squad. He played junior soccer with Westside, Pine Hills and Mitchelton FC. He has said that there were no Aboriginal role models for him to emulate and that his passion for the game was somewhat stalled because soccer was off the agenda at school. There, rugby union, rugby league and Australian football were the order of the day. Soccer was an after-school activity.

Williams' natural athleticism was instrumental in him being spotted by rugby union scouts and offered a scholarship by the Queensland Reds. But he decided to follow his soccer dream and has had no regrets. He always felt that he could go further in soccer and liked it better than the other sports. As a teenager, his talent was obvious. He had trials and spent time training with Belgium clubs Anderlecht and Club Brugge and English giants Liverpool. In an interview with the *Sun Herald* in 2006 he said, 'Going to Liverpool was unbelievable. Not many people get a chance to go there, even on a trial, and not many Australians had been there before. It was a great experience to train there. They didn't offer anything but said I would be in the reserves and I'd be better off going to another club and working my way up from there.'

Williams returned to Australia and signed for the Queensland Roar towards the end of the inaugural A-League season in 2006. He played only two impressive games as a substitute for the Roar. 'It was unbelievable. My first professional football game was in my home town in front of my family. It was a privilege and a great way to start my career.'

His time with the Roar was short-lived as he was quickly signed by top Danish club Brondby on a three-year contract. His coach at the time with the Queensland Roar, Miron Bleiberg, wished Williams the best: 'If Australian football benefits from him taking this course we will be very pleased. We hope he can continue his progress over there and further his career. Craig Moore took a similar path when he was young and went on to achieve great success. Hopefully David will enjoy the same level of success.'

Initially, it was a wise choice for the rising star to move to the Danish club as his stepping stone to European success. The *Sun Herald* reported, 'Brondby is certainly not one of Europe's contemporary giants but it has been a nursery for some of the greatest names in European football. Danish legends Peter Schmeichel, Michael and Brian Laudrup, and John Jensen are Brondby alumnae. Blackburn Rovers American goalkeeper Brad Friedel also spent formative time at the club.' Williams got off to a whirlwind start and was an instant sensation. Australian news reports had him as a near cult figure in Copenhagen after a handful of games for the Danish club. The Brondby fans had 'taken to the Australian and ... composed a terrace song for their new hero. Admittedly, its lyrics extend only as far as repeating "Super David Williams" over and over, but any song is better than none.

It was little wonder that fans were singing his praises. Playing in Brondby's youth and reserve teams, he scored twelve goals in five matches and was soon promoted to the senior squad. Williams was philosophical about his lightning success: 'Take the opportunity when it comes, because it might not be there next time ... Work hard and keep your head down. Australians are known for hard work, and that's what gets them places ... I like being from Australia [in Europe] because we all work hard and try to get what we want. A lot of the players here take a lot of things for granted.'

Moving to Europe and being away from home and family might have been a problem for others, but not David Williams. While some felt they weren't always treated well and struggled to make friends, Williams found it was completely different for him. The transition to being a professional European-based player went off without a hitch. In an interview with the *Sun Herald* he said, 'It wasn't too difficult to leave home. I'd been away with the [Australian] under 20s and under 17s a lot last year so I wasn't home much anyway. I know that my friends and family aren't going anywhere and that they'll always be there. I do miss everyone when I'm over here, but I don't get homesick.' Language and a different culture and climate had their challenges, but nothing was too extreme that he could not overcome: 'I can understand more Danish than I can speak. I do Danish classes. I know what the reserve team coach is saying, and the first team coach is Dutch and has lived in England, so things get translated if I don't understand.'

Following in the footsteps of namesake Harry Williams was a proud legacy that David Williams was acutely aware of: 'It would be great to follow in the footsteps of Harry Williams. There's not too many Aboriginal players who are professional so it's good to be one.' He was also aware of his role in inspiring other young Indigenous players, saying, 'I guess I am a role model for some people.'

Williams broke through to Brondby's first team in the Danish Superliga when he was just eighteen. This sudden elevation was an early career highlight, and doing it so quickly marked him as a player for the future. In one of his early games for the first team, he came on as a substitute from the bench and nearly scored a winner in a 1-1 draw against Aalborg. Williams recalled the game for the *National Indigenous Times*:

It was a pretty interesting game. It was good to get a game in front of a full house of 14,000 people. It was a good atmosphere but not as good as playing at home when you have your own crowd behind you. Everyone wants to beat Brondby and rises up to do better against them because we're the biggest team

in the league. My first touch was a through ball and we nearly scored from that.
And then my second one hit the post. They were my only two touches.

Over the next two seasons Williams played 34 times for Brondby's first team, scoring four goals. His first for Brondby was in a home game against Silkeborg IF. In a Royal League game against Swedish side Hammarby IF, he scored two goals in Brondby's win. He also scored against German outfit Eintracht Frankfurt in the UEFA Cup.

Williams started the 2008–09 Danish season where he had left off, scoring another goal in the UEFA Cup. His form for Brondby was instrumental in him being called up by Socceroos coach Pim Verbeek for the 2010 World Cup qualifying game against China, and he came on late in the match.

Unfortunately, Williams' great run of form for Brondby was derailed by a knee injury in a training mishap. After he overcame the injury and returned to fitness, he fell foul of the new Brondby coach, Kent Nielsen, and found himself sitting on the sidelines. His frustration erupted in a public outburst, in which he demanded that the club either play him or he would leave for fresh challenges within a three-week timeframe. Williams was adamant in an interview with *The Courier-Mail*: 'I'm in a difficult situation. I have to play football. I have not developed in the last six months.' Brondby weathered the Williams storm and exiled him to trials with South African club Bidvest Wits in June 2009. Williams' representatives advised him against this move. They felt it would be best if he came back to Australia to revive his career.

Brondby subsequently allowed Williams to join the new A-League franchise North Queensland Fury on a one-year loan deal for the 2009–10 A-League season. The move looked a promising one as the Fury also signed former Liverpool star Robbie 'God' Fowler as their marquee player. The club signalled its commitment to encouraging the game within Indigenous communities when Williams was joined at the Fury by two other Aboriginal players, Paul Henderson and Freddy Agius. Fury coach Ian Ferguson was delighted in his signing and told the *Koori Mail* that Williams:

was an exciting prospect who would bring goal-scoring ability and speed to the
squad. He's played for his country at under-age levels and for the Socceroos in

*a World Cup qualifier against China last year. David's got a great reputation
even at his young age and being an under-21 player and hopefully he'll continue
to develop as a player. It's great to have a young player of his talent in the squad
... He's been playing in Denmark with Brondby IF since 2006. We heard the club
had lent him out for a trial in South Africa and thought we'd make a play for
him and it's paid off.*

The Fury did not get off to a great start and for a period they languished on the
bottom of the table. Results certainly went against them, including a 5-0 thrashing
by Gold Coast United. Williams' form in the early part of the season was patchy and
at one point coach Ian Ferguson had him coming off the bench as a substitute.
'I think David has to concentrate a bit more on his final ball. Everything else has
been great, his work rate, getting up and down the wing, taking people on. I think
it's just his distribution, that final thud, he's got to be a bit more deadly in that area
so we make that pass count and hope that Fowler can get on the end of it.'[88]

Ferguson admitted, however, that he did not want to place enormous
expectations on his young player. 'He's a young kid and I just think expectations
sometimes are too high on him, he's just coming back from overseas, he's got to
adapt to the weather, he's got to adapt to the A-League.' Williams himself felt he
just needed the opportunity to show what he had under the bonnet. 'It's what you
play football for, you don't play to sit on the bench the whole time ... I would love a
permanent starting position. I know I'm capable of it, I just have to get some game
time to get the confidence I need and just get back into the flow of things and I'm
sure it will kick off from there.'

As if in answer to Ferguson's request, the Fury, with Williams, began to develop
better cohesion and understanding from playing together. They achieved a run of
draws and a two match-winning run that lifted them clear of the bottom of the table.

In a return clash against fellow Queensland new boys Gold Coast United, who
had humiliated the Fury 5-0 earlier in the season, the media highlighted the
presence of Aboriginal stars Williams and Tahj Minniecon in the two teams.
Williams and Minniecon had been lifelong friends, as both their families were

88   Sportal, viewed 14 August 2009 <sportal.com.au>

heavily involved with the church in Brisbane. They had played together at the Queensland Academy of Sport and both had originally signed for the Brisbane (previously Queensland) Roar. Tahj Minniecon told *Sport Gold Coast* before the match: 'Speed is a huge part of both our games and we'll both be looking to unlock the defence. I haven't seen David play for a while but he's a fantastic talent … When he gets the ball, he's always on fire. We're very similar players. It will be interesting to see who wins out.' The match showed that Williams' form had completely turned around and he, along with Fowler, terrorised the Gold Coast for a revenge 2-0 victory.

Late in the season Williams regained his shooting boots and the Fury had some notable victories over top-six qualifiers the Newcastle Jets and the Gold Coast. His performances saw him gain another cap with the Socceroos against Indonesia, where they qualified for the 2011 Asian Cup. By season's end the Fury had climbed the table to finish a credible seventh in their first season in the A-League.

However, the following season, 2010–11, was a very difficult one for the Fury. Financial woes and constant doubt over whether the FFA would keep them in the competition, once the World Cup bid was lost, undermined confidence and support. Several players, concerned about their future, signed with other clubs. With morale low, the losses on the field mounted. Through it all, the performances of David Williams were remarkable. He was the Fury's leading marksman, with five goals, and was initially included in the Socceroos' Asian Cup squad for Qatar. Despite missing selection in the final 23-man squad, he was nevertheless kept on standby in case of injury.

Ange Postecoglou, coach of then Australian glamour team Brisbane Roar, indicated that Williams was one player he would love to have in his team. Postecoglou coached Williams at Australian under 17 and under 20 level and described the Fury star in an interview with *The Courier-Mail* as 'one of the most talented players I've ever coached.' There was media conjecture that if the Fury went under, there was every likelihood that Williams would return to his home town of Brisbane and link up with the Roar.

After enduring a season spent hanging over a precipice, the Fury were finally put out of their misery. The FFA told the club that it had not met the financial requirements of $1.5 million necessary to stay afloat, and its A-League licence was revoked.

Initially, Williams signed a short-term six-month contract with Sydney FC to play in their Asian Champions League campaign. He made his debut for Sydney in a hard fought 0-0 draw against South Korea's Suwon Bluewings. The draw was a good result considering that Sydney lost captain Terry McFlynn when he was red-carded after only 34 minutes of play. Williams impressed his new home fans with an outstanding game. After the match, he was critical of the Koreans' incessant diving during the game. He told *The Daily Telegraph,* 'It was difficult to play a physical game. It's not a soft sport. If you can't handle it in the right sense of the rules, then you're in the wrong sport.'

Sydney FC failed to make the second round of the ACL and, in late June, it was announced that David Williams had signed a one-year deal with Melbourne Heart. In the 2013–14 season he was named Melbourne Heart FC Player of the Year, Supporters' Player of the Year and John Aloisi Golden Boot Winner. In 2014 Williams featured in the A-League All Stars games coming on as a substitute for the legend Alessandro Del Piero in the 63rd minute. It was Del Piero's last game in Australia after two seasons with Sydney FC.

During that 2014 season David Williams shared an historic moment with three other Indigenous star players Jade North, James Brown and Adam Sarota when all four players were on the field at the same time in a clash between Brisbane Roar and Melbourne City. City won the game 1-0 and Williams could not contain his excitement of the occasion and significance of the moment after the game:

I was talking with Browney about it and then I spoke with Adam (Sarota) after the game... Jado (North) had mentioned it as well so it was pretty special for all of us... We all realised it and knew that it wasn't something that had happened in the A-League before.

Indigenous players have been a big part of Australian football for a long time in the past and the present and this was a nice little thing to be a part of.[89]

Despite being the record goal scorer at the time for Melbourne City at the

89   John Greco 11 December 2014 https://www.a-league.com.au/news/williams-hails-historic-moment

conclusion of the 2016 season he was released. In the hopes of resurrecting his international career Williams signed with the Hungarian first division team Szombathelyi Haladas. He outlined his reasons for the move:

> *For me it was all about an opportunity to get myself back in Europe and be playing football freely and the way that I like it... I didn't come for the money, I didn't leave Australia because I was sick of it, it was just to try and help my football go to another level. You always want to make yourself better and I would love to play for the Socceroos again. I will definitely do all that I can to make it happen again. It's always an honour playing for your country no matter what age you are. I feel like I can do it, I just have to stop talking in some senses and perform on the pitch and hopefully if I get enough goals or I'm playing regularly then hopefully it doesn't go overlooked.* [90]

He would make 66 appearance for the Haladas club and score 20 goals but there would be no Socceroos recall. He signed with Wellington Phoenix for the 2018–19 season. Wellington under new coach Mark Rudan proved the surprise packet of the season with David Williams scoring some cracking goals. On reflection it has been a roller-coaster ride of a career for David Williams. In some cases bad luck through untimely injuries as well as poor decisions on club choices has stunted his chances of more appearances for his country. Like Jade North and Travis Dodd, he should have a prominent role to play in the future development of Indigenous participation and opportunities with the World Game.

Adam Sarota – In Pole Position

Adam Sarota signed with Brisbane Roar in 2008 and was named the National Youth League Player of the Year for 2008–09. Another exciting young Indigenous prodigy, Sarota was on the verge of fulfilling his early promise. His soccer-loving father is Polish and his mother Aboriginal. The family moved from Cairns to

---

[90] John Davidson 21 November 2016 – https://theworldgame.sbs.com.au/williams-eyeing-socceroos-recall

Brisbane with the sole aim of him playing soccer at a higher level. The decision, and the level of support from his family, paid off - he represented Queensland at the junior national titles and won an education scholarship to Kelvin Grove College.

Subsequently, Adam's father contacted former Queensland State team coach George Pagan and pressed to have his son join one of Pagan's specialist coaching soccer clinic tours of Germany. Adam's father wanted to see how his son would measure up against top European opposition. Adam and his father joined the tour and, as a result, Adam had a trial with top Bundesliga side Bayer Leverkusen. The club is recognised as one of the best in Germany and is renowned for its top-class youth soccer development programs. Adam obviously impressed the Bayer coaching group as the Sarotas were invited to extend their stay and for Adam to further his development. Despite the enticing offer, the family declined because they saw the importance of Adam completing his schooling before following his soccer dream.

Adam Sarota was signed by Brisbane Roar, and broke through to the senior squad during the 2009–10 season. He played a number of impressive games for the Roar during the A-League season. In early 2010 he and two other promising youngsters, Tommy Oar and Michael Zullo, signed with Dutch side FC Utrecht.

Sarota became a big talking point in the wake of the 2010 World Cup in South Africa and Australia's team rebuilding efforts for the 2014 World Cup. Sadly, it was not because he had been selected by new Socceroos coach Holger Osieck in the squad for matches against Switzerland and Poland. Rather, it was the fact that Poland launched a dramatic bid to include the young player in their national squad that grabbed the headlines. Sarota was invited to join the Polish international squad's training camp before the upcoming friendly against the Socceroos. His father, Tony, had emigrated to Australia from Poland about 30 years before. This gave Adam Sarota dual citizenship and, through that, the possibility of playing for Poland. At the time he made no firm decision one way or the other about his intentions. For his part, his father, Tony, continued to encourage his son to pursue his dream of playing for the Socceroos. He told *The Courier-Mail* in 2010, 'We would prefer Adam play for the Socceroos as he grew up supporting them and has always dreamed of playing for them. But if they don't want Adam in the Australian squad for the qualifiers for the [2014] World Cup in Brazil, maybe

Adam should play for Poland. Why should he miss out on the chance to maybe play at a World Cup?'

Sarota got off to a quiet start with Dutch club FC Utrecht. But he, alongside other young Aussie star Tommy Oar, were named on the bench for Utrecht's Europa League match against Scottish heavyweights Celtic. He later came on as a substitute against Liverpool at Anfield in England and nearly scored the winner.

Frank Farina, former coach of the Socceroos and Brisbane Roar, was adamant that Sarota had missed out on selection in the Australian under 17 and under 20 squads because of his trip to Germany when he was seventeen. He told *The Courier-Mail* in 2010, 'Adam went away at a young age over to Germany. Whether he decides to wait for Australia or take up the Polish offer, it's going to come down to what he wants to do.'

The situation was resolved favourably when then Socceroos coach Holger Osieck included Sarota in his squad to play Germany in March 2011. Although Sarota did not get game time, he was on the bench for this historic match, he saw the Socceroos come from a goal down at half-time to defeat the three-time World Cup winners. As the *Newcastle Morning Herald* reported, Osieck said, 'Now we have clearly indicated, yes, we are interested. He did well in the camp so far, he is OK in training and he showed a level of commitment'.

Adam Sarota played 48 times for FC Utrecht between 2010 and 2016. He made the first of his three Socceroo appearances against Wales in 2011 but was overlooked for the Brazil 2014 World Cup squad. An ACL tear undermined his great start with FC Utrecht. In 2014 he was loaned to the Brisbane Roar to gain more game time. On his return to Holland he moved to Go Ahead Eagles and had played 13 games for the club before a serious ankle injury disrupted his progress: 'the midfielder suffered a spiral fracture which left his ankle sitting 90 degrees to the rest of his leg'.

He eventually returned to Australia and Cairns to try to resurrect what was at one time such a promising future. He was undertaking a specialised hard training and rehabilitation program. But this was combined with an unorthodox fitness regime that included spear fishing, hiking and camping in the wild. Sarota was philosophical 'I'm desperate to get back. When you're not injured you forget just how much you love the game. You really don't know what you've got until its gone.

It's been an incredibly difficult time but because I love the game so much, I keep working hard to get back to that professional level'.

In late 2018 Adam Sarota signed for NPL club Cairns and was reported as likely to play against Sydney FC in a round 16 clash of the FFA Cup. Sadly, injury ruled him out of a return to the game. A resolute Cairns team went down in a fighting performance 2-1 to Sydney FC and one was left to ponder the impact a player of Sarota's class may have had on the game. At this point in time Adam Sarota remains lost to the game and the sickening run of injuries appear to have completely derailed a very promising career.

CHAPTER 6
The Islanders – Frank Farina, Archie Thompson, Tim Cahill and Mary Fowler

Frank Farina - Fingerbone

Frank Farina, one of Australia's greatest players, seemed to be on the move from the time he hit the ground. He was born in Darwin, in the Northern Territory, lived for some of his young childhood in Papua New Guinea and was raised in Cairns. He developed a love for the game from an early age and played with his older brothers and friends in makeshift games on the street, in paddocks and in the backyard. His father Paolo an Italian immigrant from Faenza had played the game back home in Italy and played in local competitions mostly in small country towns when he first came to Australia. His father was an encouraging inspiration in developing a love of the game in the young Frank Farina.

Frank's mother Bess grew up in Townsville. But her family like many Aboriginal and Islander families of northern Queensland had been previously interned on Palm Island under the strict control of the government. Frank may have inherited some of his mother's sporting prowess. She was a very good squash player and reportedly still plays the game in her seventies. Frank's mother's family were originally from the Torres Strait. His father Paolo was a carpenter and the family followed his pursuit of work across Queensland, Northern Territory and New Guinea.

Frank's first competitive game was played in New Guinea when aged seven. The Farina family moved to Cairns when Frank was aged ten. Sadly, his mother and father separated, and it caused an upheaval in his young life. He played all his junior soccer in Cairns. As a young teenager he was given the nickname 'Fingerbone' because of his long hair that resembled the mane wore by David Gulpilil in *Storm Boy*.[91] He wasn't recognised early as a star player and was never picked for the Queensland state junior teams. His breakthrough came when he was encouraged to play with Mareeba United in the then Queensland State League. He was just sixteen when he came into their first-grade team. He was selected for an Australian Institute of Sport (AIS) Scholarship based in Canberra in 1982.

Frank stated it was a stroke of luck for him to get to the AIS. The AIS intake were to be selected from the national state championships and he was not even in the Queensland squad let alone the team. A Level 2 coaches' clinic was being conducted in Brisbane at the same time and Frank was one of the young players asked to play for this coaching group. Jimmy Shoulder a former coach to the Socceroos and at the time head coach at the AIS was one of the coaches running the coach's program. Shoulder was impressed on the spot by Frank and was amazed that he was not a member of the Queensland state team. Shoulder offered him an AIS Scholarship on the spot.

Frank and a fellow north Queenslander Ray Junna drove all the way to Canberra and the AIS in Frank's father's Sigma some 3200 kilometres. It was an exciting first year for a seventeen-year-old. Frank Farina was selected in the Australian Youth team and played qualifying games for the 1983 World Youth Cup in Acapulco, Papua New Guinea and Costa Rica.

At the AIS the routine was pretty regimented but was focused on football. It was up at 6am then out to the AIS for running and weights at the indoor stadium (still freezing cold in winter). Then it was back for a shower and hot breakfast before school. It was back to training straight after school with mostly ball work. Frank would later reflect on the success of the AIS program and that it was 'virtually like being a professional player but having the opportunity to finish school as well'.[92] Being based in such a professional setting provided these young players every opportunity to succeed including access to doctors, sports medicine and physiotherapists. The AIS was a very tough and disciplined environment and one had to work hard to succeed.

91   Farina, F, *Farina – My World is Round,* Vox Peritus, Sydney, 1998: pp15
92   Farina, F, 1998: pp15

Initially again left out of the Queensland side for the 1982 Australian youth championships some good fortune played a part in Frank getting a late call up and start. AIS coach Ron Smith rang the Queensland state coach, Fred Robbins and pushed him to include Frank Farina in the squad. Frank was not likely to play at all until striker Steve Glockner broke his ankle days before the team were to take part in the Championship. Farina got the role and Queensland won the title with Frank scoring six goals and leading scorer of the tournament. Subsequently Frank was picked in the Australian youth team to travel to Acapulco in Mexico to take part in the first Joao Havelange Cup. Eight teams from Argentina, Australia, Brazil, Costa Rica, Israel, Mexico, USA and the USSR took part. Australia had a great tournament including a 2-2 draw with Brazil in their opening game before going on to take third place and the Bronze Medal.

This tournament proved a great lead up for the 1983 World Youth Cup qualifiers. In the first stage the Australian team overcame New Zealand, Fiji, Tahiti and New Guinea fairly easily to reach the final qualifying round in Costa Rica against Israel and Costa Rica. Despite losing their first match against Israel 3-1 Australia eventually finished top of the tournament to qualify for the 1983 World Youth Cup finals to be held in Mexico City.

On his return from Costa Rica Frank was placed on loan from the AIS to National Soccer League team the Canberra Arrows. He had a dream start scoring on debut against Adelaide City in Adelaide. The euphoria was short lived. He was badly injured in a training incident and would be out for eight weeks, and his chances of making the Australian team for the 1983 World Youth Cup was under serious threat. Frank played only a handful of games before the team was chosen for Mexico and he was adamant his form was not that great. He was on pain killers and anti-inflammatory tablets to allow him to play but managed to make the squad.

Australia performed credibly at the Mexico World Youth Cup Finals. Drawing with the hosts Mexico 1-1, beating Scotland 2-1 and losing to South Korea 1-2. The first game against Mexico is remembered with great affection by Frank Farina. Played in the famous Azteca Stadium that holds 110,000 people with an electric atmosphere was an experience never to be forgotten especially when he scored the equaliser to stun and silence a packed stadium.

In 1984 at age nineteen Frank Farina was first selected for an Australian squad by new coach Frank Arok. This team would form part of Arok's plan to qualify for the 1986 World Cup in Mexico. Several international club teams visited Australia in 1984 to play the Socceroos including Manchester United, Nottingham Forest, Glasgow Rangers, Juventus and Iraklis. Frank played several games mostly as a substitute but was gaining invaluable experience.

Later in the year the Socceroos went on tour to China and Europe all part of the preparation plan. Frank was by this time playing for Sydney City in the NSL and his performances on the world tour must have made an impression as he was offered an eight-week trial by English second division club Portsmouth. He played only three trial games for Portsmouth mostly because poor weather conditions abandoned matches. On his return the Socceroos played in a World Series event in Australia against Tottenham Hotspurs, Vasco de Gama, Udinese and Red Star Belgrade. It was common in those years for the Australian team to play against visiting club teams. They also played a three-match series against China and of the eleven games played the Socceroos won eight and lost three games. The team was beginning to jell.

Australia overcame its Oceania qualifying group against New Zealand, Israel and Taiwan to reach a final World Cup qualifying game against Scotland. This Scottish team was a cracker that included the likes of Graeme Souness and Kenny Dalglish. The Socceroos were overwhelmed by a rampant Scotland in Glasgow 2-0. The return match in Australia would confirm which team went to Mexico. Frank Arok was a master tactician and beseeched the Australian Soccer Federation (ASF) to play the return match in Darwin and also put in a request to Australian Liverpool star Craig Johnston to join the Australian team. Sadly, the ASF ignored Arok's request to play the game in hot and steamy Darwin and scheduled it instead for an evening game in Melbourne - scheduled perfectly to suit the Scots. Craig Johnston probably still to his regret turned down the invitation to pull on the green and gold jersey.

Australia played extremely well and had some great chances to win the game, but it ended 0-0 and Australia were out. One still wonders what may have happened if the game had been played in Darwin with Craig Johnston in the team. Following the disappointment of missing the 1986 World Cup Australia took part in the 1987 President's Cup in South Korea. Seven other teams including Morocco,

Egypt, Chile B, Shamrock Rovers, Fortuna Sittard and South Korean A & B teams participated. The Socceroos made the final losing on penalties to the South Korean A team 5-4. Frank Farina had a good tournament scoring four goals but had missed a penalty in the shootout.

Frank enjoyed two good seasons with Sydney City. They won the northern zone competition in 1985 and the NSL Cup in 1986. In the Cup final Frank scored two goals to down West Adelaide 3-2. By the end of the 1986 season, the financial backer of Sydney City, Frank Lowy, wanted out of the NSL competition unless an independent NSL body was formed to which the then Australian Soccer Federation would not agree. Frank was sold to Marconi for $30,000 and Lowy pulled his Sydney City team out of the competition a few weeks into the 1987 season. Frank Farina was given immediate hero status with Marconi through his father's Italian heritage. In his first season with the club he was the leading scorer and was also voted the NSL Players' Player of the Year (equivalent of the Johnny Warren Medal today), which he won again the following season also. He was given a trial by Dutch first division club Roda JC and was signed on a two-year deal for $400,000. Sadly, the deal fell through because he could not gain a work permit.

In his second season with Marconi they won the championship and the grand final beating Sydney Croatia on penalties after finishing 2-2 at full-time. At the season's end Frank was besieged with overseas offers from Holland, Belgium, Croatia, Italy and England but decided to wait until after the 1988 Olympic Games in Seoul before making a decision on where his playing future would be. Australia had qualified for Seoul by topping the qualifying group of Israel, New Zealand and Taiwan. It would be the first time since the 1956 Olympic Games in Melbourne that Australia would feature in the Olympic Soccer Finals.

Australia prepared for the Olympics by hosting a Bicentennial Soccer tournament that included world champions Argentina, Brazil and Saudi Arabia. Australia went down in their opening game against Brazil 1-0 to a goal scored by superstar Romario. The tournament remains memorable for the fact that Australia beat Argentina 4-1 including a stunning 35 metre strike from captain Charlie Yankos. The Australian team made the final going down again to Brazil 1-0. In Seoul at the Olympics Australia made the quarter finals including a memorable win over Yugoslavia in the group game 1-0 with the goal scored by Frank Farina. Australia were beaten 3-0 by eventual winners the Soviet Union in the quarter finals.

Despite the disappointment of losing in Seoul, Frank Farina was offered a trial with top Belgium team, Club Brugge. The trial went well, and he was signed by a top European club. He joined the club mid-season and finished with eight goals from fifteen appearances. His position with the club looked precarious into his second year with a change of manager and he had dropped down the pecking order. During the early pre-season he was mostly an unused substitute and had even asked his agent to organise a move. Frank even had words with new coach George Leekens but was finally given an opportunity in a Belgium Cup match. He scored twice in a 3-1 victory and had convinced Leekens of his worth. Club Brugge would eventually go on to win the Belgium championship with Frank scoring 24 goals in 33 appearances. He was the top scorer in the Belgium League and named the top foreign player. There was immediate interest from Italy and both Bologna and Genoa had expressed interest but Club Brugge would not let him go. Frank was disappointed but focused on another good season. The Club finished fourth in his second season and he bagged twelve goals from 26 games.

There were some incredible highlights including a European Cup tie against an A.C Milan side containing the like of Ruud Gullit, Marco Van Basten, Frank Rijkaard, Paoli Maldini and Frank Baresi. They held A.C Milan to a 0-0 draw at the San Siro and were unlucky to go down 1-0 in the return. But the culmination of the season saw Frank score in a 3-1 over Mechelen in the Belgium Cup Final. It was already known before the close of the season that Frank Farina had been signed to play for Bari in the Serie A in Italy for the 1991–92 season.

At international level during this period Australia had catastrophically been eliminated from the 1990 World Cup qualifiers. Having initially beaten New Zealand 4-1 at home and then achieved a wonderful 1-1 result with Israel in Tel Aviv Australia looked in the box seat. But a 2-0 loss to New Zealand in Auckland and a 1-1 draw with Israel in Sydney saw the team eliminated. The complications of having a high number of its best players, including Frank Farina, now playing in Europe had in some ways contributed to the Socceroos downfall. Farina like many in Europe had missed half the games.

The move to Bari initially got off to a good start. Farina was playing and scoring goals in the pre-season in a side that included England captain David Platt, Joao

Paulo from Brazil and Boban from Croatia. But the early signs turned sour and poor results and a lack of goals saw the coach replaced and Frank Farina frozen out of the team once this happened. An offer by Sheffield Wednesday, then in the English first division, after only eight appearances for Bari seemed a godsend. Sadly, Bari reneged on the deal and increased the transfer fee and the deal fell through. He was finally allowed to play on loan with Notts County in England playing five games before the season's end. He ended up signing a three-year deal with Strasbourg in the French first division. He scored eight goals in twenty appearances in his first season somewhat hampered by an ankle injury and playing for the Socceroos in World Cup qualifiers.

The Australian team now boasted a number of internationally recognised stars including alongside Farina the likes of Mark Bosnich, Ned Zelic, Robbie Slater and Graham Arnold. The Socceroos overcame New Zealand comfortably 1-0 and 3-0 with all of the overseas based players in the team. The next hurdle was to be Canada. In the away game Australia went down 2-1 after keeper Robert Zabica had been sent off. The tie was levelled after the Socceroos won the return match 2-1, Frank Farina scoring the first with a bicycle kick. Australia progressed after winning the penalty shoot-out with Mark Schwarzer saving two penalties and Farina scoring from the spot to secure the win. Frank would miss the first game of the next tie through copping two yellow cards against Canada.

The qualifier would be against Argentina with Diego Maradona making his return to the Argentinian team and would ensure a sell-out crowd in Sydney. The Sydney Football Stadium was packed with 44,000 people. Argentina scored first through Balbo from a Maradona cross and Aurelio Vidmar equalised close to halftime for the Socceroos. Australia could not add a winner and had to travel to Argentina for the return held in a packed River Plate Stadium. They went down 1-0 from an Alex Tobin own goal.

After three unsuccessful World Cup campaigns Frank Farina announced his retirement from international football. He was given the opportunity to play one more international game against Ghana in Sydney in 1995. It was to be his official testimonial game and he was given the honour of wearing the captain's armband for the match and the Socceroos won the game 2-1. He was given a rousing standing ovation from the crowd and added that playing for his country was 'an absolute pleasure and privilege'.[93] He had one more season in France signing with Lille playing twenty games and scoring eight goals. Despite interest from Belgium he decided it was time to come home. He signed with the Brisbane Strikers and had a very successful first season back at home. The Strikers finished fifth and lost to Sydney United in the semi-finals. He scored 20 goals from 30 appearances during that first season back home.

Bruce Stowell the Strikers coach was informed before the start of the 1997–98 season that his services were no longer required. Frank was approached on taking on the dual role of captain/coach. This was to be his first foray into a coaching/manager's role and he could not have asked for a better start. Despite ranked as 66/1 outsiders before the season began the Strikers finished second in the league with Frank scoring twelve goals from 25 appearances. They made it through to the grand-final against old rival Sydney United. A home grand final with a capacity crowd of just over 40,000 to cheer them on created a memorable atmosphere. Frank scored the opening goal in a 2-0 victory. He later recalled that win with the whole of Queensland watching was a very 'special memory that not many footballers have the opportunity to savour… It's right up there with anything in terms of atmosphere and sense of achievement'.

He was also realistic enough to recognise that in achieving such success there was only one way to go and that was down. The 1997–98 season saw the Strikers finish twelfth. Frank only scored one goal from 18 appearances. There were issues over non-payment of his salary at the seasons end and he opted out and joined Marconi as their coach for the 1998/99 season. They achieved a respectable semi-final berth. Frank only played two games that season scoring no goals and it was to be his last as a player.

The Socceroos boasting a team labelled the 'Golden Generation' and coached by legendary Englishman Terry Venables seemed assured of making France 1998 but were eliminated after a 2-2 draw with Iran in Melbourne having led 2-0. The disappointment within Australian soccer circles was devastating. Despite achieving incredible success Venables left as head coach of the Socceroos. The Australian coaching job was inundated with applicants but after only three seasons as a coach

[93] Farina, 1998: pp121

in the National Soccer League Frank Farina was appointed in August 1999 as the man to end the long wait since 1974 to have Australia qualify for the World Cup.

There certainly were some initial very good signs in 1999 they drew and lost matches against a second-string Brazil and then with all of their European based players in the squad Australia demolished Hungary 3-0 in Budapest. In 2000 the Socceroos won the Oceania Nations Cup and qualified for the 2001 Confederations Cup in Japan and South Korea. Australia achieved wonderful success in this tournament including beating world champions France 1-0 and Mexico in the group stage before losing to Japan 1-0 in the semi-final. They took third place however by beating Brazil 1-0.

The Socceroos under Farina's guidance won through the Oceania qualifying stages of the 2002 World Cup before again sadly being eliminated 3-1 on aggregate by Uruguay and missing out on the 2002 World Cup finals. In 2003 Australia defeated England 3-1 in London in one of the most memorable Socceroo victories the England team included the likes of David Beckham, Paul Scholes, Wayne Rooney, Rio Ferdinand, Frank Lampard and Michael Owen.

In 2004–2005 Australia easily qualified through the Oceania stages of the World Cup. The 2005 Confederations Cup in Germany was to be the end of Frank Farina's reign as they lost all three games. Frank at the time felt he was being targeted by the Australian soccer media and his position undermined. He was replaced as Socceroo coach by the legendary Dutchman Guus Hiddink who guided Australia to qualify for the 2006 World Cup finals in Germany in the final two play-off games against Uruguay.

Frank Farina's coaching managerial career after the Socceroos has been somewhat turbulent. He held the reigns briefly at both the Brisbane Roar and Sydney FC before being dismissed, The Brisbane sacking precipitated after a drink driving charge. He was also national technical director and briefly coached national teams in Papua New Guinea and Fiji.

In 2000 he was recognised receiving an Order of Australia Medal for his service to soccer as a player and coach.

Frank Farina deservedly is recognised as one of the great Socceroo players and a pioneer in playing in top flight European football competitions. Frank has also given his time to encouraging Indigenous development in the World Game.

During his five years in charge of the Socceroos he gave caps to two young Aboriginal players in Kasey Wehrman and Jade North, both of whom he signed at Brisbane Strikers years before. In 2004 Frank Farina took himself into the outback to spread the word, advice and encouragement of the game to remote communities in western Queensland. The FFA supported Farina's remote coaching directive by providing old kits and balls to the communities. If only this program had been given adequate financial support and encouragement 14 years ago and continued.

Whatever the future holds, Frank Farina has cemented himself as one of the true Indigenous greats of the Australian game.

Archie Thompson – The Bush Bullet

Archie Thompson was born in New Zealand to a New Zealand father and his mother was from a remote region of New Guinea. The family moved to Australia when Archie was only three weeks old. Like Frank Farina before him, Archie Thompson did not come through the traditional Australian urban city soccer route but was constantly on the move. The family lived in Liverpool in western Sydney until Archie was four then relocated to Lithgow then to Wodonga on the Murray River. They finally settled in the regional district of Bathurst.

His junior football career started at the age of four playing for the Lithgow Rangers. When the family moved to Wodonga, he joined the Twin City Wanderers Soccer Club and retains very fond memories of his years playing for that junior club. Both his parents were passionate about the game and Archie's mum even took up the game and was reputedly a very good player including winning the best and fairest award in the local women's competition for Albury Wodonga. Archie had an insatiable appetite for the game from a young age and would practice non-stop 'before school, after school' and during school.

When they moved to Bathurst his football skills saw him selected to train with the NSW Football Academy which meant his father driving him down from Bathurst twice a week for training. He played for NSW Country and remembers some of the top players he went up against in those championships including Vince Grella, Brett Emerton, Danny Allsopp and Harry Kewell. Archie recalled how competitive it was during those junior years, but his ability was obvious to some as he was invited to be a part of the Australian Under 12 and Under 13 squads. He was again selected for the Under 14s squad but turned the opportunity down. Archie has reflected that he was not ready for the commitment nor the pressure and expectations of being in those squads. He gave the game away and lost his way and took two years out.

His life and football career were nearly ruined during this difficult teenage period. Making wrong decisions, hanging with the wrong crowd and finding trouble looked a recipe for disaster. He was rebelling against the world; finally leaving school and taking a job in a Chinese restaurant. He kept some interest in the game playing for the local Bathurst 75 club in the first division competition. He did not train because he could not get time off work but simply turned up on the weekend to play. In that first season he scored nine goals in just fifteen appearances. But he was not at all focused on football it was just an interest as he was in full on 'party mode'.

He thanks Harry Kewell for influencing a turnaround in his life and football. One-night working in the Chinese restaurant as a kitchen hand he looked up at the old black and white portable TV they had in the restaurant and an English Premier League game was on featuring Leeds United. There was Harry Kewell who he had played against and been in Joeys squads with starring on the pitch with Leeds United. He started running to and from work to get fit, cut out hanging with the wrong mob, and decided to have another crack at being a real footballer. He gave up the job at the restaurant because of the hours. He took a job at the Blayney abattoir. The pay was okay, and it was good for his fitness.

The downside of course was that he was up to his arms in cow shit all day. But the additional time allowed him to focus on football training. This rise in fitness saw him promoted to the Bathurst 75 state league side. He was now fit, hardened and his passion for the game reignited.

Political correctness was certainly not a part of the coaching or football fraternity in those days and Thompson was designated the nickname 'midnight'. His performances were picked up and he was offered a trial with the Gippsland Falcons in the NSL. The man conducting the trial was none other than Australian football coaching legend Frank Arok. Instead of having the players trialling on grass Arok held the trial in the club carpark on bitumen, gravel and cement. Archie threw himself into the game chased, ran, tackled and got the nod from Arok that he was now a professional footballer. In only his second game against Sydney Olympic he was praised by Johnny Warren on a segment of the *World Game* on SBS for a top game. He enjoyed playing under a coach like Arok despite the fact that could not understand a lot of what he said.

Arok had a strong message 'work hard' that influenced Archie. He remains forever grateful to Arok for the opportunity and trust in him as a player that Arok bestowed. His time with the Falcons was also significant in him being recognised wrongly as an Aboriginal player.

He gained the nickname as the 'bush bullet' whilst with the Falcons. It was also during this time period that fans started bringing Aboriginal flags to the games. His wife even overheard one spectator 'sprout about how they knew me well and I was Indigenous, from one of the tribes up north'. Archie stated that even the ABC and a Human Rights and Equal Opportunity website stated that he was in fact Aboriginal. Archie Thompson was forthright that nothing would have given him a source of more pride 'but the simple fact is: I'm not!' [94]

His mother of course was from New Guinea. He spent three years with the Falcons making 43 appearances and scoring ten goals. Going with the mistaken identity story he was often mistaken for Anthony Mundine. He initially did not think there was much of a resemblance himself until he opened a paper one day and thought they had an article on him with a picture until he read that it was in fact Mundine.

In 1999, Archie Thompson transferred to Carlton for $40,000. He was to play under the Socceroo great Eddie Krncevic who had played at the highest levels in Europe and for a short spell had played with Archie for the Falcons. In his first game for his new club Archie bagged four goals in a thumping 5-2 win at home over Brisbane. He was an overnight fan favourite. Carlton boasted some incredible young talent at the time including Mark Bresciano, Vince Grella, Josh Kennedy and Simon Colosimo. Carlton made the preliminary final and with

[94] Thompson, A *Archie Thompson – What Doesn't Kill you Makes you Stronger,* Victory Books, Melbourne, 2010: pp50-51

the class of players should have made the grand final but went down to the Wollongong Wolves.

Carlton sadly sank into financial problems. Eddie Krncevic resigned and took the coaching position with Marconi in Sydney. Archie Thompson had established himself scoring 23 goals in 53 games for Carlton. Krncevic obviously recognised a talent and took him north to Marconi.

During his short stint in the harbour city Archie was ecstatic to make his debut for the Socceroos in a friendly against Colombia in Bogota. Frank Farina subsequently selected him in the Australian squad for the 2002 World Cup qualifiers. He scored his first goal for Australia coming on as a substitute in a 22-0 victory against Tonga. Only two days later Australia recorded a record scoring victory over American Samoa 31-0 with Archie Thompson also gaining a spot in the Guinness Book of Records by scoring 13 goals in the match (a record he still holds). It was an auspicious start to his international career. Thompson enjoyed his time in the harbour city with Marconi and scored six times in just thirteen appearances before European opportunity came knocking through offers from Belgium.

Belgium had been the springboard for several Australian star players including Eddie Krncevic, Tony and Aurelio Vidmar, John Aloisi, Graham Arnold, Frank Farina and Paul Okon. Anderlecht, one of the most famous clubs in Belgium, offered him a trial but in the first instance he had to miss out through sickness. Then for a second opportunity he had only just flew back in from the Socceroos World Cup qualifiers in the Pacific and was jet-lagged. The trial did not go well, and Anderlecht turned him down. Fortunately an official from Lierse was present and they offered him a chance and he signed a four-year contact.

Adapting to the living, training and playing conditions in Europe was an immense hurdle to get over. Archie reflected that sometimes 'it would be minus 10 degrees at training and you had to wear different boots because the ground was frozen'. He would be rugged up for training in 'multiple layers of clothing starting with thermals and finishing with a padded duffel jacket'.[95]

He did not set the house on fire in the beginning and it took ages for him to score a goal. This was rather disappointing to the fans who took on board that this

[95] Thompson, 2010: pp61

was the player who scored thirteen goals in one international match. A change of coach before the beginning of his second year and a knee operation put him further on the outer. Archie found himself frozen out of the first team. He was demoted to the thirds team. Lierse were struggling financially and into his third season he was still in playing limbo. The second team gained a new French coach and he gained a promotion back into that squad. Several first team injuries saw him reluctantly recalled to the first team and he scored immediately. He held his place in the first team until the end of the season and was cheered to see the departure of coach Emillio Ferrera before the start of his final season. He finished up scoring fourteen goals and helped them avoid relegation. There were opportunities to move to a bigger European club but being on struggle street for four years saw him and his young family wanting to return home, and the beginning of the new A-League was the perfect vehicle.

He was contacted by Gary Cole and the new Melbourne Victory franchise and with signings like Danny Allsopp, Kevin Muscat and coach Ernie Merrick he could not sign quick enough. It was a difficult first year. Despite good crowd numbers, the team slumped to seventh place on the ladder and missed the finals. In that first season Allsopp and Thompson as the strike force only scored eleven goals between them. Archie did contend with some distractions during the season including being taken to PSV Eindhoven in the Netherlands by supercoach Guus Hiddink who had taken over as coach of the Socceroos. Hiddink had a high appreciation of Archie Thompson and wanted him under his guidance at PSV. An injury shortly after his arrival curtailed Thompson's PSV opportunities only making two appearances off the bench and he was returned to the Melbourne Victory.

In season two of the A-League there were new recruits and an improvement in attitude. One big plus was the signing of Brazilian midfielder Fred a genius of attacking creation. Melbourne Victory took the Premiers Plate and the Grand Final double beating Adelaide 6-0 in the decider. A crowd of over 55,000 saw Archie Thompson bag five goals in the Grand Final. Archie was awarded the Joe Marston Medal for the best player award for the Grand Final, but he thought Fred was unlucky in that he set up four of Archie's goals. At the season's end Danny Allsopp and Archie Thompson had nearly tripled the goals return of the previous year bagging 27 goals between them.

2006 would be a memorable year for Archie Thompson on the international arena. Guus Hiddink had replaced Frank Farina as coach of the Socceroos for the final hurdle of World Cup qualification against the mighty Uruguay. Thompson was very impressed with Hiddink and his methods of motivation. The first match against Uruguay was to be played in Montevideo with huge and fanatical support for the home team. It was a huge leap of faith by Hiddinck to play Archie upfront against Uruguay and demonstrated the Dutchman's appreciation of his worth. It was a massive boost in his self-confidence to play in that game, even though Australia went down 1-0.

The return match in Sydney at the Olympic Stadium was a sell-out and saw Australia triumph 1-0 and win the tie in a penalty shoot-out with John Aloisi scoring the winning penalty and taking Australia to their first World Cup Finals for thirty-two years. Archie Thompson was an unused substitute in this history making match but recalls he was one of the first to reach the galloping and celebrating Aloisi. He recalled the Australian dressing room after the game which included the likes of John Travolta and Olympic swimming legend Dawn Fraser joining in the celebrations.

He was subsequently chosen in the Australian squad that went to Germany this team achieved wonderful success in Germany beating Japan 3-1, losing 2-0 to five-time champions Brazil and drawing 2-2 with Croatia to reach the last sixteen round. The team hailed as the 'Golden Generation' were eventually defeated 1-0 by eventual champions Italy through a controversially awarded penalty kick. Archie Thompson sadly did not get to take the field in Germany but regards being a part of the squad at the World Cup as a career highlight.

In the wake of the 2006 World Cup euphoria Melbourne Victory having lost the mercurial Fred to D.C. United in the United States did not live up to their achievements the year before and failed to make the finals.

He was once more a part of the Socceroos squad when he played in the 2007 Asian Cup and also the Olyroos team that played in the 2008 Beijing Olympic Games. Both tournaments were something of a disappointment for the Australian teams. In the Olympics the Australians could only finish third in Group A and missed on making the next round. In the Asian Cup Archie played one match against eventual winners Iraq. Australia were eventually defeated by Japan in the quarter finals on penalties after Vince Grella had been sent off.

In 2008–09 Melbourne Victory were again crowned the A-League champions winning the Premiers Plate and Grand Final double. They again defeated Adelaide in the decider this time winning 1-0 in front of 55,273 fans. The following season the Victory again made the grand final, but it would not be remembered fondly by Archie Thompson. He was carried off after only twelve minutes tearing knee ligaments. Victory would eventually lose 4-2 on penalties to Sydney. The pain increased for Archie with the knowledge that he would be out for some time and it would take a lot of physio and rehab to get back. He was now out of the 2010 World Cup squad for South Africa and he would have to follow it from his couch at home.

He returned the following season after knee reconstruction surgery. The Thompson trophy cabinet was not complete, and Melbourne Victory had another all-conquering season in 2014–15 again winning the Premiers Plate and Grand Final double. They defeated Sydney 3-0 in the grand final and Archie Thompson gained a cameo coming on as a late substitute.

In early 2016 it was announced that his contract with Victory would not be renewed for the upcoming season. After eleven seasons he finished with 224 appearances for the club, scoring 90 goals. He remains a Melbourne Victory legend and a fan favourite and was justly recognised by being made a club ambassador.

Initially he signed a short two game contract with Victorian State League Heidelberg United. He would eventually sign for a season in 2017 with Murray United FC back in his old home town of Albury Wodonga. In 2018/19 he began making appearances on Fox Sports A-League show and has become a regular favourite.

Archie has confessed he enjoyed playing up to the crowd during his career especially opposition supporters. He had no problems copping a bit of stick in good humour but had no time for racist abuse. He admitted he had been racially verbally abused by players on the pitch in the past, but the game's administrators had cleaned that negative element out of the game as it is just not tolerated. He revealed there was a lot of racial abuse in his time in Belgium from rival supporters but he 'just had to let it go and play to the best of my ability'. He felt he was toughened for the racial abuse overseas because he had been hardened to it from a young age playing in Australia as a kid. He remembered the parents of opposing teams along the sideline screaming 'kick that blackie'.[96] He reflected that at times it was 'very full on' for him and his brothers and sisters.

Looking back over a playing career that stretched over twenty years he achieved wonderful success including playing for his country on 54 occasions and scoring 28 goals.

Tim Cahill - Legend

Arguably the greatest player to ever pull on a Socceroos jersey, Tim Cahill was born in the soccer heartland of Western Sydney to an English/Irish father and a Samoan mother. His father met his mother in Samoa and 'had to steal her off the island' before Tim's grandfather could catch him.[97] Tim's mum Sissy's father and grandfather were both chiefs of the village of Tufuiopa, Apia in Samoa. The young couple ventured to Australia and a new life. Although many of his family were rugby league or union players, Tim's light frame and small stature saw him encouraged to play soccer.

The Cahill's were a working-class family with four siblings three boys and a sister. They were tough days for Tim's parents scratching to make a go of things and provide for their young family. Tim was instilled with a love of football from his dad who was a mad West Ham supporter. He was always playing up a grade or two for his age and by eight or nine his skills ant technique had improved sharply particularly developing a love of heading goals.

From the outset Tim was highly motivated and passionate about the game with an insatiable drive to work and improve his game. As a junior he played with Balmain Police Boys Club, Marrickville Football Club, Lakemba Soccer Club and Plumpton/Oakhurst Soccer Club.

At the age of ten he made the Canterbury representative team and felt like he always had a ball at his feet. It was a full-on schedule Lakemba games on Saturday, Canterbury Reps on Sunday and indoor games with Banshee Knights on Thursday night. The indoor game further developed his skills and close control. Tim's father

---

[96] Thompson, 2010: pp107
[97] Cahill, T, *Tim Cahill – Legacy,* Harper Collins Publishers, Sydney, 2015: pp23

took a keen interest and would conduct training sessions for him and his brothers, dribbling through cones, doing sprints and intricate passing drills and importantly heading practice.

At the age of seven Tim Cahill was very fortunately introduced to Johnny Doyle who was a local, much respected, coach in the area where Cahill lived. Doyle had been born in Ireland, but his football skills were nurtured in northern NSW and the footballing nursey ground of Australia, Newcastle. Doyle originally played for Lake Macquarie before moving to glamour Newcastle club Adamstown Rosebuds. In 1968 Adamstown won everything pre-season Daniels Cup, Minor and Major premiership and included top players like Colin Curran, Ken Whitmore and Trevor Smyth. Doyle initially went to Europe and trialled and trained with Arsenal before coming back home. He moved to Sydney with Croatia and was picked for the Socceroos 1970 World Tour. This was the initial team selected by Rale Rasic when he took charge and was preparing for the 1974 World Cup qualifiers. Doyle only made a few appearances for the Socceroos but his career in Sydney continued with moves to Pan Hellenic, APIA Leichhardt and Canterbury Marrickville Olympic.

Doyle moved on to coaching after his career ended and he built a reputation as someone who could bring out the very best in young players. It was one-on-one training with Doyle or sometimes in small groups of three. Doyle was a perfectionist who really emphasised one of the key components of his own game great close ball control. Doyle impressed Timmy Cahill immediately and displayed great confidence and faith in the young player. Doyle worked on Cahill developing him into a two footed player and most of all targeting his ability in the air for very special attention. Tim was making an impact and was selected in the Sydney Olympic under 12 side. If you made either the Sydney Olympic or Marconi youth teams of that era you were a young player with a future. Tim Cahill immediately started banging in goals for Olympic. Tim also experienced the excitement of Sydney Olympic's senior team acting as a ball-boy at home games.

Tim and his family were extremely proud of their Samoan heritage. He had been there a few times from a young age to connect with family and cultural ties. At the age of 14 Tim's grandmother in Samoa became ill and at the same time both he and his brother Sean were selected in the Samoan under 20s team for a tournament. This trip really immersed the young brothers for the first time in their rich cultural heritage, something they immediately grasped. Whilst the brothers assisted with their grandmother's health, they also trained with the rep team in preparation for a tournament in Fiji.

The team went to Fiji but did not perform well losing every game. Tim being only fourteen was only used in a couple of games as a late substitute. He had no idea at the time how those few minutes on the pitch with a Samoan youth time nearly cost him his Australian international career. He also had to overcome some critics who were adamant that he would never make it in the professional game as he was regarded as too small and light to make it to the top. Tim did not see size as a handicap and just knuckled down and worked harder.

Tim Cahill faced a setback when he failed to gain selection with the Sydney Olympic youth squad and was informed that he 'was too small and not fast enough'.[98] He trialled with another Greek backed club Belmore Hercules two divisions lower and gained selection. He was by far the youngest player in their under 18 squad, aged only fifteen. He had a sensational first year scoring goals at will. After one particularly good game he was asked to also play in the under 21 team. Tim was beginning to gain press coverage in the local Greek newspapers one report noting 'Cahill jumps like a kangaroo'.[99] All the heading practice and training had him like a coiled spring ready to shoot into the air and outjump much bigger defenders and send in powerful headed goals.

One day he played for the under 18s but was told he would not be required today for the under 21s. Tim could not hide his disappointment but was then informed the coach wanted him for the first-grade team. Tim Cahill remains today the youngest player at fifteen to ever play for the Belmore Hercules team. It was late in the match when he was sent on to the field as a substitute and the team had just received a corner. As Tim recalls: 'The ball came over from the right, I jumped with three other defenders – men who were much bigger than me. I managed to climb out of the pack: not using vertical leap, but proper timing of my run'.[100]

As would happen countless times throughout his career, head connected with ball and it flew into the net. The team secured the league title in that game and he

98 Cahill, 2015: pp68-69
99 Ibid, pp73
100 Cahill, 2010: pp74

was an instant celebrity. He now feels that despite the heartache and sense of failure after being cut from Sydney Olympic it was probably the best thing that could have happened to him.

The success he achieved with Belmore did not go unnoticed and he was picked up by Sydney United, a Croatian backed club with a proud history in the NSL. He was given a lot of playing time in the under 21 side despite being still in high school. Midway through that first season with Sydney United Tim's father dropped a bombshell informing him he had made contact with a couple of English clubs and there was an opportunity to trial with Nottingham Forest and Millwall. The Cahills had relatives in England, so he would have a family connection in the UK. His parents insisted it was to be his choice. He weighed up the options and thinking of the preference in Australia for big burley forwards full of muscle it was an easy response 'I'll never make it here, dad. I won't get a chance to play in Australia. I want to go to England and at least give it a go.'[101] It was a major sacrifice by all members of the Cahill family to get Tim to England for a trial and it was something he certainly appreciates.

In late 1997 he bade a tearful goodbye to his parents at Sydney airport. It was an exciting moment to be jetting off across the world to hopefully fulfil his dream to become a professional footballer. He was met by his family's Samoan relatives at Heathrow and transported to their home in Dartford. He was immediately made a member of the family and it helped overcome homesickness.

He was still to overcome the weather and really felt the cold in the first few weeks. He was training on his own in a park near their home to keep fit for the trial. He was running and kicking a ball about under grey thick skies with perpetual rain streaming down and bitterly cold. It was six weeks before the trial chance came up with Millwall. The trial lasted seven weeks with drills, exercise and games. He was nervous and over excited to begin with but settled and began to shine, helped by the fact that he formed a strong friendship with another young trialist Paul Ifill. At the end of the trial period he was informed that he was to be offered a contract and paid £250 a week. Tim would later reflect that if they had offered him two Australian dollars a week, he would have jumped at it. Out of the blue he was

---

[101] Ibid, pp82

informed that two other offers had come in from Nottingham Forest and Queens Park Rangers with more money on the table. He only took a few days to think on the offers but felt a tug of loyalty to Millwall for the chance to trial they had offered him. Despite his young age Tim Cahill was a realist and he felt that staying with Millwall would give him the perfect springboard to start his career and offer him chances faster. He immediately was placed into a flat with a couple of Irish players near the Millwall training facility. His life as a youth player and apprentice footballer was underway including cleaning the boots of the professional players and cleaning the ground and facilities.

The training intensity was nothing he had ever experienced back home. Through that first season he played with the youth and reserve teams and was also called up to train with the first team. He quickly established a reputation as a fierce competitor. He was fortunate to have another young Australian player, Lucas Neill, in the first team at Millwall and Neill made sure to give time and encouragement to Cahill.

It was at the end of twelve months and aged 18 that he was brought on as a substitute for his first game with the senior team against Bournemouth. Tim had throughout the year given 120% of himself in everything: training, games, attitude and professionalism. He was intense, focused, passionate and he likened his attitude as the 'Samoan warrior' side of his character coming through. He was totally fearless on the pitch. He was offered a new contract and he had no hesitation in re-signing with Millwall with a tidy £5000 fee that converted to A$14,500, plus £1000 a month. He sent all of the signing on fee back home to his parents. He paid a deposit for a family home back in Sydney and Tim was on his way. The Millwall fans were from the outset a source of great inspiration to Cahill and he recognised their intimidation on opposing teams and their fans. 'The Den' as the Millwall ground is called was a fortress of fear and fan adoration for their team. He was a part of the Millwall squad that captured the English Football League Second Division Championship in the 2000–2001 season.

The first three years with Millwall were not without setbacks through injuries including a broken foot; then he did his ACL, and both saw him have long spells off the field. Off the pitch his girlfriend from Sydney, Rebecca eventually moved to England to be with him and they soon had their first child on the way as well as acquiring an £80,000 apartment in Bromley.

He worked tirelessly on the ACL rehabilitation and was soon back. From that point on became a regular first team member. The greatest moment of his Millwall career was the incredible FA Cup run the club had in 2004. Millwall beat Tranmere Rover 2-1 to make the semi-final of the most revered club knockout cup competition in the world. The semi-final was to be played at Old Trafford against Sunderland. This was a massive game and occasion for Tim particularly being played at the 'Theatre of Dreams'. Manchester United had been his team from a young age and to play on their ground at Old Trafford was immense. It also held significance in that Paul Ifill, who he had first trialled with at Millwall, was also on the pitch with him. It was after a mazy run and shot by Ifill that the ball came back off the goalkeeper into the penalty area and there was Timmy Cahill arriving on the spot to send in a screaming volley past the Sunderland keeper.

Tim Cahill went on a galloping run and celebration the length of the Old Trafford stadium. It was extra special as his mum, dad and brother Sean were in the stadium also going delirious with the excited Millwall fans. When the game kicked off again Kevin Muscat the Australian captain of Millwall was injured and forced to leave the field. Millwall and their players dug deep and fought over every blade of grass of the famous pitch to achieve a wonderful victory and make the FA Cup Final. Tim still rates the semi-final goal against Sunderland as one of his greatest goals. The full impact for Tim Cahill of that goal and getting to the FA Cup Final was the fact that he was now under notice of the Australian selectors for the Socceroos, with the Final to be played at the Millennium Stadium, Cardiff in Wales against his childhood team, Manchester United.

The 2004 FA Cup Final for Millwall was anti-climactic and there was to be no fairytale end to their Cup run ended in a Manchester United triumph, 3-0. This was an outstanding United team a virtual galaxy of stars that included Ryan Giggs, Roy Keane, Paul Scholes, Gary and Phil Neville, Cristiano Ronaldo and Ruud van Nistelrooy. The press described Millwall and its players valiant in defeat going down to two goals from van Nistelrooy and a header by Ronaldo.

In the wake of Millwall's heroics in the FA Cup run and Tim Cahill's personal high form, Australian coach Frank Farina had no hesitation in calling him into the Socceroos training camp. Farina was immediately contacted by FIFA and informed that Cahill was in fact ineligible because he had represented Samoa at under 20 level. It was a shock to Farina, Tim Cahill and the Australian soccer officials. Tim offered his explanation of his grandmothers' ill health, that he was in fact only fourteen at the time and had no idea that coming on as a sub in this match could rule him out of Australian team selection in the future. It all came down to a legal wrangle involving FIFA, Australia and the Oceania Football Confederation. Tim was adamant he had been born in Australia and learnt all his football skills on the parks of western Sydney. In early 2004, after substantial work to argue the case by Farina and his offsiders, FIFA changed its eligibility rules on kids capped at junior level and thankfully he was now free to represent his country.

He was called up by Farina immediately into the Socceroos squad for a friendly match in London against South Africa. He would come on in the 74th minute replacing goal scorer Mark Bresciano. It was a very proud moment for Cahill and he acknowledges the persistence of then coach Farina in fighting to get him cleared to play for the Socceroos. This particular Socceroos squad would go on to achieve phenomenal success and gain the nickname of the 'Golden Generation'. The squad included the likes of Mark Schwarzer, Lucas Neill, Craig Moore, Stan Lazaridis, Josip Skoko, Mark Bresciano, Scott Chipperfield, Brett Emerton, Harry Kewell, Mark Viduka and John Aloisi.

Tim Cahill was retained for the Oceania Football Confederation Nations Cup and World Cup qualifying tournament to be held in Adelaide. I was fortunate to be living in Adelaide at the time and attended all of the Socceroos games in that tournament against New Zealand, Tahiti, Vanuatu, Fiji, and the Solomon Islands. Tim Cahill finished as the leading scorer in the tournament scoring six goals and signed a program for my son Ganur.

His form with Millwall had attracted the attention of offers from four clubs from the premier league and he was now faced with the option of leaving Millwall. It was no easy decision, but he eventually opted for Everton and was sold on the deal by the manager David Moyes. He had played 217 games for Millwall and scored 52 goals.

One condition on signing with Everton was that he would be free to play for Australia in the 2004 Athens Olympic Games. Australia drew its opening game with Tunisia 1-1 before thrashing Serbia 6-0 with Cahill scoring twice. In the final group game, they went down to eventual gold medal winners Argentina 1-0 with an outstanding Carlos Tevez in their side. Unfortunately, Australia lost 1-0 to Iraq in the quarter finals with both Tim Cahill and Craig Moore suspended through copping two yellow cards in the group stage. After the Olympic exit, it was back to Liverpool and a new footballing life with Everton in the Premier League. In only his second appearance for Everton he felt the highs and lows of the game. In the first half he received a yellow card through a scuffle, he scored in the 60th minute through a trademark header and tore off on a celebration run earning another yellow card, and was sent off for ripping his shirt off. Fortunately, Everton held on for the win. He established himself in the Everton team that first season, scoring regularly and ended the season as the club's top scorer. Additionally, and showcasing his acceptance by the Everton fans he was voted the 'fan's player of the season'.

The year 2006 would mark a very special year for both Tim Cahill and the Socceroos at the World Cup in Germany. Despite having knocked out Uruguay in the qualifier and with Guus Hiddink as coach, no one really gave Australia much of a chance. Tim Cahill recalled that the training regime that Hiddink and his assistant Johan Neeskens installed pre-cup was the hardest he has ever experienced. The Australian team would be able to run through brick walls and the discipline he instilled was regimental much like an army barracks. They were prepared 'scientifically, tactically, strategically, mentally'.[102] Hiddink made it clear there were no egos in his teams and certainly no certain starters.

Tim Cahill rightly or wrongly was under the impression he was in the starting line-up for the opening game against Japan. Hiddink for whatever reason changed his mind on the morning of the game. Tim was devastated to find himself on the substitutes' bench but took the news calmly. It may have in fact fired up Tim Cahill if the chance came to come off the bench.

The game against Japan will always be remembered as the first game Australia won at the World Cup finals and the first game in which Australia scored a goal at the World Cup. It was in every sense a remarkable game. After a couple of chances to Australia they went behind in the 26th minute after a clear foul on Mark Schwarzer. After 60 minutes Hiddink went to his bench and brought Cahill on to replace

102 Cahill, 2015: pp207

Bresciano. Australia swarmed forward in waves of attack for the next twenty minutes, but the Blue Samurai wall of defiance held. In the 80th minute a Kewell shot was blocked, and it fell to Tim Cahill who fired a low hard shot into the corner of the net. The pressure valve was released, Tim tore off for his customary boxing the corner flag routine and Australia and its team was in pandemonium. Only eight minutes later another ball into the Japanese box finds the foot of Cahill, and in a precision like move he dissects the crowded goalmouth to fire in a second goal in off the post. The Australian team and fans were delirious with joy. But it was not over, as John Aloisi sealed the victory for Australia in the 90th minute. Australia had won 3-1. The second game of the group stage was to be up against defending champions Brazil ,with players like Ronaldinho, Rivaldo, Robert Carlos, Cafu, Kaka and Ronaldo. It was a mighty performance from Australia to be 0-0 at halftime. Brazil took the lead after 49 minutes, but Australia pressed forward and Cahill, Viduka and Kewell all had chances to equalise. Brazil scored a second goal after 90 minutes to win the match 2-0.

The loss meant that Australia would have the chance to progress to the round of sixteen if they could achieve a draw with Croatia in the final group game. It certainly did not begin well, and Australia were one down after only two minutes. Australia equalised after 39 minutes from the penalty spot. Croatia again took the lead following a goalkeeping error by Zeljko Kalac. Australia again pressed forward with a number of chances. It was finally Harry Kewell who fired Australia level in the 79th minute.

The end of the match was bizarre. Australian born and educated Croatian defender Josep Simunic should have been sent off earlier for receiving a second yellow card eventually receiving his third card and expulsion near the end. Mark Viduka scored a good goal that was disallowed at the very death of the game. But Australia had qualified for the last sixteen and up against heavyweights Italy in the knockout phase. The Socceroos performances had witnessed an incredible surge of interest in the game and thousands of supporters back home in Australia watched these games on big screens at fan venues throughout the country.

The game against Italy - another team with a cavalcade of star players like Fabio Cannavaro, Alessandro Del Piero, Francesco Totti, Andrea Pirlo, Gennaro Gattuso and Luca Toni would be a match to remember. Australia were holding their own and then received an almighty boost when just after halftime Matterazi was shown a straight red card for a tackle on Bresciano. Australia were on top and had a number of chances to convert, but the Italians, even with a man down, held possession and locked up their defence.

Hiddink and Australia were looking to extra time and the fact that the fitness of the Socceroos and a man advantage would crack the Italians open. Sadly, it did not get to extra time. In a rare excursion upfield Italy through their fullback conned a penalty out of the referee when Grosso took a dive and fell over Lucas Neill's outstretched leg. Totti scored the heartbreaking winner from the spot and the heroic Australian team were beaten 1-0. In the final analysis the Australian performance overall was outstanding throughout the tournament. Italy would go on to lift the World Cup making the Socceroos performance even more memorable. It had been a remarkable experience for Tim Cahill and he was hankering for more. He was nominated for the FIFA Ballon d'Or in 2006 to cap off a wonderful year.

He would experience a further six great years wearing an Everton shirt including another great FA Cup run in 2009 including a penalty shootout win over Manchester United in the semi-final at Wembley. Tim Cahill would experience disappointment at Wembley in the final when after going ahead to a Louis Saha goal after only 25 seconds (the fastest ever Cup Final goal) Everton lost to Chelsea 2-1.

In the aftermath of the 2006 World Cup Finals Guus Hiddink left to take over the reins of Russia, and Graham Arnold was placed in charge as interim manager. An early exit from the Asian Cup saw the appointment of another Dutchman Pim Verbeek as the Australian manager. The Socceroos under Verbeek had a wonderful World Cup qualifying run to the 2010 finals in South Africa. Additionally, during Verbeek's reign, they had some impressive wins over Holland and the Republic of Ireland.

In South Africa the Socceroos were in a tough group comprising Germany, Ghana and Serbia. In their opening match against global heavyweights Germany Australia were over run by a skillful team full of running and power. The Socceroos were 2-0 down after just 26 minutes. Then Tim Cahill, ever the 110 percent commitment man went in for a fifty-fifty ball with German midfielder Bastian Schweinsteiger. Schweinsteiger was collected and went down like he had been shot. Tim was shown a direct red card. He was out of the match and also the following game against Ghana. The Socceroos went down 4-0 to the Germans with only ten men on the pitch and the negative goal difference would prove significant.

Against Ghana Australia were again down to ten men when Harry Kewell was given a red card. Brett Holman scored but Ghana equalised to end the game 1-1. Australia were in a must win situation against Serbia in the last group game and needed to win well. Australia were two up, including an outstanding header from Tim Cahill and went close to adding a third but a late goal from Serbia saw the game end 2-1 to the Socceroos. Sadly, it was not enough to progress to the last sixteen.

The following year, under another new coach Holger Osieck of Germany, Australia performed exceptionally well going down to old rivals Japan in the Asian Cup Final 1-0.

Tim Cahill has drawn strength from his Samoan cultural background during his career, including having a traditional tattoo placed on his left arm. It was done in 2008 in tribute to his recently deceased grandmother and was done in Samoa by a renowned Samoan tattoo artist. The artwork represents Tim and his family and their lifelines and cultural connections. The tattoo would provide Tim a sense of security and a deep knowing that he would forever be under a cloak of his grandmother's protection.

Just prior to the start of the 2012 season Tim Cahill's agent contacted him on a potential move to New York Red Bulls in the USA Major League Soccer (MLS) competition. He had spent 15 years in British football including eight seasons with Everton in the Premier League. It was a major decision for both Tim and his family to relocate to New York.

One of the great memories of his time with the Red Bulls was in scoring the fastest goal ever recorded in the MLS. Straight from the kick-off, Thierry Henry played the ball back to Dax McCarty who played an immediate long ball down the field that Tim ran onto. He brought it down off his chest and smacked it cleanly into the net.

Meanwhile Tim was enjoying himself with the Socceroos regularly scoring goals in friendly and World Cup qualifying games for Brazil in 2014. An ageing Australian team under the guidance of Osieck were struggling through the qualifying stages of the World Cup. They only just scraped through but two friendly games against

Brazil and France brought down the curtain on Osieck's time in charge, both resounding 6-0 losses.

Australian Ange Postecoglou was named as Osieck's replacement. Postecoglou had established an enviable track record of success in both the Australian NSL and the A-League, particularly in latter years with Brisbane Roar. Postecoglou came in with a fresh broom and many of the great stars of the Australian team over the previous ten years were either left out or decided to retire. Overnight the team known as the 'Golden Generation' were a part of history. Players like Tim Cahill and Mark Bresciano would have to prove their worth and earn their place in this new environment. In one of Postecoglou's early games in charge the Socceroos were beaten in London by Ecuador 4-3, but Cahill scored two goals. Postecoglou remarked after the game 'Timmy comes into every camp and trains harder than anyone. He treats every game in the Socceroos' shirt like it's his last'.[103]

The 2014 World Cup Finals in Brazil marked the changing of the guard for the Australian team and the instilling of a new philosophy and approach to the game. Australia again did not fare well in the draw and were placed in the so-called group of death with top class sides Chile, the Netherlands and reigning world champions Spain. In the opening match against Chile, the Socceroos were nearly blown away by the speed and interaction of the Chilean inter-passing and found themselves two down before they knew what had happened. Australia knuckled down and fought their way back into the match with Tim Cahill scoring with another superb header before halftime. The game had completely turned around and Australia were dominating the match and pressing forward. Tim Cahill again got to a cross at the near post and his header hit the net. Unfortunately, the linesman's flag was up for a very close offside call. Australia had another outstanding opportunity to equalise before Chile scored their third goal to seal a 3-1 victory.

Their second match would be against a rampaging Holland who had just smashed reigning champions Spain 5-1. No one gave Australia any hope in the game and expected a massacre. The Socceroos pressed high and harried the Dutch from the outset. Holland scored against the run of play through an individual goal from Arjen Robben. Then came a goal from Tim Cahill right out of goal scoring

---

[103] Cahill, 2015: pp297

heaven. I was at the stadium close to the front when Ryan McGowan played a 40 metre dissecting pass high and through the back of the Dutch defence. For me in the stand that day, and so close to the action, for a moment it felt like time stood still. The ball arced over, Tim Cahill was onto it, and caught the ball perfectly on the volley and it screamed into the Dutch net past a clawing goalkeeper.

Tim Cahill wheeled away and ran to the corner flag for his boxing routine and towards where I was seated. It sent the Australian section of the stadium delirious with celebration. I just look back at that goal with the sheer audacity and precision involved to conjure such a goal. Australia were now really in the game and uplifted through such a magnificent goal. Australia were awarded a penalty and skipper Mile Jedinak stepped up and cool as you like put Australia in the lead. It seemed as if a football fairytale was unfolding but the young Australian team lost their focus and the Dutch scored through van Persie and Depay to take the lead back. Australia chased hard for another equaliser but were down and out of the World Cup, 3-2.

Tim Cahill had picked up another yellow card against Holland, his second of the tournament, and would miss the final group game against Spain in any event - an anti-climax seeing Australia could not progress. Spain duly won the game 3-0 through goals from David Villa, Fernando Torres and Juan Mata. The 2014 World Cup would be remembered for the young Australian team that was blooded in the fierce competitive space of World Cup finals football, Tim Cahill's magnificent goal against Holland and the fact that he had now joined an elite group of players who had scored goals in three successive World Cup final tournaments.

Thoughts were now turning to the 2015 Asian Cup to be held in Australia. Tim Cahill's time with the New York Red Bulls was up in the air. They had made the MLS play-offs but went down to the New England Revolution and Thierry Henry announced his retirement. Tim focused his attention on the Asian Cup and, at the age of 34, trained with even greater intensity. The form of the Australian team in the lead up to the tournament was questionable and the critics were already out. The doomsayers were answered in the first game when from a goal down Australia swamped Kuwait 4-1 in Melbourne. Australia defeated Oman 4-0 and were given a jolt by South Korea going down 1-0 in the final group game. The quarter final clash with China saw Tim Cahill score two outstanding goals including an overhead scissor kick to see Australia through to the semi-finals. The Socceroos overcame the UAE in the semi-final 2-0 to book a spot in the Asian Cup final against old foes South Korea.

The final witnessed an intense, exciting and uplifting match. The game flowed back and forth during the first half with both sides having chances and prepared to break at speed on the counter when defending. The deadlock was broken just before halftime when Massimo Luongo found space and sent in an unstoppable shot from the edge of the area to put Australia 1-0 up. South Korea intensified their efforts after the break to find an equaliser. Tim Cahill copped a couple of bruising tackles and was clearly a passenger, and was subbed off in the 62nd minute. The Socceroos defended their lead with resolve for the next 30 minutes and seemed assured of lifting the trophy until a defensive lapse in the second minute of injury time saw an opportunity fall to Son Heung-min and he dispatched the equaliser. The stadium had been silenced and the Australian team so close to victory were now to face extra time and a very uplifted South Korea. The Australian team lifted and in the 14th minute of extra time Tommy Juric concocted an opportunity that fell to James Troisi to slam Australia back in front. The Australia team fought for every ball through the second period of extra time and ran like men possessed. The referee blew the whistle and Australia were champions of Asia and had claimed their first major international trophy. Tim Cahill was ecstatic and has reflected on the euphoria that engulfed the Australian group after the game and during the presentation ceremony. He was at that point unsure if the game may well have been his last in the green and gold of Australia.

The aftermath of the Asian Cup witnessed a major shift for Tim Cahill. He moved from the United States to China and signed with Shanghai Shenhua for one year with an option for extension. He was not prepared for the Chinese supporter's enthusiasm for his signing with over one thousand fans turning out to greet him at Shanghai International Airport. He stayed and played with Shanghai throughout the 2015–2016 seasons making 28 appearances and scoring eleven goals. The team made it to the Chinese FA Cup Final but went down in extra time to Jiangsu Suning.

When informed that he was not a part of new coach Gregorio Manzano's 2016–17 season plans Tim gained a release and joined Zhejiang Greentown also in the Chinese Super League. He would make 17 appearances for Zhejiang Greentown and scored four goals. Tim Cahill's club playing future from the time he left Everton has resembled something of a short-term global travelling minstrel footballer. The main focus for Tim in heading to China was gaining as much playing time as he could to remain a part of the Socceroos squads for the World Cup qualifiers for Russia 2018. It was plain that he remained a part of Ange Postecoglou's plans, simply by the fact that he continued to score goals for the team despite the age of 37. The qualifying rounds to the World Cup finals in Russia ran into difficulties early on and Australia struggled. Coach Postecoglou became a target of the media and critics. Tim Cahill for his part continued to come up with valuable goals including scoring his 50th goal for the national team in a 2-1 win against Syria.

At club level he left China and elected to return home and signed a lucrative three-year deal with Melbourne City in the A-League. Initially everything went well as City won the FFA Cup Final against Sydney City with Tim Cahill scoring a trademark header. Another highlight was a spectacular 35 metre volley scored against arch rivals Melbourne Victory in a 4-1 Melbourne derby win. But a clear differing opinion on the team with new coach Warren Joyce saw Tim Cahill spending a lot of time on the bench which, with the World Cup approaching, was causing Tim no end of frustration.

The Socceroos failed to gain qualification direct from the Asian Confederation for the World Cup finals, and had to take part in an inter-continental play-off for the final spot, which saw increased pressure and criticism levelled at the team and coach Postecoglou. Tim Cahill had endured enough at Melbourne City and was granted a release from his contract to return to Britain and his first club overseas, Millwall. Tim made his debut as a late substitute for the team and was given a standing ovation from the Millwall fans.

The Socceroos eventually booked their ticket to Russia with a two-leg win over Honduras, but coach Ange Postecoglou had taken enough of the media criticism and resigned as Australian coach. Sadly, this certainly put the Socceroos at a significant disadvantage going into the World Cup. Dutch coach Bert van Marwijk was announced as the interim coach.

The Millwall move was also frustrating for Tim Cahill he made only ten appearances for the club, all as a late substitute. This was not the ideal preparation for a player at the age of 38 on the eve of his fourth World Cup tournament.

The 2018 World Cup Finals were to again prove a frustrating tournament for

Australia. They were drawn into a very competitive group including France, Denmark and Peru. In the opening game they were drawn up against a star-studded French team that would go on to win the tournament. Australia put in a magnificent performance to be level with France until a very lucky late Paul Pogba goal. The second match saw Australia draw 1-1 with Denmark, but it was an uninspiring game. Tim Cahill had not gained a minute on the field in the opening two games. The final game against Peru needed Australia to gain a convincing win to progress but it was not to be, going down 2-0. Tim Cahill was given the chance to make his mark on football history coming on in the 53rd minute but sadly could not come up with a goal. Australia would finish bottom of the group and Tim Cahill immediately announced his retirement from international football. But befitting his status and achievements he was brought back for one final cameo appearance for the Socceroos against Lebanon in Sydney in late 2018. He was greatly honoured to make 108 appearances with 50 goals.

He signed with Jamshedpur in the Indian Super League for the 2018–19 season and made eleven appearances and scored two goals for the club. On March 28, 2019 he announced his retirement from the game.

How can one adequately sum up Tim Cahill as a player? Flamboyant, driven, inspirational quite simply a super talent.

Mary Fowler – There's Something About Mary

The Matildas' youngest player leading into the 2019 France World Cup was 16 year old Mary Fowler. Mary, one of five siblings, is the daughter of an Irishman and a Papua New Guinean mother. Mary learnt to kick a ball on the sands and beaches around Cairns.

Mary had represented Queensland at under 12 level aged just ten and all were amazed at her skill level. Former Matilda player Sonia Gegenhuber coached Mary in the representative team and was glowing in her estimation as a complete package: 'She has the footballing brain and the skill level, first touch, body position, vision, athletic ability.' [104]

[104] *The Weekend Australian* 8-9 June, 1991: pp41

She had training and trials whilst her family was based in Holland. On their return to Australia the family certainly did it tough in supporting the kids sporting careers. They stayed in caravan parks and tents and struggled to make ends meet. The family even had a nickname for the family car "Hotel Tarago" because of how often they all had to sleep in it. [105]

Mary Fowler would go on to make her debut for the Matildas against Brazil aged just 15 in 2018. She later came off the bench in matches against England and France. Former Matildas' coach Alen Stajcic who was in charge for her debut game described her as one of the most gifted players he'd seen in the women's game. [106]

Mary was very proud to be chosen as part of the Matildas squad for the France World Cup. Coach Ante Milicic was adamant that Fowler was 'chosen not on potential but on current ability'. She had already had a good tournament with the Asian Qualifiers for the Asian Cup in Myanmar with the Young Matilda'. In one of those games, an 11-1 thumping of Nepal ,she scored five goals. Milicic added that her selection for France was still a learning process and 'what better place than going to a World Cup'. [107] Sadly she suffered a hamstring injury shortly before the World Cup began. She was on the bench for the game against Jamaica and Norway but will be all the better for the having experienced a World Cup. She is certainly a star player in waiting.

[105] *The Daily Telegraph,* 8 June, 1991
[106] *The Sydney Morning Herald,* 15 May, 2019: pp52
[107] *The Sydney Morning Herald,* 15 May, 2019: pp47

This 1862 etching, by artist Gustav Mützel, depicts a young Aboriginal man balancing a ball on his foot in a Ronaldinho-like pose. Mützel used the notes from pioneer scientist, William Blandowski, as the basis for this work.

Quilp with the Dinmore Bush Rats, Ipswich, Queensland, 1910

Willie Allen was a Larrakia man from the Top End, a World War I soldier and all-round sports star.

Goalkeeper Walter Ernest 'Bondi' Neal (centre of picture) with the Balgownie Rangers, c.1921

Children playing football at Cubawee Aboriginal School near Lismore, New South Wales, 1930

Charles Perkins' invitation to attend Old Trafford for a training session "with your boots", 1959

Charles Perkins playing for Adelaide Croatia in 1961

The South Australian state football team, 1960, with John Moriarty (front row, third from left) and Charles Perkins (front row, fourth from right)

John Moriarty playing for Adelaide Juventus, 1960

Gordon Briscoe, 1970

Harry Williams was the first Indigenous Australian to play at a World Cup and was part of the first Socceroos World Cup squad, West Germany, 1974. Williams played 43 games for Australia between 1970 and 1977.

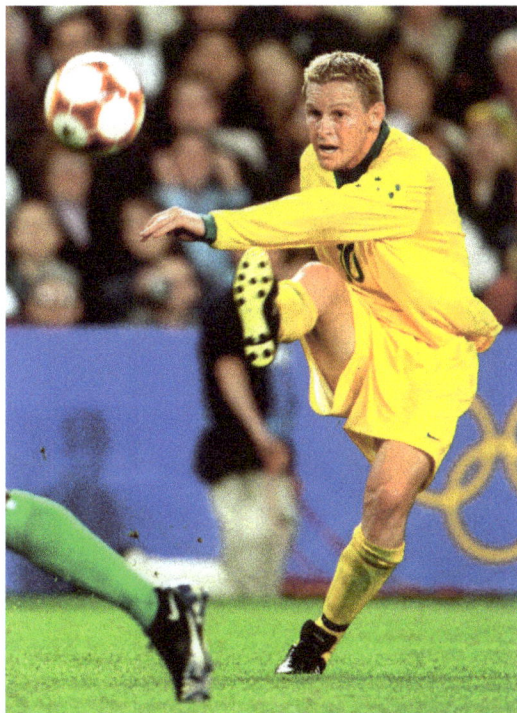

Kasey Wehrman played
14 games for the Socceroos
between 1998 and 2006

David Williams in action for North Queensland Fury, A-League, 2010.
He played two games for the Socceeroos between 2008 and 2010

Adam Sarota played three games for the Socceroos in 2011 and 2012

Adelaide United captain, Travis Dodd, Club World Cup final v Gamba Osaka, 2008. He played two games for the Socceroos in 2006

Jade North played 41 games for the Socceroos between 2002 and 2013

Frank Farina played 67 games for the Socceroos between 1984 and 1995. He was also coach of the national team from 1999 to 2005 presiding over 60 games

Tim Cahill is the Socceroos all-time leading goalscorer with 50 goals from 108 games between 2004 and 2018, while Archie Thompson played 55 games for the national team between 2001 and 2013

Paul Henderson, Leicester City, 2008

James Brown, Melbourne Heart, A-League, 2012

Tahj Minniecon, Western Sydney Wanderers, A-League, 2013

Karen Menzies was the first Indigenous woman to play for the Matildas, playing 9 games from 1983 to 1989

Kayleen Janssen played 27 games for the Matildas from 1991 to 1995

Bridgette Starr was an outstanding Matilda who played 59 games for Australia between 1994 and 2002

Kyah Simon is still an active Matilda with an international career that began in 2007

Lydia Williams is still an active Matilda with an international career that began in 2005

Phoenix Cerda of Mildura United celebrates a goal

The world at her feet? Shadeene Evans of Borroloola in the Northern Territory

CHAPTER 7
Playing on the Fringe – Emerging Talent and Unfulfilled Expectations

The sudden and unexpected acceleration of Aboriginal involvement in soccer initially proved a very positive development. There have been some outstanding Indigenous soccer players who broke through to the highest levels of the game. But for bad luck, injuries, lack of support or understanding of cultural differences, some of these players did not go on to reach their full potential.

The disappointments along the way include a complete failure to observe sometimes subtle but nevertheless important considerations when dealing with Indigenous players and issues. While these may be slight, they can in some cases mean the difference between an Indigenous player succeeding or failing.

Tom Sermanni, twice the coach of the Australian women's soccer team, the Matildas, was one who had shown insight and been able to recognise what is needed to ensure Indigenous players succeed. Obviously, good support is crucial, and Sermanni was forthright in *Australian Football Weekly:* 'The critical thing is how you manage [Indigenous players]. You have to allow a little bit of leeway and a bit of freedom to get the best out of them. Their approach to the game is great; they play very seriously, but they need that freedom, too.'

Tahj Minniecon – The Gun

Like his friend David Williams, Tahj Minniecon was a soccer prodigy blessed with blistering pace and great ball control. Born in Cairns, of Aboriginal and Islander descent, with 'connections to the Kabi Kabi and Wiradjuri mobs and Vanuatu'.[108] He grew up in Brisbane and Canberra, where he learned his soccer skills. He went to Cavendish Road State High School and Carbrook State School and played junior soccer with Loganholme Lightning Football Club.

Minniecon was a standout during his junior career and was picked up by the Queensland Academy of Sport and subsequently the Australian Institute of Sport. In 2003, when he was just 16 years old, the English club Blackburn Rovers invited him to spend several weeks at their academy. Being noticed by state and national selectors firmly planted the idea in the young player's mind that a soccer career was on his agenda. He told the *Koori Mail,* 'Hopefully, I've got the goods for that. I've been to England already and it gave me a good insight into how they play there and how they make it in the [English Premier League]. It wasn't very different to what I was used to here. I coped pretty well with it.'

In 2007 Minniecon was signed by Brisbane Roar (then Quensland Roar) from the Australian Institute of Sport. He was excited: 'This is my hometown club and ever since the A-league started, I always wanted to start my career with Queensland Roar. My family and friends are in Brisbane and I can't wait to get started.' He played twenty-four games for the club during the 2007–08 season, scoring four goals.

Minniecon was selected in the Australian team that played in the 2007 Youth Olympics in Sydney. He scored the crucial goal that secured Australia the bronze medal. He had already tasted international success and was hungry for more. He had been a part of the Young Socceroos team that won the Weifang Cup in China. They beat Uzbekistan 1-0 in the final game of the tournament and finished top of the tournament - one point ahead of hosts China, and Iran. The young team won four of their five matches and given that they played five games in ten days, this was a testament to their stamina, especially as all the matches were played in stifling heat and humidity. Tahj Minniecon was selected by the media as the Player of the Tournament. This success capitalised on his earlier performances when selected to represent Australia in Japan in 2005 at the Niigata Youth Tournament. There, he scored the winning goal against Hungary to bring home the cup. After the initial

....

108 *Koori Mail,* 15 August 2007, pp94

breakthrough, things cooled with the Roar and he was put out on loan with Redlands United in the Queensland Premier League where he scored nine goals from just fifteen appearances.

A little surprisingly for some, Minniecon signed with the new A-League franchise Gold Coast United for 2009–10. It has been suggested that money was his prime motivator, but Minniecon told *Australian Football Weekly* there was much more to the decision. 'I don't think the money was too much of a factor, to be honest. I know a lot of people are saying that it is, but in all honesty it wasn't. [Gold Coast] are forming a great team and it 'll be good to learn off the likes of Jason Culina - if he arrives - and Shane Smeltz and Paul Okon; it's definitely going to be a step up in improving my game.

Minniecon was Gold Coast United's youth marquee signing and he was regarded as one of the hottest properties in the A-League. A club spokesman had no reservations in stating that 'searing explosive pace and power' made him one of the League's most difficult opponents. The conclusion was that 'the best is yet to come from Tahj.

Towards the end of the 2010–11 season, he gained a place in the Gold Coast team that reached the play-offs. Although they lost out to the Central Coast Mariners in the elimination semi-final, Tahj Minniecon was beginning to grow in confidence and fulfil his undoubted potential. He was unquestionably an exciting young prospect and, like David Williams, had the potential to play a major part in the Socceroos post-South Africa 2010.

Sadly, in his four seasons with Gold Coast United, Minniecon wasn't able to establish a regular first team berth. Admittedly, he'd been up against some stiff opposition, with established international star strikers like Shane Smeltz and Bruce Djite in the squad. Initially he looked like gaining a move to the Newcastle Jets in a trade deal for Chris Payne but the move fell through when he suffered an injury in a youth league game against Sydney FC.

Sadly, the career of Tahj Minniecon unravelled and derailed as the Gold Coast club folded. He moved to the Western City Wanderers where he again struggled to break through for a regular position in the first team. He made 16 appearances over two seasons without scoring a goal.

It appears that Australian teams do not encourage off-the-cuff, flair, skill and speed as Minniecon struggled to gain acceptance in more regimented strict defensive formations. He left the Wanderers and played ten games with Rockdale City Suns in the NSW Premier League before moving to the Philippines with Loyola Meralco. He scored on his debut for the club in a 3-2 victory over Manila Jeepney in 2015. The club changed its name to FC Meralco Manila when it joined the Philippines Football League in 2017. Minniecon's bad luck continued when the club was dissolved in early 2018. He returned to Australia and played for Nunawading FC in the Victorian State league where he scored two goals and made 23 appearances. Now something of a journeyman footballer, Minniecon joined Davao Aguilas in the Philippines Premier League in late 2018. At the age of 30, Minniecon can reflect on a career that offered so much but his skill, speed and flair was not something prized or encouraged in the Australian game.

Freddy Agius – The Wonder Boy

Freddy Agius was a prodigious young talent, although he had had his share of stops and starts in a career that had always promised so much. He started playing soccer when he was five years old and fell under the spell of the world game. He initially followed along behind his older brother Raymond, who was playing for the local Brahma Lodge Junior Soccer Club in Adelaide. He played both soccer and Australian football until he was ten years old, at which point he chose soccer over Australian football.

Agius comes from a respected South Australian Aboriginal family and he draws support from them. They include uncles Vince Copley and Ross Agius, a former prominent Australian football player in the South Australian National Football League, who won premierships with the dominant Port Adelaide Magpies during the 1980s. But undoubtedly his number one fan was his grandmother, Auntie Josie Agius, and to her he always carried the fond nickname of 'Freddy Frog'. In an interview with the *Adelaide Sunday Mail* in 2004 he said, 'Nanna is my number one supporter. She's always been there for me from day one when I first played soccer and I'm glad my family is right behind what I do.'

Vince Copley was impressed from the beginning. Speaking with me in 2004, he said:

Freddy's brother Raymond was pretty good as well, as young boys they had all the skills, it was like seeing Johnny [Moriarty] and Charlie [Perkins] again ... His grandmother, who is my sister, said come out and have a look at him. So, I did and said, 'Look, he's wasting his time here.' He made the Joeys [Under 17s World Cup team and all of his team-mates with the Joeys squad are players now playing at the very highest [European] level. I said to Freddy this thing has already taken you half way round the world and Aussie Rules won't do that.

From his early days on the primary school pitch, Agius was a sensation, impressing teammates, opponents and spectators alike. Between 1998 and 2000 he played for the South Australian Sports Institute. His talent and performances were of such a high quality that he gained selection in the Australian under 17 World Cup squad that travelled to Trinidad and Tobago to contest the Under 17 World Cup in 2001. He was a standout in the Australian team and was judged by many as one of the most gifted technical players of the tournament. He scored a wonder goal with a spectacular free kick, gained Man of the Match honours with his performance against the hosts, Trinidad and Tobago, and certainly grabbed the attention of the scouts.

The World Cup delivered many wonderful memories including being invited to cricket legend Brian Lara's home for dinner after his cracking performance against Trinidad and Tobago. At the time the big names that surfaced as part of the under 17 World Cup were Fernando Torres, Carlos Tevez, Pablo Zabaleta and Niko Kranjcar. Freddy Agius' name was right up there with them as one of the most exciting talents of the tournament. [109]

On his return from the Caribbean, Agius was seen as a young player with a future full of untapped potential, who was already gaining heady comparisons as the new Harry Kewell. The *Adelaide Sunday Mail* reported that, 'the Aboriginal and Torres Strait Islander Commission named Agius as the junior sportsman of the year. Agius had dreams of making a move to play in the English Premier League and he was fast becoming a role model for young Indigenous Australians. Several European

109 *The Advertiser*, April 22, 2016.

sides including Swiss club Basel and French outfits Paris St Germain and Olympique Marseille were keen on Agius.' As part of the young Australian team, he also visited England, the United States, Italy, New Zealand and Asia. This certainly broadened the young player's horizons.

Agius was one young player with a great knowledge of the history of Aboriginal soccer players, who took the exploits of Charlie Perkins and Harry Williams as his inspiration. As he told the *Adelaide Sunday Mail,* 'Charles Perkins was my mentor he took me under his wing when I was young and got me through the hard stuff after I was away from my family for long periods of time.' On Harry Williams, he said, 'I met Harry a few times. He gave me some good tips and it was great to meet the first Indigenous player for the Socceroos. I think Harry has paved the way for a bigger crop of Indigenous players who might be playing for the Socceroos including myself.' He was respectful of those who had gone before him, telling the *Koori Mail:* 'If I can get close to the heights those two got to, then I want to be that someone who young people can look up to as I looked up to them.'

In retrospect, after the Under 17 World Cup, Agius should probably have taken an opportunity with an overseas club that had a good young player support system. Such support was unheard of at Australian clubs at the time. Instead, he returned to Adelaide and played three games with Playford City before being signed almost immediately by the ambitious National Soccer League (NSL) club Sydney Olympic Sharks. It seemed things could not be better for the young player whose heroes were the 'Brazilians Rivaldo and Roberto Carlos alongside Anthony Mundine and AFL star Michael Long.'

In the space of twelve months it all came crashing down. Agius was put into hostel-style accommodation, without support or guidance. He found it very difficult being away from his family when he was so young. This meant he had trouble settling with the club and maintaining his motivation and focus. Overwhelmed by his predicament, Agius eventually buckled under the pressure. He packed up and returned to Adelaide, seeking the comfort of his family and familiar surroundings. The *Sun Herald* reported at the time:

Aged 17, Agius played four games and scored one goal during the Sharks championship fling last season, but the attacking midfielder fled Sydney as the club closed in on its historic title.

According to coach Gary Phillips, Agius was called into the Sharks squad for its NSL finals campaign but never showed up for training. 'I spoke to Fred to tell him he'd been included but never saw him again ... I don 't know where he is right now.'

It was reported that the Sharks had torn up his contract. Ironically, the Sharks at the time boasted other Indigenous players - Jade North and Morgan Cawley, son of tennis legend Evonne Goolagong Cawley.

Agius' move to Sydney was probably not well thought through, and his uncle, Vince Copley, spoke with me about this in 2004: 'Freddy had all the skills. We got him to Sydney at the age of 16 and he was signed up but there was nothing in place for him, no support. We should have recognised that he would need family support.'

The late Martyn Crook, a former coach of Agius while technical director for the South Australian Soccer Federation, reflected sadly, 'We didn't know that he'd come back to Adelaide and didn't even know that he'd been delisted by Olympic. He was a huge talent, but it was always on the cards that something like this was going to happen.'

What was blindingly obvious at the time was that soccer clubs in Australia simply were not equipped to provide adequate support and direction for young Indigenous players. And yet there was a subtle underlying inference in the comments made about Freddy Agius, redolent of that old, unfounded idea that 'blacks can't cope and will eventually go walkabout.'

Back in Adelaide, Agius initially decided that he needed a complete break from soccer. In 2003 he started playing Australian football for Central Districts in the South Australian National Football League. He went on to win a premiership medal in the reserve grade team in his first season and thoroughly enjoyed his year of Australian football. But as he told the *Koori Mail*, 'Two weeks after our footy grand final ... [Adelaide] United rang me and asked if l wanted to play again, I said yeah, and they invited me to train with them. It helped that I knew most of the players and admin staff there. It was perfect timing that United rang me.'

The opportunity to play for his hometown team in the NSL held special significance for Agius. Coach John Kosmina told The Advertiser that his new

THE ABORIGINAL SOCCER TRIBE

signing was quickly back to his best: 'He's a hell of a skillful kid. He's got a natural instinct for the game, which you don't see all that often. There are other [youngsters] we'll have a look at in due course, but they lack experience whereas Freddy's actually played national league ... Freddy's a creative player who has got a nose for goals and that's what we're looking for.'

Agius was an immediate favourite with the Adelaide fans. The *Sunday Mail* described him as 'winning the hearts of the United faithful with his electric speed, impeccable left boot and his willingness to contest every ball in the attacking midfield role.' He made an impact so significant that Socceroos and Olyroos coach Frank Farina admitted to keeping a close eye on his progress. Agius said, 'Hopefully my first goal for Adelaide is not too far away and then we'll take it from there. Anything is possible, and I hope that I can make an impression on the right people.' Agius and Adelaide had a great 2003–04 season. They defeated Brisbane in the minor semi-final and reached the preliminary final, which they lost to eventual grand final winners Perth Glory in what was to be the final season of the NSL.

In the first leg of the minor semi-final against Brisbane, played in Adelaide, they demolished their opponents 3-0. The major role Agius had in that victory is clear from the article in *The Advertiser*:

> *Wonder Boy Fred Agius scored one of the goals of the season and veterans Carl Veart and Michael Brooks each struck priceless goals to give Adelaide a 3-0 win in a fiery elimination final against the Brisbane Strikers ... Agius struck the second goal with a magnificent shot with the outside of his left foot in the 67th minute ... Agius the darling of the Hindmarsh crowd picked the right moment to score his first goal for United, sending the crowd into a frenzy ... Substitute Brooks iced the match for United with a header in the 92nd minute after a cross from Agius.*

Agius' performances that season gave him an outside chance of making the Olyroos team for the 2004 Athens Olympic Games. Frank Farina selected him for a match against Tunisia and Agius was overjoyed. In an interview with *The Advertiser* he said, 'I can't wait to get over there and have a good game. I'll try to stay fit and play as well as I can and try to press for a spot in the Olympic squad ...

I'm getting a game [against Tunisia] so I will play what Frank [Farina] wants me to play and you just never know. It's good to have another Nunga in the team. With the Joeys I was the only Nunga. Having Jade [North] in the team is a bonus for me. We actually had to mark each other in the [United v Glory] preliminary final.'

Agius' success opened up another area of great interest to him - promoting the game within Aboriginal communities. He was involved with national Indigenous soccer programs and visited outback communities on northwest Queensland with the then Socceroos coach, Frank Farina.

But sadly, Agius did not make selection in the final Olympic squad for Athens in 2004.

Then there was a long break when the NSL finished and competition at a national level went into recess for a year and a half. This further derailed Agius' progress. The new A-League competition replaced the NSL in 2005, but the A-League's Adelaide United franchise did not pursue his services. Agius was deeply disappointed to be overlooked by Adelaide United. He went back to play for Adelaide City in the South Australian competition from 2004 to 2009, which marked another long period of waiting in the wilderness for a chance.

Then in 2009, new A-League franchise North Queensland Fury signed him for their first A-League season. Agius was joined by other prominent Indigenous players David Williams and Paul Henderson, alongside Liverpool legend Robbie Fowler. He gained plenty of game time in the pre-season and took a starring role coming off the bench on a return to Hindmarsh Stadium, up against Adelaide United, in an exciting 3-3 draw. But opportunities throughout the season were scarce and his time on the park limited. In his two seasons with the Fury, Agius only made five appearances. By 2010 he was back playing in the South Australian Super League, and in 2011 he signed with Indonesian club Cendrawasih Papua FC, which plays in the Indonesian Premier League. He played 16 times for Cendrawasih Papua scoring three goals. He returned home to Adelaide and continues to play for his local amateur team Brahma Lodge. In 2016 Freddy was working for Metropolitan Aboriginal Youth Services in Adelaide. The love of the game was still burning strongly in his new role 'I want to help the boys get into soccer. I love working with them'. He hinted at possibly moving into coaching in the future:

And once I finish playing, I want to get into coaching. But the boys I look after all love the AFL and I'm trying to convert them over to soccer and there has been a huge increase in the last two or three years.[110]

The Advertiser article remined readers of the sublime skills of Freddy Agius, 'His sweet left foot is still breathtaking and his vision and ability to thread a through ball or take brilliant set pieces are still on show.' [111]

By any measure, Freddy Agius remains the enigma of Australian soccer and a story of 'what might have been.' The football authorities could do no better than look to support Indigenous development in the game by employing Freddy Agius in a coaching development role.

James Brown - Dancing to the Soccer Beat

At an early age James Brown was regarded as a junior soccer sensation. He may share his name with an African-American soul music icon but he moves to a different beat. His dream from the outset was to gain selection for the Socceroos.

Brown started playing soccer when he was seven years old, with a Bilambil team, near Tweed Heads in New South Wales. Later, he switched to Kingscliff and then Burleigh Heads, just over the border in Queensland. Initially, he attended high school at Palm Beach Currumbin State High School but was happy to return to Tweed Heads and go to high school at Kingscliff.

Brown's performances on the soccer field gained him selection to the Queensland Academy of Sport (QAS). His family was full of praise for the Australian Sports Commission for the financial support it gave him, telling the *Koori Mail* that without it, 'James would not be in the position he's in today.' These early experiences shaped Brown's soccer path and development, and he was quick to also acknowledge the support of his grandfather when speaking with *News Gold Coast:* 'He ran me all over the place, up the coast to train with rep teams and also to Brisbane to the QAS. Anything I achieve will be down to him.'

---

[110] *The Advertiser (Adelaide),* 22 April 2016
[111] Ibid.

It wasn't just this young player's name that suggested comparisons with the 'Soul Man', James Brown. Gold Coast youth soccer maestro Pat Hedges, who had worked with Brown since he was twelve, said that the rising soccer star was 'endowed with natural footballing rhythm and footwork the great man himself might have appreciated. He's got a lovely flowing approach to the game and his natural instinct is to get forward and use his skills at every opportunity. I have no doubt he will be in the mix for a starting spot once the season begins.'

In early January 2006, aged 15, Brown was well and truly on course to fulfil his goal, when he gained selection in the Australian under 17 training squad that took part in a four-day camp in Sydney. This team would be the first Australian team to compete in an Asian Football Confederation tournament after Australia was elected as a member of the Asian Confederation. A run of injuries temporarily derailed his progress and would become an all too regular feature in the years ahead. He continued his youth representative honours as part of the Australian under 20 side in Saudi Arabia that qualified for the Under 20 World Cup finals, to be held in Colombia in late 2011. His potential and talent was enough to ensure that he would spend time at both the Queensland Academy of Sport (QAS) and Australian Institute of Sport (AIS).

At the age of 18, Brown signed with the new A-League franchise, Gold Coast United - his hometown team - for the start of the 2009–10 season. He looked on the signing as a stepping stone in his dream of being a role model for young Aboriginal kids. He had his own idols, including Jade North and Travis Dodd. But his dream was 'to see a stampede of Indigenous kids flocking to ... "real football".' On the day he put pen to paper with the Gold Coast club, he told *News Gold Coast:* 'I have a long way to go but it would be great if I'm able to break through into United's first team so that local Aboriginal kids like me around the Gold Coast might see what I am doing as worthwhile and want to follow me into the sport. Down on the Tweed there's a sizeable community and most are into rugby league and touch ... it would be great if I was able to change their minds.'

Once fully fit, Brown was spending time with the QAS while awaiting the start of pre-season training with Gold Coast. He was taken by surprise when contacted by Gold Coast United billionaire owner Clive Palmer in person. Palmer, who had reportedly donated millions of dollars to support Aboriginal communities in the

Pilbara region, was equally enthusiastic about his young signing and said, 'It's great to have a local Gold Coast kid with an Indigenous background in our squad. He's a terrific player and will be a credit to himself, the club and his community.' Palmer's injection of major funding to support Indigenous community health would later be revealed as unfounded and unsupported.

The future looked very bright for James Brown indeed. But he suffered a major setback to the start of his career with the Gold Coast after breaking his right fibula in training in 2009 and spent eight weeks on the sideline.

The youngest player at the time on the Gold Coast books, Brown once recovered from injury made his debut for the club in a 0-0 draw with Wellington Phoenix in October 2009. Gold Coast officials said that big things were expected from him in the future. During the 2010 season he had some extended runs in the first team, scoring a couple of goals. Playing with high-profile Socceroo Jason Culina clearly helped his development. Brown broke through with the Gold Coast in 2011 and in a young exciting team became a standout player. He was noted for scoring a number of spectacular long-range goals. He looked every inch a future Socceroo in the making. Internal and external problems with the club surfaced in 2012 and the FFA revoked owner Clive Palmer's A-League license and the club lost their place in the competition.

James Brown joined the Newcastle Jets where over two seasons he made 28 appearances but did not score a goal. Brown's time with the Jets saw him constantly battling injuries and recovery.

He had also joined another club that descended into turmoil following the takeover by another mining magnate Nathan Tinkler. Trying to rekindle the spark and form of his time with the Gold Coast he moved once more to Melbourne City. Again, Brown was plagued with injury problems and over two seasons with City only managed 16 games scoring one goal. Brown was revealed to be undertaking a unique fitness recovery program with ballet as the medium. Brown had looked to be cementing a place in the City team in 2015 including scoring a decisive goal in a 1-0 win over Sydney FC away when a week later he went down with a foot injury. The injury saw Brown out of action for nearly a year. His coach at the time John van't Schip remained supportive and felt that Brown was 'over it mentally, he is happy, he is feeling great, he is running'.[112] Despite the optimism and the mental and physical determination that Brown displayed he could not break back into City's future plans and he was released.

In mid 2016 he joined Avondale in the Victorian Premier League but only stayed a month with the club. Another move this time internationally saw him in August 2016 join new South African Premier League club Cape Town City but after only making three appearances he left the club and returned to Australia.

The situation must have been devastating on Brown. The injury toll and slow recovery rate over the previous five seasons must have had his confidence at rock bottom. He joined Nunawading City in the Victoria Premier League and for the first time in five seasons Brown appeared to be back to full fitness and he played 37 games for the club and scored nine goals. In 2018 he moved again to Hume City playing a further 15 games and scoring another three goals in the Victorian Premier League. He remains on the books at Hume City.

James Brown must wonder where his career may have taken him except for the onset of injuries that plagued him across the past several years.

Paul Henderson - Have Gloves, Will Travel

Paul Henderson was born in Sydney in 1976 and grew up in the harbour city, a member of a large, close -knit family. He started his soccer career in the New South Wales Premier League, making his debut for Sutherland in 1996. He signed with NSL club Northern Spirit in 1998 and played 134 matches for the Spirit in the old NSL before deciding to make the big leap and try his luck in Europe in 2004.

Henderson initially arrived in England to have a trial with Ipswich Town, but a chance meeting with a goalkeeping coach put him in touch with an agent who had connections with Bradford City. He signed with Bradford and played 40 games for the club before his performances drew the attention of scouts from bigger clubs. Nottingham Forest was one that took a genuine interest in his form. Unfortunately, their scouts attended a game where Bradford performed poorly, and Bradford City were beaten 4-1 by Milton Keynes Dons, and this defused the Nottingham interest.

[112] *The Age,* 25 Febuary, 2016

Then Bradford manager Colin Todd decided that the transfer speculation was responsible for Henderson's below-par performance.

Despite continued impressive performances for Bradford, Henderson rejected the club's offer of a three-year contract and instead joined Leicester City on a trial basis. He performed well during the trial period and subsequently signed a two-year deal. Henderson felt right at home at Leicester as they had a host of Aussies on their books, including Patrick Kisnorbo and Danny Tiatto. He was initially signed as cover for their regular keeper, but stated that he was 'willing to fight for his place' and that he felt Leicester was a club 'moving in the right direction.' First team keeper Robert Douglas had a bad run of form and received constant criticism from fans and officials. This gave Henderson his chance. He played 15 games in the first team under new manager Rob Kelly during the 2005–06 season. With this performance, he installed himself as the first-choice keeper for the 2006–07 season.

Leicester spent the season in a battle of survival to avoid relegation from the English Championship. Their defence was leaky, to say the least - they conceded 36 goals in twenty-eight games. But they survived. Henderson's form again attracted the interest of other clubs, including Wigan, Aston Villa and Norwich City, during the January transfer window. He decided against a move and re-signed with Leicester for another two years. But he spent much of the 2007–08 season on the substitutes bench; he managed to play 14 games, conceding 16 goals and holding five clean sheets. Leicester was relegated at the end of the season to League One level.

At the start of the 2008–09 season, Henderson was again in a battle for the number one keeper's jersey, this time with another loan signing, David Martin. Henderson started the first game of the season playing against Milton Keynes Dons, where he kept a clean sheet in a 2-0 win. He was the hero in a 3-1 victory over Lincoln City in late 2008, saving two shots in a penalty shootout. Leicester lost their next match against Rotherham United, which drew a savage rebuke from manager Nigel Pearson, who described it as the team's worst of the season. Henderson lost his spot to David Martin, but Martin's poor run of form saw Henderson reinstated as the number one keeper. He suffered a bad groin injury in February 2009 and Leicester subsequently took on three Premier League keepers on loan to cover his absence. Leicester went on to win the League One title and, despite his absence through injury, Henderson was still presented with a medal.

During the off-season, reports circulated that Henderson and fellow Australian Patrick Kisnorbo were surplus to requirements as Leicester prepared for their Championship League campaign in the coming season. The rumour was that both players would need to look for other clubs. Henderson decided it was time to head back to Australia, and he was quickly signed by new A-League club North Queensland Fury for the 2009–10 season. He was adamant that the decision to come home was an easy one, particularly with a growing young family. He told the *Koori Mail* in 2009, 'I was looking forward to coming back from playing overseas and I'm a big family man so being only a three hour flight from Sydney is a big help.'

Henderson played in the historic season opener against Sydney FC, in which the Fury lost 3-2 in what was an exciting game. Henderson's form in the early round drew harsh criticism from fans and commentators as he made a couple of highly visible errors of judgment. He regained his form, and some outstanding performances in a victory over Gold Coast and a loss to the Newcastle Jets saw him installed as the number one keeper for the Fury. But his form fluctuated throughout the season and he was in and out of the side. He was not retained by the Fury for the 2010–11 season.

Initially Henderson signed with a short-term contract with former glamour Sydney club Sydney Olympic in the state competition, but he gained an A-League lifeline from the Newcastle Jets, with a one-year contract to fill in for their injured keeper, Neil Young. Early in the season Henderson switched to the Central Coast Mariners, again as an injury replacement, but he was unable to force his way into the team, which finished the season as runners up to the all-conquering Brisbane Roar. He returned to Sydney Olympic and was part of the team that won the club the NSW Premier League title in 2012. He rightly gained the Goalkeeper of the Year Award in 2012 after an outstanding season. In 2018 at the age of 42 the evergreen Henderson was still in the Olympic squad.

The Luckless Ones, Missed Opportunities, Disappointment and Tragedy

Several Aboriginal players have shown very high potential as soccer players but for a variety of reasons, including injury, bad timing, bad luck and lack of support, have failed to fulfil their early promise. Aboriginal sporting involvement has a long history of people gaining a degree of support and recognition in the wider sporting community that was conditional upon them winning or performing at a high level, otherwise they quickly finished on the scrap heap.

In recent decades, in other codes, there is strong evidence that when an Aboriginal sporting career ends, the opportunities to gain work in the media or other related areas, which are available to non-Indigenous players, are usually not there. The AFL and to a lesser degree rugby league have sought to remedy this and now provide some guidance for life away from the sporting arena. Clearly, in the 21st century any Aboriginal person involved in a sporting career should be encouraged to gain educational qualifications, to ensure that they have a life after the cheers fade and the backslapping parade has filed away.

Some Aboriginal players whose soccer careers never fully blossomed deserve recognition. **Morgan Cawley** had the unenviable task of following in the sporting footsteps of his mother, tennis great Evonne Goolagong Cawley. Morgan Cawley was nevertheless intent on making his own impact and was a gifted sportsman. He was a very good soccer player and a product of the Queensland Academy of Sport, where he impressed. He played a number of games with the Sydney Olympic Sharks in the NSL in 2001. Sadly, Cawley suffered a number of crippling knee injuries that curtailed his career. He made a number of attempts to resurrect his career in New South Wales and Queensland but was undone by injury.

Tallan Martin held a scholarship at the Australian Institute of Sport in 2000 and 2001 and was a young player of considerable talent. During his time there, he was coached by Steve O'Connor, who described Martin as a 'player blessed with good physical attributes - a talented athlete with a good engine'.[113] But injuries, constant moves between clubs and bad luck stalled his progress. One writer lampooned his injury-plagued and nomadic career, saying he'd had 'more clubs than Jack Nicklaus'.[114] Martin had stints with Newcastle United, Wollongong, Marconi and Bankstown City. In 2007 he had a brief stint with Sydney FC as an injury replacement, but luck just did not come his way.

....

[113] Fogarty, M, *Indigenous Athletes at the Australian Institute of Sport,* Australian Sports Commission, Canberra, 2005
[114] *Four Four Two,* May 2008

Lawrence Gilbert - is a proud Bundjalung man from Cabbage Tree Island from the far north coast of New South Wales. He originally started his football career at Margate FC and now Peninsula Power FC, going on to play for NSW and Australia. Lawrence's speciality was futsal and was first introduced to the small game at the Australian Indigenous Futsal Championships in 1992 and was subsequently selected for NSW and the Australian Indigenous Futsalroos between 1992 and 1998. In 1994 and 1995, he was selected to play for the National Futsalroos, touring Mexico and South America playing mini-world cups against America, Peru, Brazil and Mexico. Lawrence played over 30 games for Australia either for the national Indigenous Team or the national Australian team. Since then, Lawrence has worked at all levels of government driving change for Indigenous peoples and is now a key organiser, advocate and administrator in the Indigenous football arena. Lawrence is passionate about how the world game can change lives and believes that this is something that can be introduced to the Indigenous peoples of Australia. [115]

Another young player with a great deal of promise was **Ramone Close**. In 2005 he gained selection in the Australian Schoolboys under 19 side that toured Great Britain. He was also a member of the Queensland team that played in the National Youth Championships in Sydney, where the Queenslanders finished runners up. He was awarded the Nike Golden Boot Award as the leading goal scorer at the championships. The performances of Close and teammate Tahj Minniecon at the National Youth titles resulted in them both being invited to join the Queensland Academy of Sport. There, the two developed an uncanny, almost telepathic understanding of each other's play, which brought opposing defences undone. Both Ramone Close and Tahj Minniecon would join the AIS in Canberra for a time. Somewhat similarly to Tallan Martin's experience, Close has been a player on the move, playing for Wynnum Wolves, Redland City Devils and the Townsville North Queensland Razorbacks in the Queensland State League. After a season in the state Premier League with the Razorbacks, Close was encouraged to head overseas to Europe.

He initially spent four months in 2011 with the Portuguese first division club Associacao Academica de Coimbra before moving to Belgium where he spent the

115 Information as provided in personal correspondence by Lawrence Gilbert

rest of the season with the club Royal Racing Montegnée, scoring five goals from 12 appearances. He subsequently moved on to Poland becoming a star attacking midfielder for the Drawa Drawsko club. During his time in Poland, he was invited by Frank Schaefer, the football manager of FC Kohn to trial with the famous German football club.

In looking back on his European adventures Ramone was adamant that it 'was a great learning curve, where he gained experience, knowledge and understood more about the finer techniques of the game'. He added that 'Football in Europe is totally different to here in Australia. The sport is loved by millions and is almost a religion. The players are more skilled, the coaches are more demanding, and the supporters are much more passionate'. The locals in the small Polish village took to him and he 'became a celebrity. They all thought I was Spanish but were bewildered when they discovered I was an Indigenous Australian'. It was tough at times 'not only on the football pitch, but in training and within the community through the constant cold weather and language barriers'.

On his return to Australia Close joined Redlands United FC in Brisbane. In 2017 he signed with Peninsula Power and they earned promotion from the third tier of football in Queensland to the Queensland National Premier League after an undefeated season in 2018. It is clear that Ramone Close is now fixated on assisting in promoting and developing the game within Indigenous communities and this commitment is his main priority.

Ramone was named as Football Brisbane's new Indigenous Ambassador in 2018. He was heavily involved along with Lawrence Gilbert in setting up a new National Indigenous Football Championship that kicked off in Logan, Brisbane in November 2018. Close was critical that the football authorities had not been successful in implementing pathways for Indigenous players into the game. He stated that the new initiative was about setting up a pathway ourselves and then have Football Federation Australia hopefully get on board.

Ramone had also established a grassroots Goori Football program to develop football skills for Indigenous kids. He had played a major role in establishing the Brisbane Warrigals Indigenous team that had won the initial National Indigenous Football championship in Nowra in 2016 and were runners up in 2017. Ramone felt the game offered unlimited opportunities for young Indigenous players: 'I'm a big believer that we can find the next Lionel Messi within the Australian Indigenous community, but I also believe the opportunities football can offer worldwide are tenfold on that of the other sporting codes can provide… Raising awareness and increasing the participation of Indigenous players in the game is of great importance to me. Seeing more Indigenous players succeed here in Australia or overseas would make me extremely proud. Recognition of Indigenous footballers will hopefully open doors to more young Indigenous people taking up the sport.

The story of **Evis Heath** offers a tale of triumph beyond the sporting arena. Despite being a fine soccer player, he did not get the lucky break into the soccer big time but has instead developed a career as an outstanding artist. He is from the Dunghutti and Biripi peoples of the New South Wales mid North Coast. He started his junior soccer career in Newcastle and the game quickly had a grip on him. In an interview in 2009, he recalled, 'It was the skill required to play the game. I am a creative person and soccer is a mind and creative game.' He played for Newcastle Austral and made his first-grade debut with Hamilton Olympic in 1997.

At the same time Heath was studying for a Bachelor of Graphic Design at the University of Newcastle. He was a gifted student who won commissions to design artwork for books, CDs and posters and also illustrate a series of Awabakal Dreaming stories.

Heath successfully combined his university studies with his passion for soccer. He was a member of the Newcastle Breakers Youth team in the old NSL in 1996–99 and made his NSL debut in a match against Queensland during that period. He later re-joined Hamilton Olympic in the Northern New South Wales Premier League before going to Melbourne, where he played for the Port Melbourne Sharks.

Heath returned to Newcastle and captained Hamilton Olympic to the Northern New South Wales Premier League title, honoured with the premiership's Player of the Year Award. He was also a member of the all-conquering University of Newcastle soccer team that triumphed at the National University Student Games in Adelaide during 2002. He was selected in the Australian Universities Merit Team but eventually decided to hang up his boots and take a break from the game, focusing instead on a successful career as an artist and graphic designer. Evis then took a career change of course and went into body building and became a qualified personal trainer who runs his own gym and boot camp program all year round . Heath retained his passion for and interest in the game and has always looked for ways to contribute to the growth of soccer in Indigenous communities.

Sheffield Shield Cricket and soccer star **Roger Brown** is another clear example of the multi sporting talented nature of Aboriginal sportsmen and women. Brown was recognised until the arrival of Jason Gillespie as having played more first class cricket matches than any other Indigenous player; 31 games for Tasmania between 1984 and 1987. Brown was a talented opening bowler who also toured Zimbabwe with an Australian under 25 team in 1985–86. He was selected to play for Prime Minister Bob Hawke's XI in the same year. Brown was additionally a talented soccer player with the Launceston Juventus side.[116]

Tate Russell – son of NRL Legend Ian – made his debut for the Western Sydney Wanderers against Melbourne Victory during the 2018–19 season with regular right back Josh Risdon away playing for the Socceroos in the Asian Cup. The 19 year old's impact was impressive. A confident, strong, fast, clever and creative defender he really looked the goods. He would cement himself a place in the side and his performances brought back memories of Harry Williams and Jade North. Tate's father Ian Russell was a top class rugby league player with the Illawarra Steelers including being named as the 1992 Dally M Lock of the Year. Ian Russell himself had been a soccer player up until the age of 18. Tate's debut against the Victory saw him produce a standout performance against one of the most prolific and dangerous forward lines in the A-League – James Troisi, Kosta Barbarouses and Ola Toivonen. Newspaper coverage noted that his proud mum and dad were in the crowd for his debut. 'The 19 year old was comfortable on the ball, his decision making clear and his defensive work almost without fault'. His coach Markus Babbel was full of praise:

> *Now he is seven months with me, and he has improved a lot... now was the time to bring him in. Because I was not happy with some of the players in the last game. It was time for the youngsters... I was hoping for this type of*

---

[116] Tatz, C & Tatz, P, *Black Pearls – The Aboriginal and Islander Sports Hall of Fame,* Aboriginal Studies Press, Canberra, 2018: pp81

performance… He has been doing the right things at training, especially with the tactical sessions. He is a smart guy, clever and he is learning quickly.

The young player had first signed for the Wanderers in 2015 from the South Coast Wolves. He had started playing the game in 2003 for the Wollongong Olympic Junior Soccer Club. He spent five years with Olympic before he was included in Football New South Wales Project 22 in 2008. He then joined the Illawarra Skills Acquisition Program in 2010 before spending a further four years with the South Coast Wolves winning two state titles in 2013 and 2014. He joined the Wanderers Youth team in 2015–16. He was even included as a 17 year old in a 21-man Wanderers squad to play against English heavyweights Arsenal in 2017.

It is clear after his performances in 2019 that he will most certainly be a player for the future and has been included in Young Socceroo and Olyroo training squads. Josh Risdon announced that he had signed for the 2019–20 season with Western Melbourne and this will certainly provide the opportunity for Tate Russell to make a fullback spot with the Wanderers his own.

The Tragedy of **Lancelot "Buddy" Newchurch.** No story in this book comes even remotely close to the tragedy of "Buddy" Newchurch. He was a young Aboriginal soccer prodigy of the early 1970s. Buddy had initially played AFL in Whyalla but switched to soccer at about the age of ten. The game quickly took a grip on the family as his brothers, Clem, John, Charlie and Glen all took up the game. He was spotted as a 16 year old by Chelsea's assistant manager Ron Suart who had been on tour in Australia in 1971 with the English Football Association side. Suart must have been impressed because he immediately offered Newchurch a three month trial with Chelsea in London. Chelsea of course had won the 1970 FA Cup final over Leeds United after a replay with players like Peter Osgood, Peter Bonnetti, Eddie McCreadie and Charlie Cooke.

Buddy Newchurch flew to London with the assistance of the local Whyalla community who raised over £500 to support his trial opportunity. He additionally received a soccer scholarship awarded by the Aboriginal Sports Foundation.[117]

He spent three months in London training at Chelsea's Mitchum complex.

---

[117] *The Canberra Times*, 27 July 1971: pp22

The biggest hurdle to cross from the outset for a 16 year old Aboriginal boy on the other side of the world surfaced only 48 hours after landing – acute homesickness. 'I cannot put my mind to football. I'm missing my family and mates'. Despite this Suart and the coaching staff were confident: 'Buddy shows promise ... He's homesick now but he's only been here two days. He is going to settle down alright'. Buddy was described as quiet and in his private time just ate, slept, watched TV and wrote endless letters home.

The football, players and facilities certainly made an impact on young Buddy. The standard was high, and the training had improved his game 'I've learned a lot faster here, it's a lot different'. He was described as being '5ft 3in and with trendy long hair'. He commented that the level of training was something he had not experienced. 'All I knew about training until yesterday was having a run with the boys once a week and then the game on Saturday'.

Buddy's doubts seemed to be the clear symptoms of severe homesickness. At the conclusion of his three months despite acquitting himself well at training and playing in a couple of trial games it was decided the best move was to send him back home to Australia. Chelsea officials were adamant that he 'showed tremendous improvement during his time' with the club.[118] The decision for him to return home to Australia was taken after he held discussions with Chelsea coaches and staff. Sadly, one can't help thinking that Buddy was crying out for home and could not get there quick enough. If only he had the support to stay on and make it over there it may have saved his life. Buddy returned to Australia, his family and football back home. He would play for Whyalla teams Croatia and Wanderers.

The real tragedy of his story is not the missed opportunity of playing in England but that ten years later he was brutally murdered at the age of just 27 in 1982. He had been bashed to death outside the Westland Hotel in Whyalla. His death remains an unsolved crime with a $200,000 reward still standing for information that leads to an arrest. The local Whyalla community commemorated his memory by naming a Whyalla street after him - Buddy Newchurch Place.

The reports indicated that the crime consisted of Buddy being assaulted by two men with sticks or bars. He was beaten about the head and body and had

....

[118] *The Canberra Times,* 26 October 1971: pp18

been severely kicked. He was conveyed to the Whyalla hospital with severe head injuries but was pronounced dead on arrival. Two suspects were charged with the murder, but the matter did not proceed to trial. The court ruled at the committal proceedings that there was insufficient evidence on which a jury could reasonably convict beyond any reasonable doubt. It appears there had been great difficulty in getting any eyewitnesses to provide evidence. This had stalled the prosecution case. It is important to note that it has been stated that one of the suspects later committed suicide. The death of Buddy Newchurch visibly affected many people in the local community.

Some personal insights placed on Ian Syson's website [119] have revealed more on the short life of Buddy Newchurch. He was described as a very 'skilful left-sided midfielder/striker' and 'a real gentleman'. One commentator felt that the Chelsea experience had seen Buddy struggle with the weather and homesickness. In his young life he had attended Eyre High School in Whyalla and that he 'was a popular all round nice guy, friendly and well liked at school'. He had married young with a wife and kids. Another wrote 'Buddy was a great guy, funny, always up for a laugh, very kind with a big heart. He was a fantastic player'. Buddy was another young player who clearly had the ability but had needed the support particularly being so far from home.

Soccer is a game that offers unparalleled riches to those that reach its elite level and play in the lucrative overseas leagues. Some years back, the two greatest rugby league players of the time, Andrew Johns and Brad Fittler, were making around $700,000 a season in the NRL. But it was said Harry Kewell, then with English Premier League team Liverpool, could make that amount in six weeks! When compared with the world game, rugby league and the AFL are minnows in both a global and financial sense.

The future is bright for Indigenous involvement in soccer and there has been some outstanding success stories, but progress has been slow. Some of the players discussed show that raw talent alone is not enough. Of course, players need extreme dedication and a great deal of luck on their side. Injury and misfortune can quickly end the most promising careers. Young Aboriginal men and women

[119] http://neososmos.blogspot.com/ – Ian's site offers well informed information and discussion.

in soccer - as in all sports - must be well prepared and equipped from the very beginning for life after sport.

Education and sport, for most of the past two hundred years, did not offer Aboriginal people a level playing field of opportunity. As an Aboriginal man, I experienced educational disadvantage and indifference, but I finally built up the courage at the age of 40 to take myself off to university and apply myself in gaining a belated education. Today, sport and education offer Aboriginal people opportunities never before imagined. Combining the two gives our sportsmen and women something they never had in the past: a life of financial security, health and wellbeing - for themselves, their families and communities.

CHAPTER 8

The Aboriginal Matildas – The World Game and Indigenous Women

Women's soccer in Australia took off during the mid 1970s and can be linked to a rise in interest due to the Socceroos qualifying for the 1974 World Cup finals in West Germany. A series of women's trans-Tasman challenge matches were organised in 1974 and three New Zealand Women's teams - Blockhouse Bay, Eden Saints and Papakura Bay - visited Sydney. Coinciding with these matches, the New South Wales Women's Soccer Federation was formed under the leadership of Pat O'Connor.

O'Connor was a visionary and a committed campaigner for women's soccer in Australia; she had been secretary of the Sydney Women's Soccer Federation before the state body was formed. From that point on, the game for women spread rapidly throughout every state and territory and has now established an international profile thanks to the achievements of the Australian national women's team, the Matildas.

Interestingly, the game for women in Australia has a much longer history than many might imagine. In 1929, more than 7,000 people paid to attend the State Women's Soccer Final, played under floodlights at the Sydney Sports Ground, and witness the victory of an all-Northern New South Wales final, won by Speer's Point over Weston, 1-0.

Aboriginal women's involvement in the game coincides with the surge of interest during the 1970s. There are several Indigenous women soccer inductees to the Aboriginal and Islander Sports Hall of Fame. This is a staggering achievement for Indigenous women in the round-ball game. Players such as Bridgette Starr, Lydia Williams, Belinda Dawney, Leanne Edmundson, Felicity Huntington, Kayleen Janssen, Kyah Simon and Karen Menzies have achieved national, state and representative honours.

Nevertheless, soccer as a game for Indigenous women, despite some obvious success stories, is still in its infancy. At the grassroots and wider community level, not enough is known about the success and opportunities for Aboriginal women in the game. Soccer has a great opportunity to play a key role in encouraging Aboriginal women to succeed on and off the field. Football Federation Australia need to capitalise on the success of Aboriginal women in the game and step up their outreach programs to Indigenous communities.

The stories in this chapter provide inspirational insight into the careers of a number of Aboriginal women players. Unfortunately, there is more information available on some players' careers than others, especially the more recent players, which is a reflection of the changing status of women playing the world game in Australia today.

✻ ✻ ✻

The game for Aboriginal women certainly stretches back. **Magdalene (Maddie) Verberg McIntosh** was born in Darwin in 1934. She was the daughter of a Dutch immigrant Edwin Verberg and a 'fullblood' Aboriginal woman Anmilal (also named Magdalene Verberg) of the Kungarakan people. In 1952 her father took his daughter on a trip to Holland and showed her where he was born and introduced her to their Dutch family members. Edwin Verberg was a strong-willed individual who passed on to his children, including Maddie, a deep sense of pride and an attitude of 'do what you think is right and that is it'. On her return she met and married a white miner from Queensland Lorry McIntosh whose family originally opposed the marriage. She had two daughters Dannylynn and Lynda Louise.

As her girls grew up, Maddie took a deep interest in sport and encouraged her girls to participate in softball and hockey. Then in her thirties she began to play competitive sport as well and was convinced of the need to play sport alongside your kids. She reflected that soccer seemed to take off in Darwin during the 1960s and 1970s and there were women's competitions as well. She recalled agreeing 'to play soccer in a team and we used to put on charity games. Later, we played in competition soccer and won one grand final as well as the Ampol Cup'.[120]

Following on from Maddie Verberg-McIntosh's example it appears that Darwin and the top end offered opportunities for Aboriginal women's participation in the round ball code from the 1970s.

Louisa Collins, as described in the book *Black Pearls,* represents the sporting liberation of Aboriginal women in northern Australia. The repeal of the special restrictive policy applying to Aboriginal people considered less than "full-blood" opened opportunities formerly closed off. Like many of the women Collins was accomplished in several sports including representing the Northern Territory in both hockey and basketball. But she also played in three soccer grand finals in Darwin and was the top goal scorer for six seasons.

Karmi Dunn was another sporting star across a number of games that included representing the Territory in basketball, netball, softball and soccer.[121]

Lee McGowan from QUT is currently compiling a book on the history of the women's game in Australia and he recently and kindly passed on some information about **Leonie Young** (nee Yow Yeh). Leonie hails from a very famous rugby league family as a niece of former Redcliffe and Queensland winger Kevin Yow Yeh. Leonie herself was a talented sportswoman and had started playing soccer in the late 1970s. She is noted as being the first Indigenous woman to play in the Mitchelton Seniors and one of the first to play in the elite Brisbane Women's competition. She was also the first Indigenous woman to play for her state of Queensland between 1980 and 1983. Leonie was a key player in forming the Tiwiwarrin Indigenous Women's team who played in the Brisbane city league for almost 20 years.[122] The Tiwiwarrin team were described in the press as 'fast, agile and predominantly Aboriginal'.[123] The teams name was drawn from an Aboriginal word meaning fast. The name seemed aptly given because the girls were lightning

120 McIntosh, M and Rothwell, E, *Aboriginal History,* volume 3, 1979, pg3-24
121 Tatz, C & Tatz, P (2018) *Black Pearls,* Aboriginal Studies Press, pp129-132
122 Personal correspondence with Lee McGowan, 4 June 2019
123 *The Sun (Brisbane),* 27 April 1988

quick and the harmony within the team group was understandable seeing ten members of the side were relatives. The team's jersey was in recognition of the colours of the Aboriginal flag red, gold and black. The team attracted a lot of support. Leonie Yow Yeh stated at the time: 'We just go out to play the game. For what it is worth, I think we will surprise the best teams in the competition as I think we are certainties for the premiership'. [124]

Karen Menzies - Aboriginal Trailblazer

Karen Menzies was the undoubted trailblazer for Indigenous women soccer players in this country. Her achievements in the game are many, and her courage in overcoming her life experiences matches and, in some instances, even exceeds that of her illustrious male compatriots Charlie Perkins, John Moriarty and Gordon Briscoe.

Menzies not only had to overcome prejudice and the horrific experience of being taken from her family and being denied her Aboriginal identity. She also had to deal with being a highly competitive sportswoman at a time when the roles and choices available to women were more constrained and traditional. Plus she was openly gay.

Karen Menzies was born in Sydney in 1962 and was ·taken from her birth mother at eight months of age. She was made a ward of the state from the age of eighteen months to 18 years. First, she was placed in an institution, until she was one year old. Then she was fostered to a family who wanted to adopt a child - although despite Department of Child Welfare assurances to the family, this could never happen because Menzies' mother had never relinquished her parental rights. In an interview with me in 2004, Menzies had no hesitation in stating that she was extremely fortunate because she went to a very loving and caring family, who completely adored her. However, she grew up having no idea of her Aboriginal background. 'The family who I'd been placed with and raised with, they'd never been told about my cultural heritage. And from my own social studies and experiences at school, every time I looked in the mirror, I didn't resemble my own

[124] *The Sun (Brisbane),* 27 April 1988

kind of narrow construct of what an Aboriginal person looked like.' [125] She assumed that her heritage was one of unquestioned Anglo-Celtic descent, and she took on many of the beliefs and prejudices of the family she was raised in.

It was through her brother, who was six years older than her, that Menzies developed a love of soccer. She was a very active child, into all sports, and was especially driven to beat him at any game. They played backyard soccer and touch football, and this competitiveness forced her to extend herself at every level in sport.

Menzies was brought up in the Sydney suburb of North Ryde, which had a large migrant population and a top soccer team in Yugal Ryde. There were many soccer grounds in the suburb and local kids' interest was high. There were also lots of kids in the neighbourhood and they played cricket and tennis, but 'backyard soccer was probably the favourite with half a dozen of us.' [126]

By the time Menzies reached high school, she had still not played in an organised soccer competition. Her experience was restricted to the school playground with the boys in her class or the backyard with her brother and local children. She had started going to her brother's weekend soccer games. Nevertheless, her passion for soccer had taken hold and every spare moment was spent kicking a round ball. She was regularly caned or put on detention at school for playing soccer with the boys. As she explained, this was a time 'when there was a very clear gender distinction of what sort of game girls should play and what sort of game boys should play.' [127] Letters were sent home and she started getting lectures there, too: 'Now don't do that, don't play soccer.' Menzies rebelled against the message from the school and her parents: 'I didn't give a stuff about that, I loved the game and I wanted to play, so I was prepared, to kind of put up with getting into trouble.' [128]

During her early years at high school, Menzies' foster father suffered several heart attacks. Because she was still a ward of the state, the Department of Child Welfare started visiting the family home regularly. This undermined any sense she had of belonging and of being a real part of the family. The department was also

125   Interview with Karen Menzies, 30 September, 2004, Newcastle
126   Interview with Karen Menzies, 30 September, 2004, Newcastle
127   Ibid.
128   Ibid.

visiting the school, where she and her friends were in trouble for taking time off school. She was 13 years old and most of her friends were 16, and there were times when they'd gone to someone's house and there had been alcohol and cigarettes. The department felt that Menzies was exposing herself to moral danger, and as she was a ward of the state, she could be targeted.

She was placed in an institution with girls as old as 16 and 17, on remand from court, most having committed criminal offences. There was high security, high brick fences and barbed wire everywhere, no comfort, support or understanding, just orders to 'get out there and scrub that floor.'[129] She had come from a stable, fairly predictable family life. Now she didn't know where she was going next, nor whether she would be returned to the family. It was a very upsetting and confusing time. After three months, with no contact with the family that had raised her, she learned that she would be relocated to another institution in Newcastle, some 160 kilometres from Ryde and the world that she had known until then.

The date of her relocation to Newcastle - 27 April 1976 - and her arrival remain vivid in Menzies' memory. She met the house parents and there was a very brief discussion about the house rules. One rule was that all the kids had to play sport, and one of the sports was soccer - there was a girls' competition. Menzies remembered 'absolutely, literally jumping out of my chair and saying, "Soccer!" ... being so excited, I can even now get in touch with that feeling ... about how excited I was ... by five o'clock I was at soccer training, meeting all the players in my team, which was Merewether under 14s.'[130]

Menzies can still recall coming back to the home that night after training and 'just being absolutely over the moon.'[131] She didn't really know where she was living or who any of these people were, but she didn't care.

Life continued in a state of soccer bliss. She attended Merewether High School, which had a long and proud soccer tradition. The home was in some ways like a boarding school. 'We sort of lived at this place, and people could go out, and spend holidays with friends or relatives if you had them ... and we were all involved with the neighbourhood, all the sporting things within the neighbourhood. So, life went

---

129 Interview with Karen Menzies, 30 September, 2004, Newcastle
130 Ibid.
131 Interview with Karen Menzies, 30 September, 2004, Newcastle

on, and I had incredible success through soccer.'[132]

From her first year she was a member of Newcastle and Lake Macquarie open representative teams. By the next year, 1977, when she was aged 14, she was playing with the under 16s. Then in April of that year she was picked in the New South Wales State Open team, by far the youngest player in. the team. She would remain a member of the New South Wales State Open team for more than 13 years.

Menzies had been reconnected with the only family she had known, and she was visiting them periodically. From her perspective, everything was going well. Then out of the blue, when she was 16, the Department of Child Welfare asked if she wanted to meet her birth mother. This was something that she'd always wanted to do, and that her foster family had supported.

The authorities quickly organised for her to visit her mum and four siblings, who were living in Queensland. Menzies had grown up with a firm belief in her own abandonment and was very keen to finally meet her mother and get some answers to all her questions, including 'Did I look like her?', 'Well, why wasn't I with her?', and 'How come, you know, my mum didn't want me?'[133]

Just before Menzies was due to go to Queensland, the welfare workers showed her photos of her mother and sister Carleen and, with no warning, preparation or tact, told her she was Aboriginal. This information was far too complex for Menzies to fit within her already confused 16-year old head. The family she was about to be reconnected with were, from her perspective, nothing like her. The reunion might have been very exciting for her younger sisters, but the feeling was not mutual. In an interview with me in 2004, Menzies described herself at this time as 'a really fucking angry adolescent ... and now I'm an even angrier adolescent, because I found out all of this information in such a short space of time. [My mother] just got this absolute 16-year-old brat, who was filthy on the world, who swore and just didn't want to have anything to do with her or the other kids. It was unbearable, there was no escort or support or counselling, nothing.'[134] It was a horrible reunion, and her mother responded to her daughter's rage, hurt and searing questions with shame and silence. The reality, which Menzies would not discover for years, was

[132] Ibid.
[133] Ibid.
[134] Interview with Karen Menzies, 30 September, 2004, Newcastle

THE ABORIGINAL SOCCER TRIBE

that the authorities had also removed her mother and her mother's six siblings and that her grandmother had also been removed. The ongoing historical trauma had shattered one family over generations.

When Karen returned to Newcastle, the welfare workers decided that she would have her own Aboriginal tutor, who would visit the home after school and teach her about Aboriginal history and culture. The stigma, stereotyping and pressure of being identified as Aboriginal was at its height and Menzies had only a confused understanding of what it really meant to be Aboriginal. She reflected, 'I carried all of this stuff and it was all pretty negative.'[135]

When Karen turned 18 and was of age, she was discharged from her wardship. She began working with the Department of Sport and Recreation - a job made in heaven. She played sport, did kids' camps, played soccer with kids and with people with intellectual and physical disabilities. It was a period of healing, although she thought constantly of her mother and siblings but was too scared to make contact with them.

But through it all there was soccer. It was her life. It gave her a sporting identity, it provided her with self-esteem and confidence and got her through a very difficult period. It gave her huge satisfaction as well as an outlet to unleash a certain amount of angry aggression. She was rewarded for being so fiercely competitive. On her 21st birthday, while she was celebrating with friends in a Newcastle pub, the national coach rang to congratulate her, saying 'You've made the Australian team and will be going to Noumea to play in the Oceania Championships.'[136] Her exceptional performances at the recent National Championships had been responsible for her selection.

There were lots of such rewards: selection for state teams, the Australian team, travelling overseas. As she told me in 2004, 'There's no greater feeling than playing for your country and lining up on that field and the national anthem's played ... and looking down and sort of seeing that crest there, thinking, "Whoa, that's me ... I'm here."'[137]

The process for selection for the Australian team in those days was that a squad

---

135 Ibid.
136 Interview with Karen Menzies, 30 September, 2004, Newcastle
137 Ibid.

of twenty-four would be picked after the National Championships. On the basis of how players performed, the squad was whittled down to sixteen and those sixteen players would go on tour. Menzies was picked for the next six consecutive seasons and went on to play in three Oceania tournaments. The best success that the Australian Women's team had in those years was the Oceania tournament in 1986 played in New Zealand. They made the final and were beaten by New Zealand 3-2 in a cliff-hanger, in which one of the Australian players scored an own goal.

There were difficulties with being a sportswoman, especially financial pressures. The women had to pay their own fares - even when playing for Australia. They did receive a tracksuit but, unlike today, they had to give back the strip. 'You put your shirt on and came off the field and you handed it back ... the very last tournament, which was in 1989, we kept our strip from then.' Karen remembered making 'bucket loads of lamingtons'[138] to contribute to her trips to Noumea, the United States and New Zealand. But the disparity and inequity in how men's and women's sport was and is funded remains a gnawing issue for her.

Karen started out as a striker, 'because I could run like the wind,' and she held that position in the state team. But as she got older, she played in the midfield for both the Australian and state teams, and then as stopper or sweeper. She explained, 'As you get older and wiser you get to be a lot more strategic.'[139] She had her last game for Australia in 1989 and her last appearance for the state team in 1990, when she captained Northern New South Wales to their first-ever State Championships victory.

Karen Menzies played the opening four games of the 1991 season in the regular club competition and then broke her ankle. She never came back from that injury. Over the years there had been other injuries, including her first knee dislocation at age 14, which led to her first knee reconstruction three years later. She was convinced that she would come back from the broken ankle, but it did not happen. She recalled, 'I had such high hopes, it was devastating, just terrible.'[140] At the time of her career-ending injury she had played in nine full international matches for the Matildas. Looking back, it was the sport and the socialising that she loved

[138] Interview with Karen Menzies, 30 September, 2004, Newcastle
[139] Ibid.
[140] Interview with Karen Menzies, 30 September, 2004, Newcastle

and craved. She had had great success with soccer. On the field she was arrogant and confident, but off the pitch she had no self-confidence and erected barriers around herself.

School had been a non-event for Menzies, but she started studying for her first degree in 1991. She has gone on to acquire four university qualifications in all. She had worked at the New South Wales Department of Community Services (DOCS) since the early 1980s, working with children and families. She had read many case files and court cases and started to see an appalling pattern of Aboriginal children being removed from their families. She came to understand the full impact of the period of assimilation, and ultimately made the connection that this had been her experience. She secretly read her own file and learned what had been done to her mother and grandmother. Around 1986 or 1987, during her third year in the job, information about the Stolen Generations started to receive widespread media coverage and enter the consciousness of wider Australia. Menzies was driven to reconnect with her family once more and this time it was on her terms. She now has a wonderful relationship with her family, her mum, four siblings and all their kids as well. One of the highlights was meeting her Nan before she passed away. 'She was a woman of such incredible strength because it's hard to imagine losing one child, but she had seven children taken from her.'[141]

The years of working with children and families at DOCS was a journey of self-discovery that Menzies felt ultimately led to her own salvation. She went on to work at the Human Rights Commission and was the social worker on the Stolen Generations Inquiry during the 1990s. Her work on the Inquiry brought her and her family's experience flooding back but on a much bigger scale. 'The opportunity to hear people's testimonies, the resilience that I saw and sure there was lots of pain and suffering that I saw as well but the incredible resilience of Aboriginal and Torres Strait Islander people had such a profound impact on me.' In her interview with me, she found it difficult to explain what it did to her, but it gave her a degree of strength and 'any work or issue that I have to do or face, it's just like being on a holiday.'[142]

---

[141] Interview with Karen Menzies, 30 September, 2004, Newcastle
[142] Ibid.

From Menzies' perspective, Indigenous involvement in soccer has been affected by the lack of visible role models. She said, 'It's always been a characteristic of the AFL teams that they have Aboriginal players, and a lot of the league teams like North Queensland and Penrith. And these are not just mediocre Aboriginal players, they have these absolute brilliant and outstanding players like Matty Bowen from North Queensland.' [143]

The place of role models is so important in attracting kids into different sports. Menzies had never seen Aboriginal people play soccer and soccer was always portrayed negatively, as being an ethnic sport and typically not suitable for Anglo Australians. She felt that her involvement in soccer was a bit different to most Aboriginal players because she did not have the racial barriers to overcome. 'When I first started to play, I didn't know I was Aboriginal, and my appearance does not automatically portray that background ... so I got to live in society without discrimination.' [144]

The biggest barriers Karen experienced occurred when she made the transition from player to coach. She had taken up coaching after her career-ending injury. It was an outlet that helped her cope with the fact that her playing career was over. She coached the Newcastle Open team in the Sydney competition for the 1994–95 season. In her first year as coach, the team reached the semi-finals, and the next year, the final. In 1995 Menzies was named as one of five assistant coaches to the Australian Women's team. She was one of only three female players to have achieved a level-two coaching qualification at the time.

During the selection process to name the official assistant coach from the group of five, one of the male coaches asked her, 'Don't you feel a bit anxious being in this situation about all of the allegations that could be levelled at you?'[145] Menzies had been openly gay for as long as she could remember and was furious at this insinuation. She had been very excited at the prospect of being involved with the Australian team in the leadup to the 2000 Olympic Games in Sydney. Money was pouring into the sport and there was an incredible sense of possibility.

But Menzies walked away from the selection process in Canberra and left soccer

[143] Ibid.
[144] Interview with Karen Menzies, 30 September, 2004, Newcastle
[145] Ibid.

altogether. She felt she could never go back, to where she was vulnerable to such malicious allegations. The game she had loved for so long, which had been such a crutch during her years of torment, was finished for her. She has had nothing to do with the sport since. During her interview with me, she said, 'It was a really difficult thing to do because soccer was my foundation stone, from having a love for it and everything it offered.'[146]

On the future for Aboriginal kids in soccer and in sport, Menzies had no hesitation in stating, 'Sport does provide a foundation for life, I think it's your sports roots, it's just a wonderful opportunity to have a whole bunch of friends around you and to be able to test yourself as to what you are capable of doing ... it gives some great life skills and mixing with people, whether you become the leader in the team or whether you become the joker in the team, it prepares you to take on any role.'[147]

Karen retains her love for the game and has attended Matildas games held in Newcastle.

Felicity Huntington - Mixing Soccer and Futsal

Felicity Huntington is a Torres Strait Islander, born in Lae, Papua New Guinea, in 1968. As a junior she played a great deal of age representative outdoor soccer and was chosen to represent New South Wales and also toured New Zealand with a high school team. She switched to indoor soccer, futsal, in 1985. In 1990, she played in the International Aboriginal Cup against the Canadian Indians, both here and in Canada. She was selected for Australia's international team that toured Brazil in 1993. Reverting to the outdoor game, Huntington played sweeper for Blacktown City in the Super League in 1995 and 1996. She retired from outdoor soccer in 1996 but was still playing futsal in 2000 for Rooty Hill in the national competition run by the Australian Indoor Soccer Association.

Felicity worked for many years at New South Wales State Rail and then moved to the New South Wales Anti-Discrimination Board. In this role she worked with the Aboriginal and Torres Strait Islander Outreach Program, investigating

---

[146] Interview with Karen Menzies, 30 September, 2004, Newcastle
[147] Ibid.

and mediating complaints of discrimination from Indigenous people across New South Wales.

Bridgette Starr – A Star in any Measure

This outstanding player held the distinction of being the most capped Indigenous international soccer player until surpassed by Lydia Williams and Kyah Simon. She represented Australia on 59 occasions, including 53 A-internationals. Although born in Tamworth in rural New South Wales, Starr was a long-time resident of Newcastle. It was there that she began her soccer career in school teams and with clubs like Branxton Greta, Weston Bears, Raymond Terrace, Cardiff and Hunter Port Stephens. She signed up for an all-boys team with Branxton Greta, never dreaming it would make such a difference to her life. But her skills rocketed as a result of playing soccer with the boys and in just five years, at the age of 16, she was playing for Australia. She was a member of the Australian Youth team that won the 1993 Dana Cup in Denmark and the Australian Youth team that toured New Zealand in 1994.

Starr was a member of the Northern New South Wales team that won the 1997 National Championship, and she played for the New South Wales Sapphires in the Women's National Soccer League - then known as the Ansett Summer Series. The Sapphires won the Ansett Summer Series in 1999–2000. She was regarded as an ice-cool defender, powerful in the tackle and strong in the air. She was calm under pressure, confident on the ball, and had good distribution skills.

Starr was one of the twenty inaugural full-time residential scholarship holders in the Australian Institute of Sport (AIS) women's soccer program, based in Canberra. Her scholarship was renewed in 1999 and 2000. She found that with the benefit of full-time coaching and training, her skills, technique and fitness level improved enormously, as did the spirit and unity of the team.

A prodigious talent, Starr made her full international debut with the Matildas against Japan in 1994, in front of 40,000 screaming Japanese fans. Within weeks of her debut, she competed in the Oceania region's Women's World Cup qualifiers but missed selection in the final 1995 World Cup squad. Just a month after the World Cup, however, she was back in the Matildas, competing in the United States

Women's Cup, and went on to become a regular member of the team. Australia played and defeated New Zealand 3-1 in what was a thrilling final of the Oceania region Women's World Cup qualifiers. Starr scored her first international goal in the game, which saw Australia qualify for the 1999 Women's World Cup in the United States. She was selected in the 1999 World Cup finals team and played in all of Australia's games.

By the time the Sydney 2000 Olympics arrived - it was the first time an Australian women's soccer team had competed at the Olympics - Starr was one of Australia's most capped players. She recalled this career highlight: 'That was an experience I will never forget. I won my fiftieth Australian cap against Brazil at the Olympics'.[148]

After the Games, Starr had the honour of being chosen as a member of the World Stars team that toured the United States, playing matches against the United States world champions to promote women's soccer. She found it an amazing experience, and it helped to strengthen the women's game in the United States, which back then had its own fully professional league and often drew crowds of more than 8000 to its games.

Starr ended her international career as the tenth-most capped Matilda at that time. 'Soccer took me to many parts of the world and gave me great experiences and being in the AIS program for three years was a wonderful part of it. It improved every aspect of my game.

She gave up soccer for a while and switched to Australian football, which she also loves, playing for the Ainslie Football Club women's team in Canberra. But the lure of the round-ball game proved too much for such a talented player, and in 2009 at the age of 33, she signed with Broadmeadow Magic, playing in the Newcastle Women's Premier League. One player, Rebecca Bryant, deregistered herself to make room on the 16-player roster for Starr. Magic skipper Harmonie Attwill told the *Newcastle Morning Herald*: 'Starr would provide plenty of quality and knowledge to the side. Due to her work she can't play as many games as we'd like, but she's someone who can provide a bit more flexibility. We're looking at the defence, but she can play anywhere because she's experienced enough.

....

[148] Fogarty, M, *Indigenous Athletes at the Australian Institute of Sport,* Australian Sports Commission, Canberra, 2005.

Bridgette Starr was and remains one of the truly great Indigenous players to have graced the game in this country.

Kayleen Janssen – The Indoor/Outdoor International

Kayleen is one of the very few players to have represented her country in both indoor and outdoor soccer - a truly unique representative curriculum vitae. Indoor and outdoor soccer are two different sports, and it is uncommon for someone to be skilled and gain representative honours in both.

Janssen was born in Brisbane in 1968. She made the Australian indoor soccer squad in 1988. Her outdoor soccer career began for Queensland in 1986, and she was a regular state player from 1989 to 1995. A midfielder, Janssen made her international debut for Australia against New Zealand in 1991. She was in the Matildas side that contested the Women's World Cup in Sweden in 1995. Sadly, Australia was bundled out of a very strong group, which included China, the United States and Denmark. By the end of 1995, Janssen had represented Australia on 27 occasions, including a tour of Papua New Guinea in 1994; she has 15 official international caps, as well as twelve other appearances for the Matildas.

Belinda Dawney – The Late Starter

It is hard to believe that Belinda Dawney, a proud Bundjalung woman from Tweed Heads on the North Coast of New South Wales, was a late starter to the world game. She played touch football at school and only gave soccer a try when her friends asked her to. She'd been kicking a soccer ball around from the age of nine but did not play competitively until she was 16, when she started playing for the Tweed Heads Kangaroos and Tweed River High School.

Dawney felt as though she took to soccer naturally, and after trials in Brisbane arranged by her coach, she won a Queensland Academy of Sport (QAS) soccer scholarship while still at high school. She had to train with the QAS soccer squad after school. This was an enormous strain for her parents, who, three nights a week, for two and a half years, drove her from Tweed Heads to Brisbane and back, a 250-kilometre round trip. Dawney, a left-footed striker, is just 157 centimetres - not tall for a striker - but she scored seven goals in her first season with the QAS.

Dawney was representing Australia in touch football at the same time, so life was frantically busy. She said, 'The fundamental reason I started playing both sports was because all my friends were playing and I didn't want to be left out.' [149] She gained selection in the New South Wales under 16 touch football team when she was in Year 9 at school, and in 2001 was chosen in the Australian under 18 team for the Youth World Cup played in Auckland, New Zealand.

But having a good education was something Dawney's parents insisted on. With her soccer and touch football commitments, she decided to complete her Year 12 certificate over two years. Then she began teacher training in her home town and continued playing touch football and soccer.

In early 2000 Dawney was selected to go to the Australian Institute of Sport (AIS) for a Matildas training camp - this was part of the Matildas' Olympic selection process. After a week at the camp, the coach asked her if she wanted to come back full-time. With only seven months to go until the Sydney Olympic Games, the pressure was on to train hard, and Dawney gave it her all. But her hopes were dashed when she came down with glandular fever just before the Olympic team's selection and was forced to withdraw. This was a tragic blow and she took a year off from the game to recover.

Dawney returned to the Women's National Soccer League in 2002–03 and scored the winning goal for Queensland Sting in the grand final. Her sights were once more fixed. 'I want to win an Australian team spot. Who knows, I might even be offered a scholarship to the AIS. After all, I am still in my early twenties'. [150] She recognised the wonderful opportunities soccer provided: 'Soccer is my passion, and through it I have the chance to play professionally in the USA, and also represent my country at both the World Cup and the Olympics ... Working with the community is important too; I hold coaching clinics and volunteer at local school sporting events'. [151]

....

[149] Munro, K and Tyhuis, M, *Fresh Footprints,* Department of Family and Community Services, Canberra, 2003
[150] Fogarty, 2005
[151] Munro, K and Tyhuis, M, 2003

In 2003–04 Dawney was back in another grand final with the Queensland Stings. She scored the only Stings goal in a 3-1 defeat to the New South Wales Sapphires – she was the leading goal scorer in the Women's National Soccer League that season. Her performances again earned the notice of national selectors and she received a call-up to join the Matildas 2004 Olympic training camp.

For Dawney, this was the chance to make up for the hurt of four years before, when she got so close but was cruelly cut down by illness. In an interview with the *National Indigenous Times* before the camp, Matildas coach Adrian Santrac described Dawney as 'an exciting and gifted player. Belinda has threatened opposition defences in the Women's National Soccer League all year with her exceptional pace and mobility. This camp provides Belinda the opportunity to perform to her potential and take the first step towards selection for the Olympic qualifiers.' Sadly, on the second day of the camp she was injured, and this stopped her from fully extending herself.

On day eight, Santrac broke the news that Dawney had not made the team. She told *Deadly Vibe*, 'He told me I didn't get picked because I wasn't trying hard enough. My attitude wasn't right! I was so disappointed. I had been trying really hard, trying my best. It really damaged my confidence.' It all seemed like *déjà vu*, and more heartache. Dawney again took time off from the game to rebuild lost confidence and reassess her options. She became involved in the Soccer in the Outback program, an initiative of the Australian Sports Commission, the Indigenous Sports Foundation and the Laureus Sport for Good Foundation. In 2009 she took up the position of captain-coach for the Tweed Valley Kings in the Gold Coast Premier League - she was still a sharp shooter, scoring all three goals in a 3-2 win over Nerang. In the 2013 season she scored a remarkable 27 goals from 17 games and was still playing for Tweed United in 2016.[152]

Showcasing that her love for the game has not diminished, nor her desire to promote the game with Indigenous peoples in 2018 coinciding with NAIDOC week and the special theme of "Because of Her, We Can", Belinda, 'visited Tonga. She shared her love of soccer and touch football with coaches, players,

....

152 http://websites.sportstg.com/team_info.cgi?action=PSTATS&pID=195693847&client=
1-9389-136601-398413-25003354

and primary school students. Belinda shared her passion for promoting healthy lifestyles and her Indigenous Australian culture with coaches, players, artists and students during her three-day program... She also spoke about life in Kowanyama, the remote Indigenous community in far north Queensland where Belinda is a Year 3 teacher.'[153]

Leanne Edmundson –
Captain of the Australian Indoor Under 21s

Leanne Edmundson (now Metcalfe) spent much of her life playing championship indoor and outdoor soccer. Born in 1970 in Sydney, she first represented New South Wales in the Under 15s when they won the national title. Selected for the New South Wales Open team, she was also in the 1987 Australian under 18 side that made the semi-finals in the Dallas Cup in Texas. In 1988, she was in the all-age New South Wales side that played in a Perth carnival, and she was then picked for a national side that played the United States.

Edmundson captained the under 21 women's national indoor soccer side that toured Canada in 1990. She played against the visiting Canadian Indians in 1991 and was selected for the tour to Canada the following year. She played in the winning New South Wales Open indoor soccer team in the 1992 indoor national titles. In 1995, Edmundson was playing for Blacktown City in the Super League, the top echelon of women's soccer, but a shattered ankle tragically and prematurely ended her career that year.

Kyah Simon – Skill to Burn

This great Indigenous player has starred for several clubs in the Westfield W-League and the Women's Premier Soccer League in the United States including the Central Coast Mariners, Sydney City, Western Sydney Wanderers, Melbourne City, Boston Breakers and the Houston Dash.

Simon was a full international with the Matildas at just 16. Having accumulated

---

[153] https://www.facebook.com/australiaintonga/posts/1527918910651216

87 full caps for the Matildas and scoring 24 goals (at the end of 2018) she is our most capped Indigenous player. Her mother, Pam, is a Kamilaroi woman from Armidale and her father, Gordon, is a Biripi man from the Mid North Coast of New South Wales. She was born in 1991 and started playing with the Quakers Hill under 8 boys as a junior.

Simon took a huge leap forward when she went into camp with the Matildas in 2007. At the time her aim was to gain experience and develop her game among older players; a call-up from national coach Tom Sermanni for a place on the Matildas tour of the United States was not what the then 16-year-old was expecting. Sermanni named a 20- strong squad for the tour, which included a number of young players, and Simon was one of them. In an interview with *Australian Football Weekly*, Sermanni described her as a 'promising talent who has come into recent camps and basically got herself selected with her displays. She has great ability to unsettle defences and also possesses a natural football ability and game awareness'.

Simon's progress was rapid. From the ranks of the Australian under 17 team early in 2007, she moved to the Young Matildas (Under 20s) before making her first appearance for the senior team in an Olympic qualifier against Hong Kong. Alongside Indigenous team-mate Lydia Williams, she was a member of the Australian team that gave the world number two side, the United States, a fright; the Australians lost 3-2, with the Americans' winning goal coming in injury time. Coach Sermanni said Simon's appeal lies in some of the qualities Indigenous athletes are renowned for. 'She is quick, good athletically and has innate game skills. Kyah does things now that are uncoachable, she'll do the unexpected, pull [off] some things out of the ordinary, that you don't anticipate.'

One such moment came at the Peace Cup in the United States, when the baby of the squad netted the only goal against soccer giants Brazil. Simon told *Australian Football Weekly*, 'I have trouble finding the words to sum up that moment. Even when I finally got a DVD of the game and watched it back for the first time, I couldn't believe it was me kicking the ball into the net. It was such a great feeling with all the girls huddling around; to be a part of a history-making moment was indescribable.'

Sermanni saw similarities between the playing styles of Simon and Bridgette Starr, the former Matilda who he coached in the mid-1 990s. He thinks there are many more young Indigenous players like Simon and Lydia Williams out there, waiting to be discovered, and says only a lack of funding keeps Australian soccer from adequately exploring this Indigenous talent pool. 'We would love to expand our reach into that market, but we don't have the resources to do it in a concentrated manner as yet. It will take more than a few players going out to visit remote areas. The difficulty at present is identifying the players and then needing to relocate them into cities, where they can receive specialised coaching. Simon also feels there are many Indigenous girls who haven't been given the chance to really show people what they can do and make it, like she has done, 'But I'm hoping I can help change that.'

Simon certainly had a full schedule in 2008, as she was now in both the Australian under 20 and Matildas squads. She was training for the Australian under 20 pre-qualifiers and also playing for Central Coast Mariners in the Westfield W-League. In 2009 she moved from the Mariners to Sydney FC and was a member of the Sydney FC team that secured the club's first W-League title, beating Brisbane Roar 3-2 in the 2009–10 grand final.

Her soccer commitments disrupted her schooling, but her parents had no hesitation in fully supporting their daughter in achieving her dreams. After all, she had talked about wanting to play for Australia ever since she was eight years old. Simon had well and truly fulfilled that dream by 2009. She cemented her place in Australian soccer folklore as a member of the first Australian national team to be crowned as champions of Asia when they beat North Korea in the Asian Football Confederation Women's Cup final in 2010. This was an inspirational victory. The team had to overcome several setbacks and injuries to key players, not to mention monsoonal conditions at the Chengdu stadium, in China, to claim the title. The scores were locked 1-1 at the end of 90 minutes and extra time, but Tom Sermanni's team dug deep and won the match 5-4 on penalties. Simon netted the all-important winning penalty.

You could say that her sporting prowess is grounded in family sporting bloodlines. Her cousin Kyle Vander Kuyp is a two-time Olympian in the 110 metres hurdles, and there are a host of prominent rugby league players in the extended family. Her cousin Gema also plays in the W-League, with the Newcastle Jets. In 2009 Kyah and Gema achieved a wonderful sporting family achievement when they played together for the Young Matildas. Simon attended the inaugural

Indigenous Football Festival in Townsville in 2009 as an ambassador, an experience she enjoyed immensely. 'It was really good to see so many Indigenous kids playing football. It was a nice experience for me to be seen as a role model and it really lit a spark in me so that was good. Definitely a lot of kids at the festival have a natural talent'.[154]

Kyah Simon proved a key member of the 2011 Matildas at the World Cup finals in Germany. An exciting, very young team, they were eventually knocked out in the quarter final by Sweden. Simon scored two goals in the 2-1 victory over Denmark during the campaign and had signalled that she would be a player to watch on the world stage. It was extra special for Simon in that her mother and brothers were at the World Cup in Germany and had all cried with joy when she walked out with the Australian team wearing the Matildas jersey.

Simon was the top scorer in the W-League in 2010–11 and cleaned up in the awards that year winning the Player of the Year, Young Player of the Year and the Players' Player of the Year. She captained Sydney FC to win the W-League grand final in 2012–2013 scoring one goal and setting up another in a 3-1 win over Melbourne Victory. She initially signed for the Western Sydney Wanderers for the 2013 season, but she ruptured her ACL and missed the 2013–14 season. She returned to Sydney FC in 2014.

She had four great seasons in the USA NWSL with the Boston Breakers. She found Boston a great space especially training and playing on the hallowed fields of Harvard University. She had to deal with snow and freezing cold, but she gained a real buzz from the close proximity to such a famous learning institution.[155] She played 53 games for the Breakers scoring 19 goals.

She only just came back from injury in time to make the Australian team for the 2015 World Cup in Canada. She was a major part of the Australian team that made the quarter finals including an historic victory over much higher ranked Brazil. They won the match against Brazil 1-0 through a Simon goal. They were beaten by Japan in the quarter finals and Simon played in all of the games scoring three goals in total. On returning from the World Cup, Simon acknowledged the need to

....

154 FIFA.com, viewed 25 September 2009 <http://. fifa.com>
155 *Sunday Telegraph,* May 8, 2016: pp83

recuperate and rest both the mind and body to regain 100% health and fitness. The wear and tear and mental and physical fatigue necessitated a time for reflection and recovery.

In a self-reflective interview in 2016? Kyah Simon opened up on her family background, sacrifices and resilience. She revealed that her grandmother was a member of the Stolen Generation and one of the young Aboriginal girls removed from their families, institutionalised and placed into domestic service by the state government. She ran away from that environment at the age of 14 and found her way back to her family. She met and married a non-Indigenous man Ray, whose family proceeded to cut him off for marrying an Aboriginal girl. They eventually moved to Sydney living in a housing commission home in Seven Hills. The family came through some tough times and racism; discrimination and prejudice were a part of the lived experience for Kyah's mother and family growing up. Kyah's grandfather and his brothers fought in the Second World War and one of them interned as a prisoner of war.

Kyah Simon's parents did without to send her and her siblings to a private school. 'They figured a Catholic school would protect us from negative influences out in the community. That meant massive sacrifices at their end, which I am only just starting to understand now'.[156] They were then living in Quakers Hill and there was a lot of family in close proximity. She follows the Cronulla Sharks in the NRL as she grew up close to the Fifita boys. Kyah feels immense gratitude for everything her parents provided including the opportunity to play sport as a young girl. She knows they did without and made sacrifices to ensure her young life was good.[157]

In 2017 she signed with Melbourne City in the W-League and also played for the Houston Dash in the USA National Women's Soccer League.[158] Throughout 2018 she was mostly used as a substitute and impact player with the Matildas due to ongoing problems with an achilles injury. In January 2019 Simon was booked in for ankle reconstruction surgery and would be out for three months. She was

---

[156] *Players Voice 'The Things Left Unsaid'* – Kyah Simon, http://www.playersvoice.com.au/athletes/kyah-simon/
[157] Ibid.
[158] *The Sun Herald,* 22 October 2017: pp45

'gutted to be back in rehab again but am fortunate that I have enough time to be back 100% for France'.[159]

Simon missed the Four Nations tournament against New Zealand, South Korea and Argentina and an away friendly against the world number one side the United States in April 2019. In the wake of the upheaval over the sacking of Alen Stajcic and the appointment of Ante Milicic as his replacement, it remained to be seen if Simon could regain her position in the new Australian set-up. Sadly, Kyah missed out on World Cup squad selection for France in 2019 as Milicic considered she had not been playing sufficiently to warrant selection. She was nevertheless called into the squad for pre World Cup training as a standby injury replacement player. A recurrence of a hamstring injury saw her sent back to her US club side Houston Dash to enter rehabilitation.

Milicic was philosophical. 'Kyah has worked hard this week and shown a lot of positivity around the group ... We will continue to monitor her progress and hope she can return to the pitch soon to put her best foot forward ahead of our [2020] Olympic Games campaign'.[160] When one looks across the career of Kyah Simon it would be a brave person to bet against her coming back into calculations for the 2020 Olympics. The drive, tenacity and will power that Kyah has displayed throughout her career may well see her playing again for the Matildas at the Olympics.

Lydia Williams – The Deadly Keeper

Lydia Williams grew up chasing Australian rules footballs on the dusty red plains in and around Kalgoorlie in Western Australia but found her niche in the world game. She lived in the mining town until the age of ten and discovered soccer at school. Her mother, Diana, is an American who met her Aboriginal father, Ron, when working in Western Australia as a missionary. When her mother was offered a job in Canberra, the family moved.

By now a soccer fanatic, Williams had to make a decision in her new surrounds:

159   *The Sydney Morning Herald,* 8 January 2019
160   *The Sydney Morning Herald,* 27 May 2019: pp41

whether to play in the top Tuggeranong team as a goalkeeper or in the fourth division as a midfielder? The answer was easy: 'Mum, the top division of course.' She told the SBS Television program *Living Black*, 'I just love the sport and everything that's involved with it, like the people and the coaches and the travelling.'

Williams had tried a number of sports, mainly basketball and soccer, but also Australian Rules and cricket. As she started getting selected for state teams, she had to decide which sport she really wanted to pursue. It was soccer. Becoming a goalkeeper was not actually a choice. She told the *Koori Mail*, 'Goals was the only position left on the field. So, I sort of got stuck with it. We're the last line of defence and we have to make the decisive saves. It's probably the hardest position on the field in the sense that you have to be switched on all of the time, but I like that about it.'

Williams was accepted into the Australian Capital Territory Academy of Sport program. She missed out on making a Young Matildas team in her first trial, but six months after that, following a demanding training program with Australian keeping coaches, she made her Matildas match debut, aged 17.

In 2006, at 18 years of age, Williams became one of the youngest ever recipients of the Deadly Award for Female Sportsperson of the Year. She told the *Koori Mail*, 'I was speechless when they announced that. It still surprises me now to be thought of as in the same category as [previous winner] Cathy Freeman.'

With all that she had achieved during the previous twelve months, Williams certainly had plenty to be proud of. Not only was she a part of the Australian women's soccer squad that toured the United States and Mexico in late 2005, she also took part in the Asian Football Confederation Asian Women's Cup, which doubled as qualifiers for the World Cup. She also played in the World Youth Cup in Russia.

Since 2006, Williams has been a regular part of the Australian program. In 2007 she captained the Young Matildas. During 2008 she was a regular fixture in the Matildas squad as understudy to regular keeper Melissa Barbieri. Matildas coach Tom Sermanni told the *Koori Mail*, 'Williams was the second number-one keeper and ... she would be the next senior goalkeeper.'

There was some tragedy to deal with along the way. Her father died four months before Williams was selected to play her first game for Australia. But Williams believes that her upbringing in the West Australian goldfields has helped foster a tough and fearless attitude. In an interview with the *Koori Mail,* she said, 'I was always out travelling around with my family and playing with other kids in the bush and I was never worried about falling over and getting scratched or anything like that. I always had a bit of that fearless aspect.' It's something that has carried over to her work outside soccer, training to be a zookeeper while working as a tour guide at the National Zoo and Aquarium in Canberra.

The start of the Westfield W-League in 2008 has seen a new professionalism enter the women's game and Williams proved to be one of its stars, playing for Canberra United. They finished as worthy runners up in the 2008–09 season after being beaten in the grand final by the Brisbane Roar. The club's summary of the season noted 'It's not often that the goalkeeper is considered the key player in a side, but Canberra's results start and finish with Lydia Williams.' That is some statement of a player's worth.

Williams was a part of the Canberra team that won the W-League in season 2011–12. Lydia Williams, with Kyah Simon, was a member of the 2011 Matildas team in the World Cup Finals in Germany. Lydia played in the 3-2 victory over Equatorial Guinea. She has gained much international experience with the Matildas and playing in the United States NWSL with clubs Chicago Red Stars, Western New York Flash, Washington Spirit, Houston Dash and the Seattle Reign. Back in Australia she has played with Melbourne City in the W-League since 2016. She was part of the Melbourne City team that won both the 2016–17 and 2017–18 grand finals.

She has been the mainstay as the last line of defence for the Matildas across the past several years, including another World Cup in Canada in 2015 where the team again made the quarter finals after beating Brazil 1-0 in the last sixteen matches before losing to Japan 1-0. Williams looked back on the World Cup with fond memories. Kyah Simon's family had brought over a large Aboriginal flag and Williams said: 'To see that flag in the stands, Kyah and I had a word... it was pretty special you know, walking out onto the field and seeing that flag. It was one of the best moments.'[161] The moment was not lost on former SBS journalist Leah Cwikel.

....

[161] Leah Cwikel 'Queen of the Keepers' - https://www.sbs.com.au/topics/life/zela/article/2016/01/19/lydia-williams-keeps-giving-ahead-weekends-semi-final

'Seeing the image of Kyah and Lydia together with that flag in the *Sydney Morning Herald...* This is news,' she remembered thinking. 'These women represent the spiritual history of our beautiful land, they are heroes and bearers of hope for Aboriginal children who live in rural, Indigenous communities in Australia today'. [162]

Williams was also a part of the Australian team that contested the Olympic Games in Brazil 2016. The Matildas advanced from the Group Stage but were beaten 7-6 on penalties by host country Brazil in the quarter final.

Williams has certainly faced her tests of adversity including two knee reconstructions and coming back from the ACL injury just before the 2015 World Cup in Canada. In an interview with Cwikel it was revealed that she had 'overcome injury after injury to secure her spot on the international stage'. Cwikel was impressed by Williams self-belief and strength of character, writing that she was 'a force to be reckoned with on and off the field; a poignant female sports personality whose journey to the international stage encourages strength, belief and positivity for all who bear witness to her talent'. [163]

The Matildas performed and achieved outstanding results in 2017 and 2018. In the Tournament of Nations in the United States in 2017 they won the tournament finishing on top over USA, Japan and Brazil. In 2018 they again finished undefeated but placed second behind the USA on goal difference. Williams said that to get to the top and stay there was a rollercoaster ride of emotions that included 'a lot of excitement, tears, frustration and hard work'. Lydia moved in a new direction in mid 2019 by publishing a children's book titled *Saved,* a beautifully illustrated book it showcases the talents of Lydia away from the sports arena.

In making the Matildas squad for France, Lydia Williams would achieve a history making fourth World Cup appearance following China (2007), Germany (2011) and Canada (2015). The dismissal and disruption following the sacking of Alen Stajcic as coach of the team for France firmly placed the potential blame for any disappointing results at the feet of the new FFA Board. An opening 2-1 loss to

---

[162] Leah Cwikel 'Queen of the Keepers' - https://www.sbs.com.au/topics/life/zela/article/2016/01/19/lydia-williams-keeps-giving-ahead-weekends-semi-final

[163] Leah Cwikel 'Queen of the Keepers' - https://www.sbs.com.au/topics/life/zela/article/2016/01/19/lydia-williams-keeps-giving-ahead-weekends-semi-final

Italy did raise concern and voices over the timing of the dismissal and its impact on the Matildas squad. But subsequent victories over Brazil and Jamaica saw the team through to the last sixteen. Lydia Williams was in goal for all of the group games. In the group of 16 game against Denmark, Lydia Williams had one of her greatest games in a Matilda's jersey and made at least five outstanding saves but it was not enough as Australia were knocked out after extra time on penalties. I would not count Lydia Williams out on making another Matilda's World Cup squad in four years time and she will remain an inspiring role model for young Indigenous players coming through in the years ahead.

Other Indigenous Women Players

There are other Indigenous women players who have made a marked impact at the national league level.

Tanya Oxtoby, from the Pilbara region in Western Australia, was picked in the Australian Schoolgirls team when 17 and captained the Western Waves in the Women's National Soccer League in 2005. When the new W-League began in 2008, she was appointed captain of Perth Glory and that season was awarded the Glory Player of the Year - known as the Most Glorious Women's Player award. She was appointed assistant coach of the Football West National Training Centre in 2007 and Western Australia's under 15s women's coach in 2008.

Tashina Roma, born in Brisbane, played for the Queensland Roar in the W-League. Before joining the Roar, she was named as the Brisbane Women's Premier League Player of the Year in 2008.

Unlike their male counterparts, Aboriginal woman are currently flourishing in the round ball game with a number of young players bursting through to join Kyah Simon and Lydia Williams in the W-League.

Gema Simon is another player who has had her run of setbacks through injury. She has only recently won a place back in the Matildas squad under new coach Ante Milicic in preparation for the World Cup in France. She played a full game against South Korea in the Four Nations Championship won by Australia 4-1. She is a very sound defensive player with a wonderful left foot that she uses to great advantage on wide overlapping runs down the flank. Gema was born in

Armidale and started playing soccer from the age of five. She is the cousin of Kyah Simon. She signed on for the Newcastle Jets in their inaugural 2008–09 W-League season. She broke through for international honours in 2009 playing for the Australian under 20s team in the Asian Cup. She made her senior international debut for Australia at the 2014 Cyprus Cup against Scotland. In 2013 Simon signed with USL W-League team Ottawa Fury but suffered a serious injury only a month into her first season. She returned and recovered with the Newcastle Jets captaining the team in 2013–14 season. In 2014 she moved to the Melbourne Victory but returned to Newcastle after one season. After a great season with the Jets she played a winter season with Suwon in the Korean League. On her return to Australia she again joined the Jets and was again given the captaincy. In 2017 she spent time in Norway to play for Avaldsnes in the top tier of women's football in that country. Newcastle must be something like a homing pigeon location for Gema as she returned again to the Jets where she is currently playing. Let's hope she has a good run free from injury and enjoys a trip to France and the World Cup. Gema was very excited to be a part of the France World Cup squad and unfortunately did not get any game time in the Matilda's four games.

Jada Whyman is another rising young star player. A young goalkeeper of immense promise, she is following in the footsteps of idol Lydia Williams. She is currently a star performer for Western Sydney Wanderers in the W-League and the Young Matildas. She also plays for Sydney Olympic in the state competition.

Jada grew up in Wagga Wagga in western NSW before getting to Sydney via Canberra to follow her football dreams.[164] A proud young Wiradjuri and Yorta Yorta woman she sees herself as a role model for other young Indigenous women: 'I am a very proud Aboriginal woman and I hope that what I'm pursuing with my football will help to inspire other young Indigenous players to follow their dreams'.[165]

Jada reflected that her grandmother and grandfather had worked tirelessly in helping provide opportunities for Indigenous community members including instilling pride in their traditional culture. Her grandfather's family was another

[164] https://www.playersvoice.com.au/jada-whyman-our-home-was-tent/#YTvqzsVLqDK8X3SD.97
[165] https://www.anzstadium.com.au/footer/our-people/ambassadors/jada-whyman/

impacted upon by the Stolen Generations experience. He was one of fourteen siblings with most of them removed by the insidious government policy of child removal. On her Yorta Yorta side of the family there is a strong creative/performance connection some of her aunties were members of the famous 'Sapphires' singing group.

Jada was mad about AFL as a child but was encouraged to give soccer a go and 'I fell in love with the sport immediately'. Initially she had played in mixed boys' and girls' junior teams and had to contend with racist abuse from boys on opposing teams. Even her mum on the sidelines was racially abused but she gave as good as she got. Jada felt that some of these boys were jealous and intimidated and could not 'handle the fact that a girl was giving them a good run for their money'. After her second year of playing for the NSW Country Girls team she was asked to play for Macarthur Rams in Sydney at the age of just 13. On arrival, both the first-and second-string goalkeepers were injured, and she was pitched into the first team. She was spotted by then Matildas coach Tom Sermani who took her to Canberra and a fulltime coaching academy.

This move necessitated the entire family moving to Canberra. They stayed with relatives for a short time and then moved into a camp ground and lived in a tent. She recalled 'it cost us $200 a week to stay, but there were toilets and 20 cents would get you a shower with hot water. It was better than nothing'. It was a very tough time period for the family and Jada is another who realises the sacrifices made by the family for her to chase her football dreams. Jada's journey to the top and playing for Western Sydney Wanderers and the Young Matildas has been one of resilience and determination. She is another star of the future.

Allira Toby. currently with the Brisbane Roar, was the club's leading scorer in 2018 taking the Golden Boot Award for the season. From Ipswich, Toby is extremely proud of her Indigenous heritage.

Her career kicked off with junior football playing with the local Ipswich City Bulls. She also made the Queensland Schoolgirls team whilst attending Ipswich State High. Her love of the game developed from watching her dad Anthony play the game. Like others, Allira indicated that her family had to make sacrifices for her to pursue her football career. She originally played with Adelaide United in the 2016–17 season. She made 12 appearances for the Reds before coming home to join the Roar. She stated that she was 'the only Indigenous player in the Roar team and the only one in the Queensland W-League. I think that's something very special'.

Toby works as a counsellor at Marsden High School: 'My role here is to work with Indigenous and Torres Strait Islander students – there's a 170 plus students – and to support them if they need a person here to help with stuff and give them a positive outlook on life and with their schooling'.

She has set her goals: 'Every young woman soccer player hopes to put on the green and gold and represent her country!' She was quick to quip 'Can I bend it like Beckham? That's how it's supposed to go. It's what I aim for but I'm not sure it always works!' Well it certainly worked on the opening day of the 2018–19 season as she bagged two goals and added an assist in a 3-1 victory over Sydney FC. At just 23 Allira is a player of the future and one we will hear much more about in the years ahead. She was also named an Ambassador for the inaugural Australian Indigenous Football Championships held in Brisbane in late 2018. Toby was honoured to assist and help promote the game to young Indigenous players.

Shadeene Evans was taken to Brazil in 2014 as part of a trip sponsored by the John Moriarty Foundation. She was inspired by that experience and wanted 'to play with the Matildas and represent Australia'.

She moved to Sydney from Borroloola under a coaching program directed by former Matilda's boss Alen Stajcic. Evans was initially spotted by Stajcic at a tournament in Canberra when she was just 13 years old. She received a John Moriarty Scholarship in 2016 and has already played with the Young Matildas. She hopes to inspire other young Indigenous kids from her home community: 'If you really love something, you have to chase it and just fight through all the homesickness and stuff… it helped me and everyone in the community to look for a better future and I came down to Sydney to get a better education and explore things outside of Booroloola.

Noted as a football prodigy Shadeene Evans is someone going places. She was recently selected in the Young Matildas squad to take part in the second stage of qualification for the 2019 Asian Football Confederation under 19 tournament to be hosted in Myanmar in Burma. The young 17 year old could not hide her excitement or how indebted she was over this wonderful achievement:

When I first joined the John Moriarty Football grassroots program... I never imagined I'd go on to play an international tournament with the Young Matildas... It is creating a lot of opportunities for me and for the young kids in my community in the Northern Territory. I'm excited to be part of the Young Matildas squad and can't wait to run out on the field in Myanmar. [166]

Across the past 40 years Aboriginal women have made an indelible imprint on the world game and its development in Australia. With players like Kyah Simon, Gema Simon, Mary Fowler and Lydia Williams as members of the Matildas squad, the future is looking very positive and can only enhance the growth of the game in Indigenous communities. If the Matildas continue to climb world rankings and perform well in the Asian and World Cups, the game could ride the crest of a wave, with a spike in women's participation. Indigenous women could potentially be at the forefront of that exciting future.

[166] *Daily Telegraph,* 26 April 2019: pp83

CHAPTER 9

The Future – Awakening the 'Sleeping Giant'

Looking back to when I wrote the original book in 2010 it all looked so positive. So it is worthwhile examining that period again.

During the first decade of the 21st century soccer had made enormous progress in Australian sporting culture. With the formation of Football Federation Australia (FFA) and the influence of business tycoon Frank Lowy as its chairman, the leap had been startling. The initial appointment of John O'Neill as chief executive of the FFA was a masterstroke and he presided over the formation of the new national competition, the A-League, and of Australia being accepted into the thriving Asian Football Confederation. But it was the Socceroos qualifying for the 2006 World Cup finals in Germany that catapulted Australia onto the world stage and into the Australian public's imagination. Under the guidance of Dutch coaching wizard Guus Hiddink, Australia's performances in first, overcoming South American heavyweight Uruguay to qualify, and then their heroic efforts at the World Cup finals against Japan, Brazil, Croatia and Italy were outstanding.

The once formidable barriers to the game began to crumble and even the staunchest of supporters and commentators of other codes recognised that trying to hold back the march of soccer would be like trying to hold back a tsunami. After Australia defeated Uruguay to qualify for the 2006 World Cup finals, noted historian Geoffrey Blainey - himself a great follower of Australian football and author of *A Game of Our Own* - recognised the changing landscape, writing in *The Age*:

Like thousands of others who admire Australian rules football, I watched the remarkable end of the soccer game in Sydney with split feelings ... People brought up in Victoria - or in the three other strongholds of Aussie Rules - have long sensed the fierce competition that soccer would some day give our game.

If Australia's national soccer team performs well in the World Cup and goes on to win a fairly regular place in subsequent contests, the publicity for soccer here will be voluminous. Australian soccer then will probably attract more money than Aussie Rules and will increasingly recruit those talented youngsters who are mad about sport and have the natural football skills that both codes require.

All this - if it comes to pass - will be to soccer's credit. But the spectacular game of our own, with its rich traditions could well be the loser.

This sense of foreboding was well founded. I remember, when I arrived back in Australia after a trip to Canada in late 2009, flying into Sydney international airport. As I drove away from the terminal, I was confronted by a massive advertising billboard of Socceroo Tim Cahill promoting Sony Bravia television sets. It was impossible to miss the significance of this use of Cahill and his connection with international tourists. Rugby league and AFL players of the very highest calibre mean nothing to the millions of tourists who swarm into Australia each year, but Cahill and other Socceroos like Mark Schwarzer, Harry Kewell, Lucas Neill and Brett Emerton were instantly recognisable around the globe through their exploits in the English Premier League.

The FFA's application to host either the 2018 or 2022 World Cup sent another seismic signal of the massive change in the game's place in the national sporting mindset. The federal government, through then Prime Minister Kevin Rudd, pledged $50 million in support for the bid. Sadly, the bid proved unsuccessful and was proven to be a stain on the management of the game internationally and locally.

At the same time, there had been a heightened Indigenous presence. The current and future generations of Indigenous soccer stars can tap into this lucrative global marketplace. As shown in the first book, over the past 25 years a burgeoning group of Indigenous players have broken through to play in national and international leagues and gain national representative honours. I was convinced then that they had been the first wave of an ever-increasing surge of Indigenous players breaking through to the highest levels. Of equal importance was the fact that these Indigenous players recognised the crucial role they have to play in the game's future within Indigenous communities. As Travis Dodd told the *Sydney Morning Herald* in 2006:

> *The way the game is progressing, with the spotlight we had, hopefully we can be role models for Aboriginal kids. There just hasn't been that next step for kids to go before. AFL is in their face, so is rugby league. But now we're making some way on this. With the Socceroos, you do get noticed more - kids can see that. It's such a big stage. To do what we're doing in front of so many people, it gives kids something to aspire to. People stand up and listen to what you've got to say. I can have an influence now.*

This rise in Indigenous participation had been noted at all levels. Informed commentators remarked on this pronounced trend and the unease being felt among the other, once-dominant codes. An article in the *Sunday Age* in 2009 reported:

> *Australia's 'traditional' football codes - Australian football [AFL] and the two rugby codes - have long had their pick of the country's most promising Indigenous athletes. But this looks set to change with soccer finally waking up to the potential offered by the most athletic Aboriginal players - both boys and girls.*

The growth in talent had been tremendous and there was a real spike on the participation graph. At national championship level in soccer (2009), 24 Indigenous youngsters were involved. In Australian football, there were 61, so that was still top of the pile, but soccer had already outstripped rugby league, where there were just 15.

Training Programs Really Get Underway

Outreach programs to Indigenous communities had begun in earnest. John Moriarty was quick to secure the support of Macarthur River Mines in the Gulf of Carpentaria for soccer clinics near his home town of Borroloola. Travis Dodd, with former Socceroos John Kosmina, Alex Tobin and Craig Foster, all gave their time and support to the program. Former Socceroos star and national coach Frank Farina joined this journey to remote locations with the backing of the FFA. He visited remote communities in outback Queensland, donating old playing kits to help encourage the kids there. He told the *Sunday Age*, 'The game is free flowing and oozes the exuberance and improvisation that young Indigenous kids love and are attracted to.'

That kind of investment could only enhance the long-term future of the game in Australia. John Moriarty reflected that this commitment needed to be well planned and orchestrated from the highest levels of the game. In an interview with the *Sydney Morning Herald* in 2006 he said, 'It needs to be linked with the FFA so it's not done in isolation. We can't go on like we did with the old system. The FFA needs to be involved in a detailed structured way, to reach out to Aboriginal kids and bring them into football. It's long overdue, and I'd be happy to be involved.'

It seemed the neglect of the soccer bodies of the past, as highlighted so strongly by Johnny Warren, had finally been laid to rest. Long-term strategies and programs appeared underway or in development. John O'Neill, FFA Chief Executive from 2003 to 2006, acknowledged this to the *Sydney Morning Herald*: 'We've lagged behind the other sports in this area, and we know we have a lot of catching up to do. But we are committed to doing a lot more. We've now got some federal Government funding for Indigenous programs and we intend to do something about it.'

Harry Williams was also passionate about the development of young Indigenous soccer talent. He carried a lot of disappointment about the fact that there weren't greater numbers of Aboriginal players breaking through to the national level. 'I have seen so many Aboriginal kids with such tremendous talent, more talent than I ever had.' He felt it was a shame that more hadn't been given the opportunity to take up the game. He told the *Koori Mail*, 'They are all drawn to that funny shaped Aussie Rules ball, rather than the round ball. I would like to get involved in scouting and recruiting ... Soccer and the mates I made gave me the skills to cope with life. Mateship, friendship, comradeship, this helped us achieve what we did. It was quite incredible.'

In early 2006, capitalising on the surging interest in soccer in the wake of the

Socceroos qualifying for the World Cup in Germany, and as a consequence of his own experiences, Williams agreed to be the ambassador for a new Football NSW initiative to unearth and encourage Indigenous soccer talent. The program included the inaugural Harry Williams Cup, which was held at Football NSW's Valentine Park headquarters at Parklea in early 2006. Williams was glowing about the success of this first tournament. In personal correspondence with me, he said, 'Nineteen teams participated, including five Indigenous sides and some 80 plus young Indigenous players. We had fifteen girls for the week, but due to the lack of numbers weren't able to organise a girls' comp, but rest assured that will happen next year.'

The future looked positive and Williams hoped that the tournament would grow and develop from its initial success. Although many were committed to the cause, attracting corporate funding to support the fledgling Indigenous junior soccer development program would be crucial. At the conclusion of the 2008 tournament, Williams remained enthusiastic, telling *Deadly Vibe* that the tournament provided 'a terrific platform for any interested Indigenous player both male and female in furthering their careers as footballers. Football NSW have done a tremendous job in keeping the Cup alive as I have seen the tournament progress in more ways than one since its introduction a few years ago.'

In early 2009 Harry Williams made a plea for the various soccer bodies to take a united national approach to developing young Indigenous soccer players. He felt these players were 'missing opportunities because of isolation and lack of information.' He was also disheartened after the collapse of the Harry Williams Cup initiative because of a lack of funding and support. He didn't want yet more empty promises. As reported in the *Sydney Morning Herald* in 2009, Williams and Football NSW made a united call for the FFA to take 'a leading role in Indigenous development. For every kid that makes it, there's at least another dozen who are just as good but don't make it ... The state federations need to be on one page to deal with this. At the moment each state does their own thing. The Crawford Report suggested building a national approach to football. So there needs to be more work done there.'

They highlighted that the Harry Williams Cup had been a direct strategy to identify talented Indigenous boys and girls aged between eleven and fifteen Football NSW Technical Director Norm Boardman now felt that a more personalised approach was needed, one that focused on the regions. He told the Herald, 'Harry's long-term goal is the same as ours ... the program in its current form wasn't meeting its objectives ... and it was taking too long to find the talented, players and give them the right opportunities.' Boardman was convinced that a more effective strategy would be 'a series of identification camps ... rather than a hit-and miss competition where they may not be able to produce their best. Youngsters will be able to stay in their area instead of travelling to the city immediately.' Williams recognised that the regional focus had some merit but that certain hurdles would still need to be overcome. He called for significant change in the way the message went out 'to let Indigenous kids know there is structured coaching available ... just getting the word out there is difficult. We need to work on our database and identify where the kids are. We should look at other codes and learn how they get the kids to come through.' As a result, Football NSW redeveloped its Indigenous talent program, introducing a variety of talent identification camps across the football association branches of Southern New South Wales, the Riverina, Western New South Wales and Metropolitan Sydney.

Boardman and Williams were excited about the potential outcomes. Boardman told the *Sydney Morning Herald,* 'The long term goal is to provide opportunities for Indigenous footballers to represent their communities, regions, state and country, just like Indigenous players such as Harry Williams, Jade North, Travis Dodd and Lydia Williams.' Boardman was adamant that Harry Williams' long-held dream - for a national and united focus on Indigenous participation - was coming and was now a priority for the FFA: 'I do know that [the] FFA is bringing out a nationalised program, very focused on discovering Indigenous players and helping them to develop. We want to identify as many Indigenous players as possible to go and play in the A-League and play in our state leagues.'

One such outstanding talent was a young Gumbainggir soccer star Keifer Dotti. Keifer has strong community links to the Burnt Bridge, Kempsey and Bowraville regions on the New South Wales North Coast. He is the son of Phil Dotti, a former top rugby league player with Cronulla and Easts. Keifer first came to prominence when, at the age of twelve, he was the first Indigenous player to be selected for the Australian Elite Soccer Academy's First XI, in an international youth tournament staged in Hong Kong in 2006. This touring party was coached by former Socceroo

Aytek Genc, who initially offered young Keifer a trial at the academy. The young midfielder-defender made such an impression on the academy's coaching staff that he was invited to join the academy and the tour. He trained five days a week, and keen observers told the *Koori Mail* that he possessed 'all the skills needed to carve a path in the world game. He has good reflexes, vision, and kicking game, and is strong and physical.' Genc described Keifer as 'a fantastic prospect.'

Keifer took part in the 2007 Harry Williams Cup tournament, where he was named the Harry Williams Cup Best Under 14 Player. He was subsequently involved in Football NSW's Johnny Warren Program for talented players. In 2008, he signed with Apia Leichhardt in the New South Wales Premier League and was made captain of the under 14 team. Apia coaching staff were impressed with his game and his potential. Senior coach Alan Jones told *The Koori Mail* 'that giving him the captain's arm band was easy because he led by example and was a mature player for his age. Natural ability mixed with technical understandings of the game gives you a far greater vision and Keifer certainly has it all.' In 2009 Keifer was regarded by keen judges as the best young Indigenous prospect in New South Wales. Keifer had signed with Sydney FC and a promising football future seemed assured. He played in their youth team but opportunities of progress were limited and frustration and disappointment set in.

In 2013 he was playing for the Rockdale City Suns in a state league match against Manly United when he was racially abused by an opposing player following a tackle. Keifer took the incident further and the player was banned for four games. Phil Dotti was proud of his sons stance for demanding a sanction on the player but also concerned: 'Sadly word gets around in this game and at the end of the day who wants to sign an Aboriginal kid who put his hand up against discrimination.'[167]

But the stance drew a positive response and 'Football NSW stated the opposing player had been dealt with'. Both of the players and their families were brought together for a mediation process that resulted with a formal apology being made and accepted by Keifer Dotti.[168] In 2015 the powerfully built defender was again in the news when he made a guest appearance for the Borroloola Cyclones in an FFA

[167] https:///www.ftbl.com.au/news/keifer-dotti-rocked-by-racism-row-353047
[168] *The Liverpool City Champion,* 27 April 2013

cup tie against the Darwin based club Hellenic AC. It was no fairytale result for the Cyclones who went down 7-0. Despite the blow out score press reports stated the Cyclones were not outclassed and one player to impress had been Keifer Dotti. In 2018 Keifer achieved his proudest honour when he captained the first Australian Indigenous Football representative team. They played in a Trans-Tasman football series in New Zealand. The team won two of their three games and Keifer was awarded the most 'Valuable Player of the Series Award'. Keifer remains very proud of this moment stating: 'Captaining the first Indigenous Football team overseas is a big thrill, it's a great honour to represent my Aboriginal background, we have so many wonderful footballers out there.'[169]

Keifer has graduated with a degree in Primary School Teaching from Western Sydney University. He will unquestionably 'put something back into football' in the future as a coach or promoter of the game. For me having seen Keifer play during his time with the Sydney FC youth team I just feel he is another one of the talented young Indigenous players who needed more support and just an ounce of luck to have been a great player on a much bigger stage.

The Cyclones in the Top End

The growth of soccer in Aboriginal communities is not always such a recent development. Surprisingly, it has had support in certain areas for some time. Back in 2002, the Northern Territory Government Minister Kon Vatskalis, speaking during a parliamentary debate, reminded the parliament 'that the most popular sport in the Territory is not AFL, basketball or netball, it is soccer. Soccer is played from Darwin to Borroloola, with excellent Aboriginal soccer players. I have seen them in action, and I am very impressed. I am telling you the next soccer star is going to be an Aboriginal person from the Northern Territory.'[170]

This interest from remote Aboriginal communities and the sense of impending outback soccer success is widespread. Queensland 'Soccer Lady' Natalie Cardwell was adamant that within the next decade, outback Queensland would produce

---

[169] *The Macleay Argus,* 24 January 2018
[170] Northern Territory, Ninth Assembly, *Debates,* First Session, 26 November 2002, Parliamentary Record No. 9

both future Matildas and Socceroos. Cardwell foresaw the shift back in 2003, before the A-League had been set up and before it was being telecast on Foxtel. She told the *Koori Mail*, 'Hopefully there will be a lot more exposure of the sport on television, so that kids in the bush will be able to start watching Australian teams play, follow their favourite team, and hopefully soccer players will become household names, so it will give all kids something to aspire to.'

Two Aboriginal communities in vastly differing parts of Australia are worth closer investigation - Borroloola in the Northern Territory and Mildura in rural Victoria.

Borroloola, John Moriarty's birthplace, has had a long fascination with soccer. Back in 1997, the local school ground-keeper, Glenn Thompson, assembled what is regarded as Australia's first all-Aboriginal soccer team, the Borroloola Cyclones. He explained to the *Sydney Morning Herald* in 2009 how the craze for the game had spread through Borroloola. He had thrown a soccer ball to a couple of bored teenagers kicking drink bottles around. 'The next thing we knew everyone in town seemed to be chasing the ball ... soccer is a natural game for these kids, who are lightning fast and can turn on a sixpence.' Thompson was assisted by Rick Dank, who went on to take charge of the club.

The now historic club rapidly grew to have more than 100 players of different age groups on its books. When you consider that the population of Borroloola is only around 800 people, to have 100 kids playing soccer is significant. Dank supported the club in every way possible, from supplying the players with strips, socks and boots to giving them three daily meals when they travel for a game. Dank saw the game's potential to improve life for Aboriginal kids through a growing soccer culture. In an interview with *Soccer International* he said, 'A lot of things have failed Aboriginal kids. But with soccer they can see that they can succeed at a local level, at a state level, at any level, and compete against mainstream teams and beat them.'

The Cyclones have proven to be a very successful club. The under 15 team were the Northern Territory champions in 2001 and the club won the 2002 Outback Challenge. These achievements are even more impressive when you realise that the Cyclones only had one game during the year before the championships. The logistics they face in just getting to a game are quite remarkable. Dank explained that: 'We travel 1000 km for a game of soccer. Then another 1000 km back. We only play against ourselves and then we go straight into [the championships] at that level. We are a very isolated town of only 800 people and we've only got what we've got.'

Despite the isolation and lack of game time opportunities, the Cyclones continue to produce outstanding results, particularly when their players are selected to represent the Northern Territory at the National Talent Identification Championships each year. Dank recognised their wonderful achievements but also the potential that has gone largely untouched in Aboriginal communities: 'We're getting stronger and stronger every year and we're progressing. The natural talent is there. There are 100 Cathy Freemans out there. There are 100 Harry Kewells, but nobody sees them because they're not on the main road, they're not in the main Eastern states. They're here in the bush. The kids have the ability to play in Europe in a couple of years if they get the chance.' This was evident when the all-Indigenous Cyclones took part in the Arafura Games in Darwin early in 2009. The young squad became the Games' star attraction when they caused the upset of the tournament thrashing the under 16 Northern Territory team 4-0. Thompson laughed as he told the *Sydney Morning Herald* that the team 'went through like a category-five cyclone. They really lived up to their name.' The Cyclones later put in an outstanding performance against international opponents Macau, ultimately going down 3-0.

Thompson was glowing about their performances and adamant that soccer's dominance in Borroloola was not threatened by the AFL's nationwide program. 'The boys have made history ... Auskick people turned up in Borroloola with a heap of give-aways but it was a waste as soccer now dominates there.' Thompson, who as a young man had played Australian football in Tasmania, believes that soccer was a natural game for 'Aborigines because they are so agile and swift. I'll make a brave prediction ... soccer will eventually overtake Aussie Rules up here because it is a global game. When you make the national Aussie Rules team, where can you go? Ireland, to play some bastardised form of the game?'

One Cyclones star player, John Pluto, confessed that he gave away Aussie Rules and was completely sold on the world game. It is 'more skilful and fun.' He watched his idols, Brazilian superstar Ronaldinho and Socceroo Harry Kewell, on Austar. As he told the *Sydney Morning Herald,* 'It's a game that goes all the way up ...

everywhere in the world. The kids in Borroloola are playing it as soon as they can walk.' There are no formal teams; they are simply divided into four groups based on where they live. They toss a few hats on the ground for goalposts. It's basic but it works. As Thompson told the *Herald,* 'Getting a game of soccer up is simple … all you need is a round ball and away you go. I hear what people say about this being Aussie Rules territory and all that, but believe me, soccer will start to dominate out here.' People like Glenn Thompson and Rick Dank are genuine heroes in the way that they helped Aboriginal kids to pursue soccer glory. It is important to recognise that they were the foundation stones of the games popularity and continued success in Borroloola.

Catching the Bus to Mildura United

Another Aboriginal community where soccer is a driving passion is in the area around Mildura. The Mildura United Soccer Club had its beginnings in 1916 as a Greek-backed club. Aboriginal involvement with the club did not take off until 1994, with local man Chris Tsivoglou, a Greek Australian playing a pivotal role. Tsivoglou got out of his car in the main street of Merbein (a suburb of Mildura) one day to confront an aggressive group of young Koori kids, who were throwing rocks at his car. He changed the situation completely by asking whether he could teach the young vandals to play soccer. The response was immediate and Aboriginal kids, with encouragement, took to the game with great enthusiasm.

The club has been very successful at getting young people with a potential to stray into crime back onto the right path and, according to an article in the *Sydney Morning Herald* in 2009, 'the Mildura Koori Court often refers children there for help'. The Aboriginal Employment Agency has no hesitation in stating 'that the soccer club plays a role in giving young people life skills crucial for the workforce.'

By 2004, more than 140 Aboriginal kids were playing for Mildura United, from the under 9s to the under 17s. The massive increase in numbers can be attributed to a few committed people in the area. One of the big problems facing the kids was that they lived at the Namatjira Avenue Aboriginal settlement in New South Wales, about 30 kilometres from the Victorian border and the city of Mildura, and they had no way of getting to the club for training or games. Tsivoglou and a few other people identified several issues that were stopping the kids from getting involved: a lack of parental support, money and transport. Tsivoglou resolved that they would do something about it. 'These are kids from poor backgrounds and broken homes and maybe mum or dad don't have a car. One problem was just getting them to turn up every week.' [171]

These people took steps to overcome the difficulties, and the increase in the Aboriginal kids' participation was obvious. In an interview with the *Koori Mail* in 2004, Tsivoglou said, 'The reason we have a large Aboriginal content is that we are showing interest in these kids. We're driving around picking them up for training and games seven days a week. Simple as that... These kids are the club. For the long term some of these kids are so talented that if we had strong support, then their future in soccer would be good ... We're doing a fantastic job in keeping the kids occupied, out of trouble and off the streets. It would be a terrible shame to see the Koori kids' hopes and dreams crumble.'

But the Mildura United club was facing enormous financial difficulties trying to stay afloat. Sadly, the recruitment of Aboriginal kids to the club since 1992 had seen a steady decline in sponsorship. By 2004, only three sponsors were left providing token support, and most of the club's funds came from its canteen on match days.

Several people and organisations came to their timely rescue. An Indigenous sports development officer, Mark Williams, gave the club much-needed support and advice on ways to obtain funding. As a result, Mildura United Soccer Club was awarded a VicHealth Active Participation grant to support Aboriginal community fitness and wellbeing. The club used the funds to buy a bus to run a bus service four times a week, transporting players from the settlement to practice and games. The grant also helped subsidise bus running costs and train volunteers as drivers.

Billy Carrol, who ran the region's Indigenous Employment Program, helped throughout the funding process. He said, 'The whole idea of the soccer club's funding application was to develop the club to a point where it carries itself ... Soccer could help these kids turn the corner. Getting' VicHealth funding is the only thing that has kept us going.' Long-time Mildura United supporter and Aboriginal community liaison officer Buddy Parsons was one of the volunteer

....

[171]   Northern Territory, Ninth Assembly, *Debates,* First Session, 26 November 2002, Parliamentary Record No. 9

drivers. He said, 'If it wasn't for the soccer club, the kids would have nothing to do out here.' Parsons' frank assessment was supported by Tsivoglou: 'Playing soccer gives them stability. For a lot of the kids out here, the soccer club is all they've got.' Rob Moodie, the chief executive of VicHealth, felt that the funding body's assistance had been well placed. 'Some of these kids have amazing skills. But for most of them the main benefit is that they have the chance to participate regularly in physical activity which they enjoy and which allows them to connect with other players in a positive way.'[172]

One of Mildura United's young stars at the time was Jaharlyn Mitchell, who was ten years old in 2004, was reckoned to be the next David Beckham. Tsivoglou said at the time, 'He's our biggest goal kicker. He can't outrun them but he can out-skill them.' In 2010, aged fifteen, Jaharlyn Mitchell was selected, along with another Mildura United player, Charles Charles, to train with Manchester United in England.

The trip was the brainchild of Senior Constable Robbie Noggler of Corio police station, with support from both Victoria Police and the Western Suburbs Indigenous Gathering Place. Constable Noggler, a self-confessed soccer fanatic and a former coach at Geelong Grammar School, put together a team of fifteen players from Victoria for the overseas soccer camp. The team was made up of thirteen Aboriginal boys and two boys from European backgrounds.

The selection of Jaharlyn and Charles for the trip to Old Trafford in Manchester was a dream come true. According to Charles' father, four years before, Charles had been a wild and aggressive child. Now he was a level-headed and polite young man. His father told *The Courier-Mail*: 'Soccer gave Charles focus. He didn't know where to focus his energy. He picked soccer. I didn't want him to play contact sport. I told him he should learn how to handle himself on the field first ... He practised those skills and it helped him with school. He's in year 11 and I don't know too many black kids who are in year 11'. The Mildura United Soccer Club at the time had laid a solid foundation for these young Aboriginal players by supporting their aspirations and soccer dreams.

The efforts of many have played a significant role in helping this rural Aboriginal

---

[172] Victorian Health Promotion Foundation, 2006

community. Sadly, a decade later it is a story of lost opportunity. The boys never made it to Old Trafford through lack of funding support. By 2011 Jaharlyn Mitchell's interest in soccer either by choice or outside pressure and influence had begun to wane. He had moved to the Clontarf School in Mildura and there was no encouragement to play soccer at the new school. In fact, opportunities of playing the round ball game were virtually nil and he was forced to shift to AFL. He was later described on the Clontarf website as a former soccer star. This young player had been crying out for support, encouragement and development opportunities and was another young talent lost to the game.

A more recent newspaper report in 2014 highlighted that the club and its Aboriginal interest had not waned. Sadly, Chris Tsivoglou had been 'ill in recent years and his involvement had diminished, but still the Indigenous kids come, brought along by others such as Buddy Parsons and Gizza Finna'. Jonathan Thomas who had been involved early on came back to support the club and Aboriginal involvement prospered once more. Thompson said 'We have some of the older Aboriginal males who played here as juniors returning to play as seniors, which is a good thing. We are proud of that. The club is trusted by the community, it is seen as their club and I am proud of that.' He revealed that the former gun young players Jaharlyn Mitchell and Charles Charles were still with the club. Charles was then the senior captain. Both Mitchell and Charles had travelled to New Caledonia for a tournament. Thomas added: 'I think the talent here would jump right out at anyone coming in from one of the big clubs to look at the kids.' [173]

The Talent Lost

It begs the question how many young talented players have gone by the wayside? We know that Adam Goodes was a young soccer player in South Australia both at school and in the junior competitions. He had to give the game away when the family moved to rural Victoria and opportunities to play the game were limited and he switched to AFL. As we know the rest is history. But imagine if Goodes had continued in soccer, an athlete with such an engine. He did retain his supporters

[173] *The Sydney Morning Herald,* 4 June 2014

love of Manchester United from his junior soccer days. He reflected on the opportunities the game has for Indigenous Australians:

> *I see a huge missed opportunity when I watch the Socceroos play each year. We have an untapped resource of Indigenous talent in our communities that I think can be harnessed into our national team. I see the grassroots commitment the AFL has in community and I have no doubt that is the difference for young kids when they go to kick a ball, they choose an AFL ball...*
>
> *I don't think about what soccer can offer our people, I think about what we can bring to the game. Speed, agility, toughness, culture, connectiveness all key attributes to the making of a good team member.*

Today Adam Goodes, now retired from the AFL, is back playing soccer again.[174] He was playing for the Waverley Old Boys FC over-35 side in Sydney in 2018. Goodes return to his first great football love came about because he missed the camaraderie of the dressing room. It was also a way to stay fit. Goodes scored four goals in his first game but hamstring issues only allowed him to make six appearances. He certainly gave the Waverly club a major boost:

> *He is such an authentic and genuine guy, very humble and he's come along and just treated everyone with such humility and respect. He's just a super, nice, down-to-earth guy and just settled in with the group right away. There was just zero ego. Having someone like that in the team, yes he is just one of the guys and he is just one of the players out on the pitch, but at the same time you know who he is and what he's achieved.* [175]

Adam Goodes was in the news in mid 2019 for the release of two new documentaries that tell the story of how this legendary AFL player, two time Brownlow Medallist and Australian of the Year was forced from the AFL game in 2015 through the racist heckling and booing of crowds. Sadly, as the documentaries examine, he was not supported by the AFL or clubs at the time who have belatedly apologised over their

---

[174] https://www.indigenousfootballweek.org.au/state-of-play/q-a-with-adam-goodes

[175] https://theworldgame.sbs.com.au/got-the-goodes-afl-legend-switches-to-soccer

lack of support.[176] It was tragic to witness such a great player who had delivered so much to the AFL treated in such a manner. Adam Goodes appears to be enjoying his return to the round ball game playing on little suburban grounds without huge crowds and media attention. It again reinforces the point what if he had stayed a soccer player as a kid. What level could he have attained if his family had not moved and he was not lost to the game.

Adam Goodes is not the only Indigenous player lost to the game early on. Nathan Blacklock the great St George Dragons winger was a very keen young soccer player as a junior and used to hitch hike to get to weekend games. Like Goodes without support, encouragement or opportunities he switched to rugby league with devastating results.

Preston Campbell was another the former Gold Coast Titans star and the man most responsible for establishing the highly successful Indigenous All-Stars concept with the NRL was another keen early young soccer player. Aboriginal activist, actor and academic Gary Foley indicated to me that as a kid he also played soccer. Now that would have been well worth the admission price to a game to see Foley in dispute with a referee, linesman or opposing players over a decision.

In his book *Back on the Block* Pastor Bill Simon reflected on his young life and the family leaving the Purfleet Mission at Taree in 1953 to escape the control of the Protection Board. They moved to Kendall on the mid north coast of NSW. Bill was enrolled in school and found the 'best part of going to school was the sports, including soccer which was my favourite of all the field games'.[177]

The family were like refugees in their own country after twelve months at Kendall the family realised the government had caught up with them and they were informed they had to return to Purfleet. They again fled this time to Newcastle and set up at Platt's Estate a shanty town on the outskirts of Newcastle but with working opportunities close by in the industries or timber getting. At Platt's there was a large Aboriginal community and lots of kids and they had opportunity to play lots of games including .importantly for Bill. soccer. Bill reflected on his time at Platt's Estate as one of the happiest periods of his life. All of the Aboriginal parents at

---

[176] *The Daily Telegraph,* 8 June, 2019: 99; *The Sydney Morning Herald,* 8-9 June 2019: pp3; *The Sun Herald,* 9 June, 2019: pp8
[177] Simon, 2009: pp9

Platt's suffered through anxiety over the government and police suddenly appearing and taking the children away. All of the kids were told that they must 'run and hide' if strange cars suddenly appeared. In Bill's time it wasn't the neglect of the soccer authorities that stopped his desire to play the game. His father was away from the home timber getting and there was a loud early morning banging on the family's front door. It had all been well planned the board welfare officer and police took both Bill and his younger brother Lenny from his sobbing mother. They were placed in a car that sped off taking them into years of institutionalisation. Bill would spend time at the notorious Kinchella Boys Home. It was a site of shocking abuses and brutality inflicted onto the young Aboriginal boys. This was the reality for young Aboriginal boys it was not just lack of opportunities to play sport. Or that they were in locations in rural or remote locations but the strict enforced government policies of the day that not only removed them from their families but removed them from normal childhood activities like the pleasure of playing sport.

These experiences, and those faced in the examples of both Mildura and Borroloola, and beyond are a graphic reminder of the difficulties that still confront Indigenous people's sporting endeavours in this country in the 21st century.

If it wants to make a genuine impact within Indigenous communities, the FFA needs to understand the chronic disadvantage experienced at all levels by many of these communities, whether urban, rural or remote. The residue of the past and the intergenerational wounds are still carried today.

The stories of Mildura and Borroloola highlight the difficulties of access to training, matches, equipment and coaches - and such difficulties are not isolated to just a few locations. These stories also show ways in which the difficulties and the disadvantage can be tackled and overcome. There is one glaring point of evidence in all of this and that is the need of a national overarching approach to Indigenous involvement. And it needs Indigenous involvement and direction.

The benefits of doing so are enormous. Studies continue to show that Indigenous communities which have access to sport and facilities have much better health statistics than those that do not. These realities were very evident to me over 20 years ago when working in Aboriginal and Islander health and having the opportunity to visit and work within our communities right across the country. My own observations were startlingly clear where sport was an option the health and well-being of the community was elevated. Sport can clearly make an impact in critical areas such as alcohol and drug abuse, youth suicide and general fitness and physical and mental wellbeing. It can be the key to a rich life, full of opportunities.

There are also many examples of individuals working hard, and usually in isolation, at a local level to bring soccer to Indigenous kids and Indigenous communities. **Les Knox** of Narrabri is one such person. He fell under the spell of the world game and has continued a lifelong commitment to encouraging others to follow the journey he undertook. Knox played soccer as a young man during the 1960s, both at local and representative level in Narrabri, in northern New South Wales. In personal correspondence with me he wrote, 'Our local team had at least five Aboriginal players and two of us played rep for Northern New South Wales against Queensland under 19s in Tamworth in 1969, and we also won the premiership four years in a row (we had to travel to Gunnedah,100 km away to play in their local comp).' Knox went on to play in Sydney and coached junior teams in the Southern Districts Competition (Liverpool and Fairfield), winning premierships in successive years. At one point he gained work as the recreation officer with the Northern Territory Department of Sport and Recreation in Alice Springs. During his time there he ran many soccer clinics for remote communities throughout Central Australia and he 'was amazed at the natural ability the kids had throughout the region.' Knox is one example of the many efforts made by many individuals to introduce soccer to Indigenous communities, efforts which have been largely uncoordinated up until now.

Similarly, soccer development strategies have been conducted in different Aboriginal communities for some time. But there was never any overarching, connected strategy. Programs were, by and large, initiated and driven by committed individuals with a passion and interest in the game and a strong desire to improve life conditions for Aboriginal kids. For example, noted SBS soccer commentator and former Socceroo Craig Foster joined the outback caravan in 2007. He wrote about the experience in the *Sun Herald*:

I took a group of vibrant, healthy, strong young Indigenous Australians from the Bawaka people near Gove in the Northern Territory who had never played football and watched them adapt to the game with startling speed - in just one training session.

The grace and ease of these bare-footed players on a tough surface that would have humbled my shoeless feet was humbling. And as I made each exercise more difficult, they displayed the ball skills that would take a city kid a month to master. These youngsters took barely a minute... I came away with renewed passion to support Indigenous issues and encourage the world game into such communities. In our Indigenous population, we have a largely untapped pool of youngsters who have the gift of balance and dexterity which cannot be taught in football drills.

The introduction of the FFA's overarching Indigenous Football Development Program in 2009 promised that in the future, Indigenous strategies would have a nationally coordinated agenda.

The launch of this ten-year program amid much fanfare was a major shift for the game within Indigenous communities. The FFA's then Chief Executive, Ben Buckley, was confident for the future of Indigenous involvement and of the potential outcomes:

We believe we have a responsibility to encourage more young people of Indigenous background to play football as a way to improve their life through better health, better education and improved skills.

Indigenous players from other sports show that success in sport has a very positive effect on the local community and we want football to have the same impact.

Of course, we also hope that we will find more talented young players who can go on to play at the highest level, such as the Qantas Socceroos and Westfield Matildas, as well as the Hyundai A-League, the Westfield W-League and our other competitions.[178]

The centrepiece of the program was the inaugural Indigenous Football Festival, which was held in Townsville in June 2009. This was the first genuine national Indigenous youth soccer tournament, which brought together eight boys' teams

---

[178] *The Socceroo,* Issue 14, 10 October 2009

and four girls' teams ranging in age from thirteen to sixteen.

John Moriarty and Warren Mundine, as Indigenous soccer ambassadors, played a central role in organising the event. The *Weekend Australian* reported that over a two-month period, they 'crisscrossed the country, travelling to Moree, Dubbo, Launceston, Shepparton, Alice Springs, Port Augusta, Meekatharra, Borroloola and Townsville to spur on the teams ahead of the tournament.' Moriarty and Mundine were joined on the promotional trip by some high-profile Indigenous players, including Travis Dodd, Kyah Simon and Lachlan Wright, the national futsal captain. Part of the tour took John Moriarty back to his birthplace of Borroloola and an excited homecoming welcome. At the local school, the visitors looked on as 'boys and girls almost all of them barefoot, chased soccer balls with the gusto that gave birth to the local team's name: the Borroloola Cyclones.' Moriarty, interviewed on the banks of the crocodile-infested McArthur River, could not contain his enthusiasm for the way the game had taken off in his home town. Travis Dodd was also impressed by the passion for the game at this grassroots level. He told the *Weekend Australian*, 'When we first arrived, a young boy was telling me that when the kids are playing out on the oval and it gets too dark they actually go near his house and play under a street light. It's just a patch of dirt and the kids just set up two goals and play there until they get told to go home. To think that the kids love the game that much is fantastic.'

The tournament was a great success. More than 180 Indigenous kids converged on the tropical northern city of Townsville to take part. It was run over five days and included soccer matches, coaching clinics and team building activities. While the focus was on playing in a tournament, there was special attention given to fun and participation. Harry Williams was brought on board by the FFA and presented the medals and trophies at the closing ceremony. The FFA's head of corporate and public affairs, Bonita Mersiades, had played a central role in the new Indigenous program and was supremely confident of the future when she spoke with the *Weekend Australian*:

Above all, we hope that football plays its part in the reconciliation process. First and foremost, we believe it's one way in which we can contribute [towards improving] health, education and social outcomes for Indigenous people.

Second, we think there's probably some fantastic athletes among Indigenous communities who can fulfil their potential through becoming great players of the game.

A follow-up documentary for SBS Television titled *Outback United*, produced by Dan Goldberg, told the story of the Indigenous history of the game and the tournament's inception. The documentary featured prominent Aboriginal sportsmen and women, including Cathy Freeman, Evonne Goolagong Cawley and Adam Goodes, highlighting the opportunities that sport gave Aboriginal people. Goodes as stated had been a promising young soccer player before switching codes - to such extraordinary effect. He was insightful in saying, 'Soccer was not poaching players from other codes but offering kids another option and that's fantastic.' From the footage in *Outback United*, the kids' intense enthusiasm for the round-ball game was clear. Ben Buckley enthused over the success of the first tournament, saying it 'is a good indication of how football can help contribute to the reconciliation process in Australia.' The opportunities to increase Aboriginal involvement in the world's most popular sport appeared to be finally and belatedly underway. Warren Mundine, interviewed in the *Weekend Australian* in 2009, saw the opportunities of a global soccer future for Aboriginal kids: 'It's about opening those kids' universes that little bit more. You can travel the world. I'm looking forward to the day I can turn on my TV and see an Indigenous player walk on the field for Real Madrid or Manchester United. That will be the greatest day of my life.'

As we now know the high hopes held back in 2009 were completely unfounded. With no-one available or interested enough internally within FFA to drive the program after Mersiades' departure from the organisation in January 2010, there was no coordinated national approach and hopes of progress were completely dashed.

The Soccer Tribe of the Future

Aboriginal representation in the other stadium sports, such as rugby league, Australian football and rugby union, was much larger. Access to these stadium sports was easier and they offered the added benefit of monetary return - soccer has always been the poor relation in Australian sport. In addition, Aboriginal people may have actively pursued these other sports as a means of gaining social acceptance, because of their desire for respect and a place in the sun. Soccer, until recent times, was not a vehicle for gaining mainstream acceptance and respect - in fact, it was the exact opposite. The negative attitudes that clung to the game may have played a part in deterring Aboriginal people from playing it, as they already had enough obstacles to overcome in order to gain acceptance.

The successful early Aboriginal soccer players - men like Bondi Neal, Charlie Perkins, John Moriarty, Gordon Briscoe and Harry Williams - were fortunate that circumstances placed them in geographical locations that were soccer strongholds. The acceptance that Aboriginal players found within the post-World War II migrant communities had a profound impact on their life directions and outlook. The multicultural environment of Australian soccer after the war provided them with a haven from the prejudice and racism of wider Australian society.

Nevertheless, for this Indigenous future of opportunity to unfold, the ball was firmly at the feet of the FFA. The FFA's Indigenous program that began with much fanfare at the 2009 Indigenous Football Festival in Townsville, was not repeated in 2010.

In any case, some media analysts felt that during the 2018–2022 world cup bid process the FFA neglected the game on the home front, most notably with the A-League, which had suffered falling crowd numbers. It clearly undermined development of the game here with so much money and energy directed towards the bid and Indigenous development was clearly one of the casualties.

After a wasted ten year period, the time is now ripe again for the FFA to throw its full weight behind an Indigenous focus. It must now surely rate as a high priority. There are many Indigenous communities like Borroloola and Mildura across the country, just waiting for someone to come and promote the game to their kids. This new focus must be well organised and involve people who are committed full-time to the program. In most instances, as in Borroloola and Mildura, Indigenous involvement has mostly been driven largely by committed and passionate individuals. These are people who need the support of a fully functioning Indigenous soccer program, and it will be the responsibility of the FFA to provide the people, funds and framework for it to succeed.

This holds great significance on a number of fronts. Firstly, such a program can provide an avenue for Indigenous communities and especially their children to improve their health, education and social wellbeing. Secondly, it may well unearth a soccer superstar of the future. One young Aboriginal player from Dubbo, Dan Cox, took part in the inaugural FFA Indigenous Football Festival in Townsville and he was certainly optimistic about the future. He dreamt of playing for the Socceroos in the 2018 World Cup finals: 'Sometimes in my dream, I'm standing there wearing the green and gold and holding the World Cup.' That would truly be a dream come true. Sadly I have failed to unearth any further references to Dan Cox and if he still plays the game.

CHAPTER 10
The Future – What went wrong?

I feel like I have come full circle from my original book to this new updated version. From the original pessimism I felt in the early years of the 21st century not just with Indigenous involvement, but the game's very survival in this country, through to the seismic exciting changes to the structure of the game and the optimism of the period 2003 to 2008, with the culmination and very public announcement of the FFA focus on Aboriginal development with the game.

But we have come thudding back to earth; and in 2019 pessimism reigns again with the realisation that we have gone backwards. There has been no real plan or effort made by the FFA to generate Indigenous development with the game. The numbers of Indigenous players playing at the highest levels of the game have dramatically declined with no real effort or understanding of the cause and what can be done to alter course. In this final section I will look back at some of the initiatives of the last decade what worked, what did not and finally recommendations on what can be done to generate Indigenous numbers into the game.

Having been watching and playing this game for nearly 60 years I feel I have a well-developed appreciation of the issues that have faced the game in this country both historically and in the contemporary setting. Looking back at the influences on the game in my time it appeared after England won the World Cup in 1966 that the game in this country attempted to follow Ramsey's 'wingless wonders' recipe with a preference for the 4-4-2 system and a heavy influx of British coaches brought into the country. There was no attempt after the 1970 World Cup triumph of Brazil in Mexico to model our game on the Brazilian attacking flair. But then again it would be well-nigh impossible to emulate a team regarded by many as the greatest ever international side.

We went through another major influence after the 1974 World Cup in Germany when the Dutch model of 'Total Football' was the recipe to follow. We would witness a truck load of Dutch coaches and football directors brought into the country and their influences continue into the twenty first century.

There were a flurry of calls after France 1998 to follow Les Bleus model particularly with their academies of football. The success of Barcelona in Europe and Spain's 2010 World Cup victory witnessed a stampede to follow 'ticki tacka' possession football. In the example of the Brisbane Roar success under Ange Postecoglou this model appeared to bring results in the A-League. Across the past 50 years we have persisted with the 'sheep herd' mentality in copying and trying to emulate international tactics and methods with little thought of exploring our own style.

Ange Postecoglou recommended in his book, *Changing the Game*, that we should explore the idea of developing a model of football built on our own strengths. Whilst this model reflects the Australian 'never give in' attitude, high fitness, running and strict defensive discipline it could also encourage attacking flair, skill and an 'off the cuff' approach to the game.

This is where Indigenous talent could really make an impact. It also means coaches in developing talent recognise the importance to encourage, support and develop skill. When one looks at the other codes of rugby league and AFL in particular it is the Indigenous flair and talent that coaches in those codes encourage. They do not place constraints on skill but actually encourage the Indigenous players to do their own thing. They are the game breakers. They are the players like Jonathan Thurston, Greg Inglis, Michael O'Loughlin and Michel Long who can change a game's result in a blink of the eye. We need coaches who will recognise this sort of skill and not suffocate it by wanting our kids to just be running, tackling and fitting in to tight structures. But like the other codes encourage the freedom and flair of skill. It is the main ingredient this country has failed to develop. Tom Sermanni recognised the need to encourage the flair and skill of Indigenous players: 'You have to allow a little bit of leeway and a bit of freedom to get the best out of them. Their approach to the game is great; they play very seriously, but they need that freedom, too.'

Over the past 15 years our game has gone backwards in youth development because of the proliferation of professionally run elite squads and academies that are money making exercises. No disrespect; I am all for former players having an opportunity to set up careers after their playing days are over but the issue is great players are not found in Double Bay or Vaucluse. Aboriginal kids' families, for example, have no chance of finding the funds to pay for their kids to be a part of these high priced academies. When one looks around the world it has always been the case that great players like Pelé, Eusebio, Georgie Best and Maradona come from areas of disadvantage and poverty. In Australia the proof is in the fact that the players known as the 'Golden Generation' like Harry Kewell, Tim Cahill, Brett Emerton, Mark Bosnich and Mark Schwarzer to name but a few came from the working class suburbs of western Sydney.

The game in this country has once again reached a critical junction of its history. What happens next could well determine its future. In recent years, the instability, infighting, factions and voices of self-inflated experts and authorities have reignited internal power battles over administration and are damaging the credibility of the game. The A-League attendances have been falling, and there are whispers of Fox Sports withdrawing its coverage and financial support. Since the highpoint of 2006 the Socceroos' performances have declined. Despite qualifying for four consecutive World Cups the Australian team has failed to win a single game in their most recent tournaments in Brazil and Russia. We have failed to produce any world class players since the halcyon days of Viduka, Kewell, Cahill, Neill and Schwarzer.

Embedded within this decline has been the abject failure of the FFA to genuinely encourage Indigenous involvement in the game.

Initially with the appointment of David Gallop as CEO of the FFA in 2012 I signalled to all I spoke with that this would signal the ignition point of Indigenous development within the game. Gallop had established an enviable record of developing Indigenous involvement and promotion with the NRL. Alongside Indigenous player Preston Campbell he was recognised as establishing the Indigenous All-Stars game concept. A number of approaches were made to the FFA by Indigenous followers of the game shortly after David Gallop's appointment.

Subsequently in 2013 I alongside others like Phil Dotti, Jason French, Bernie McLeod, Lawrence Gilbert and Derrick Dank attended meetings at FFA offices in Sydney. I fully believed that Gallop would oversee and attend these meetings. Disappointingly he did not. It was as if it was not important at all. It is possible that

Gallop was receiving other advice but it was a very dismissive approach. Some young administrators at the FFA were given the role of holding these discussions and developing any Indigenous directive. Not surprisingly there was not a lot of confidence in the FFA approach to developing the Indigenous game.

When one looks back over the past 15 years there have been some highlights but all have been wasted through lack of funding and ongoing support.

The Harry Williams Cup in NSW was initially a great success and if given support and funding could have been developed into a national competition and strategy. It fell by the wayside through lack of funds. The FFA after the announcement of their Indigenous Strategy in 2008 inaugurated the first National Indigenous Football Festival held in Townsville in 2009. It would not be held again until 2012 when the second National Indigenous Football Festival was held in Alice Springs. The delay in holding the second Festival had stalled any hope of momentum and the concept was again allowed to stagnate after the 2012 event.

It would not be until 2016 that another national Indigenous Cup competition would be held. This event was a differing approach altogether and was driven at an Aboriginal grassroots community level by two individuals with long connections with the game Bernie McLeod and Lawrence Gilbert. Initially there was little interest shown by the FFA or media. But the tenacity and will of both Gilbert and McLeod in seeing this initial National Indigenous Championship come to be forced football administrators at all levels to sit up and take notice. The event was recorded by NITV including the finals of both the women's and men's games. I was one of the commentators of those games and was excited by the great crowd in attendance and the buzz created by the event. David Gallop, who did attend this event, stated after: 'I was really delighted to be at the Championships which were a true celebration of football and Indigenous culture. The atmosphere around the ground was fantastic and I am sure all who attended had a great time.' There was also a celebrity match between teams captained by Anthony Mundine and Craig Foster. Choc's team getting up 4-3 in an exciting and entertaining match. Sadly the successful partnership between Bernie McLeod and Lawrence Gilbert was a casualty of the stress and pressure both endured in getting the Championship up and running and they parted ways.

Bernie McLeod continued to host the National Indigenous Championship on the south coast as well as starting up the first national Indigenous team, known as the *Mariya* translating as Emu. The Emus played international games against a Maori side in 2018 winning two of three games in New Zealand. In early 2019 they played in a 'Clash of Cultures' tournament held in Wollongong that featured the Emus plus teams from New Zealand, Wollongong Wolves and an Australian African based select team. Former Socceroo's Jade North and Luke Wilkshire by coaching the Emus and Wollongong Wolves respectively endorsed their support.

In 2018 the inaugural Australian Indigenous Football Championships were held in Brisbane. This event was driven by Lawrence Gilbert and Ramone Close. The championship had the backing and support of Brisbane Roar, Football Brisbane, Football Queensland and the Johnny Warren Foundation. Teams came from across the country to take part with 26 sides nominated for the first championship. Again David Gallop lent support by congratulating the organisers.

As a result of this championship an Indigenous women's and men's team were selected to participate for the first time at the Arafura Games in Darwin in 2019. The Indigenous Roos and Koalas would play with the backing and support of the FFA. CEO David Gallop stated:

> *I'm excited to see first-hand our male and female Indigenous footballers play at the Darwin Football Stadium, Larakia Park and I look forward to meeting with Indigenous leaders during my visit to the Northern Territory.*
>
> *FFA chairman Chris Nikou said: We need to ensure the most participated game in the country 'the world game' works hard to support aspiring Indigenous footballers in regional and remote communities across the country.*[179]

In a stunning performance by both Indigenous teams they won the silver and gold medals respectively. Lawrence Gilbert was very excited by the Indigenous teams performances and the possibilities for the future:

> *The Indigenous Roos won the silver medal after making the final but were ultimately defeated by a strong Northern Territory Select XI, while the*

[179] https://www.ffa.com.au/news/ffa-officials-attend-arafura-games-support-northern-territory-football

Indigenous Koalas beat Singapore in their final to win the Gold Medal.

We are extending the pathway and we are partnering up with some of the State Federations now who are getting behind the Indigenous game," he said. We are moving beyond the rhetoric of goodwill and we are looking at now formalising some of the arrangements.

The AIFC will be incorporated and formalised and we will sign agreements which will create a pathway through to the Arafura games and Asia which is where our game is of course with the Socceroos and Matildas.[180]

Whilst these are great achievements having two separate Indigenous competitions and two national Indigenous sides is not a good look. We need a united approach to taking our involvement in the game forward. Factions, divisions and competing against ourselves is doing us no good.

What we do need is a National Indigenous Football Council to oversee Indigenous involvement in the game and to finally reach its full potential. Currently everything is being driven by individuals and groups with little connection or overall coordination We have the John Moriarty Football Foundation, we have the National and Australian Indigenous Championships. We have two separate Indigenous national teams and agendas. We have numerous Indigenous football coaching programs like Jade North's 'Kicking with a Cuz' and Ramone Close's Indigenous program. All of these initiatives are bringing in results but it would be far better if everything was under the one national umbrella and ideally that would be operated and supported through the FFA.

These sentiments are not new. John Moriarty said the same thing in 2006:

It needs to be linked with the FFA so it's not done in isolation. We can't go on like we did with the old system. The FFA needs to be involved in a detailed structured way, to reach out to Aboriginal kids and bring them into football. It's long overdue, and I'd be happy to be involved.

Harry Williams expressed similar sentiments in 2009:

---

[180] https://thewomensgame.com/news/indigenous-footballs-new-dawn-526007

The state federations need to be on one page to deal with this. At the moment each state does their own thing. The Crawford Report suggested building a national approach to football. So there needs to be more work done there.

A fractured and isolated approach to developing the Indigenous game will not prove successful but a united all-encompassing program FFA driven can do the job.

One of the most significant moments of Indigenous involvement with soccer was announced in early 2019 by Ken Wyatt, the Minister for Indigenous Health, in allocating $4.5 million dollars to the John Moriarty Football Foundation. It was the largest ever investment for Indigenous soccer development. Whilst the focus for John Moriarty Football in the previous decade had focused on John Moriarty's own community of Borroloola and Robinson River this new funding would allow major expansion and focus into Queensland and New South Wales.[181]

There is no one better placed than the Moriarty Foundation to lead such a program and to follow on the achievements it has made across the past ten years. This new funding eases my only criticism of the Foundation's initial focus being Borroloola. Of course it is John's own community and that makes it a natural site of focus but it was also already the only soccer mad Aboriginal community in the country. In 2008, there was no mention that Glenn Thompson and Rick Dank had developed and encouraged the game at Borroloola at their own expense and time since 1997. They provided the balls, shirts, boots and did the driving for the team they instigated the Borroloola Cyclones. These men lit the fire of soccer fever in that small community and it has never waned.

But with this new funding the John Moriarty Foundation can build upon all the achievements of the past and expand the game into new areas of Queensland and New South Wales where Indigenous kids are playing the game. In the lead up to the Australian National Championships in Brisbane I was asked by the John Moriarty Foundation to write a piece for their website that focused on recommendations for the game's future Indigenous development:

---

[181] https://theworldgame.sbs.com.au/indigenous-football-program-given-4-5-million-funding-boost

Recommendations

- Organise a National Indigenous Football Advisory Council (NIFAC). This body to sit under the FFA to co-ordinate programs to develop Aboriginal involvement with football.
- All A-League and W-League clubs to include two additional spaces for Indigenous players in their youth teams.
- Undertake a national study and report on the state of play of Indigenous involvement in the game and develop ways to expand and accelerate that process.
  A similar study was recently undertaken by Cricket Australia.
- All A-League and W-League clubs to have an Indigenous Liaison Officer employed to connect and promote the game within Indigenous communities.
- In collaboration with state and territory governments, support funding for, and access to, community sports programs that reflect the diverse cultures and traditional sporting activities of Aboriginal peoples.
- Establish an elite athlete development program for Aboriginal footballers.
- Develop programs for coaches, trainers, and sports officials that are culturally relevant for Aboriginal peoples.
- Anti-racism and cultural awareness training programs amongst Australian football clubs including the A-League and W-league.
- Enable Aboriginal people to influence and guide sport and recreation policy (leading to equal opportunities). [182]

Some of these recommendations have already been mentioned at length particularly the establishment of a National Aboriginal Advisory Council.

But I will direct attention to another area I mentioned: the establishment of an elite athlete development program for Aboriginal soccer players. In late April 2019 I was approached about an exciting development with the new A-League franchise Macarthur FC Bulls. The new club were going to announce at the time of unveiling their new name and logo that they were also establishing the country's first

[182] https://www.indigenousfootballweek.org.au/state-of-play/reconciliation-symbolism-and-football

Indigenous football academy. The club invited me to announce this exciting development to a packed auditorium at Campbelltown in May 2019. It was for me one of the most exciting moments I had witnessed on Indigenous involvement with the game. I was honoured to announce that alongside the new Indigenous academy they would also set up a separate Indigenous Board of management to oversee their Indigenous programs and community development. It was the club's directive to 'target a national Indigenous development strategy that is not just focused on sporting success, but prioritising the importance of health, education and well-being outcomes' for our communities'. I was approached and have agreed to chair the Board of this new Indigenous Academy to Macarthur FC. It is only early days but I am hopeful that this club's approach may influence the other A-League clubs to initiate Indigenous programs of their own.

When I first thought about the updated closing chapter of my book, I was intending to write a scathing conclusion of the current state of play for Indigenous involvement. But in recent months, with the proactive initiative undertaken by Macarthur FC and the funding by the Commonwealth Government for the John Moriarty Foundation to expand its programs, just maybe there is a faint light at the end of a very long tunnel.

Certainly after such a long period of jump starts and setbacks to Indigenous involvement in the world game positive outcomes seemed to come thick and fast as 2019 rolled on. The Matildas were at the France World Cup with three players Lydia Williams, Gema Simon and Mary Fowler a part of the squad and delivering great exposure of the talent of Indigenous players.

I hasten to add that the game is going through some troubled waters currently, and the success or failures of building a platform for Indigenous involvement will be tied to the long term strategies of the games future in this country. I only hope that those in the decision making roles make the right choices. I have seen much disappointment across so many decades for the game in this country.

Bibliography and Further Reading

Bellos, A, *Futebol - The Brazilian Way of Life*, Bloomsbury, London, 2003.

Blainey, G, *A Game of Our Own: The Origins of Australian Football*, Information Australia, Melbourne, 1990.

Booth, D & Tatz, C, *One Eyed - A View of Australian Sport*, Allen & Unwin, Sydney, 2000.

Cahill, T, *Tim Cahill – Legacy*, Harper Collins Publishers, Sydney, 2015.

Cashman, R, *Paradise of Sport- The Rise of Organised Sport in Australia*, Oxford University Press, Melbourn e, 2002.

Chase, A & Von Sturmer, J, *"'Mental Man" and Social Evolutionary Theory'*, in Kearney, GD, De Lacey, PR & Davidson, GR (eds), *The Psychology of Aboriginal Australians,* John Wiley & Sons Australasia, Sydney, 1973.

Cockerill, M, *Australian Soccer's Long Road to the Top*, Lothian Books, Melbourne, 1998.

Corrigan, B, *The Life of Brian - Confessions of an Olympic Doctor*, ABC Books, Sydney, 2004.

Corbould, C, *Becoming African American: Black Public Life in Harlem 1919–1939*, Harvard University Press, Boston, 2009.

Curthoys, A, *Freedom Ride - A Freedom Rider Remembers*, Allen & Unwin, Sydney, 2002.

Curthoys, A, *'Good Christians and Useful Workers', in Sydney Labour History Group, What Rough Beast? The State and Social Order in Australian History*, Allen & Unwin, Sydney, 1982.

Dean, B, *The Many Worlds of Dance*, Murray Publishers, Sydney, 1966.

Dean, B, *Dust for Dancers,* Ure Smith, Sydney, 1956.

Farina, F, 1998.

Fogarty, M, *Indigenous Athletes at the Australian Institute of Sport*, Australian Sports Commission, Canberra, 2005.

Foer, F, *How Soccer Explains the World - An {Unlikely} Theory of Globalization,* Harper Collins, New York, 2004.

Football Federation of Australia, *FFA National Curriculum*, 2010,

Gatt, R, *The Rale Rasic Story*, New Holland Publishers, Sydney, 2006.

Goldblatt, D, *The Ball Is Round -A Global History of Football*, Viking Press, London, 2006.

Goodall, H, *'Crying Out for Land Rights'*, in Burgmann, V & Lee, P (eds), *Staining the Wattle*, McPhee Gribble Publishers, Melbourne, 1988.

Goodall, H, *'Aboriginal Calls for Justice - Learning from Aboriginal History'*, **Aboriginal Law Bulletin,** 1988, Vol. 2, no. 33.

Goodall, H, *Invasion to Embassy - Land in Aboriginal Politics in NSW - 1770–1972*, Allen & Unwin, Sydney, 1996.

Grant, S, *Jack Pollard's Soccer Records*, Jack Pollard Pty Ltd, Sydney, 1974.

Grant, S, *The History of Coalfields Soccer*, Weastmead Printing, Cessnock, 1979.

Harlow, D, *History of Soccer in South Australia 1902–2002*, Bowden Printing, Adelaide, 2003.

Harris, B, *The Proud Champions - Australia's Aboriginal Sporting Heroes,* Little Hills Press, Sydney, 1989.

Harper, A, *Mr and Mrs Soccer,* Random House, Sydney, 2004.

Hemming, J, *Red Gold - The Conquest of the Brazilian Indians*, Papermac, London, 1978.

Hetherington, H, *original unpublished manuscript*, compiled in Northern New South Wales Soccer Council, *History of Soccer in Northern NSW 1884 to 2000 and Sydney & South Coast 1880–1957*, New South Wales State Library, Sydney, 2003.

Huggonson, D, *'Aborigines and the Aftermath of the Great War'*, in Australian Aboriginal Studies, AIATSIS, Canberra, 1993.

Kell, P, *Australian Sport and the Myth of the Fair Go*, Pluto Press, Sydney, 2000.

Lusetich, R, *Frank Arok - My Beloved Socceroos*, ABC Books, Sydney, 1992.

Jones, R & Moore, P, *He Only has Eyes for Poms: Soccer,*
Ethnicity and Locality in Perth, WA, *Ethnicity and Soccer in Australia,*
ASSH Studies in Sports History No.10.

Maynard, J, *Aboriginal Stars of the Turf- jockeys of Australian Racing History,*
Aboriginal Studies Press, Canberra, 2003.

Maynard, J, *Awabakal Word Finder and Dreaming Stories Companion,*
Keeaira Press, Southport, 2005.

Maynard, J, The First World War, in *Serving Our Country* Ed. Beaumont,
J & Cadzow, A, New South, Sydney, 2018.

Micaleff, P, *The World Cup Story: An Australian View,*
Philip Micaleff Publishing, Sydney, 1994.

Moriarty, J, *Saltwater Fella,* Viking Books, Melbourne, 2000.

Moodie-Heddle, E, *The Boomerang Book of Legendary Tales,* Longmans,
Green and Co Ltd, London, 1957.

Morris, B, *'Cultural Domination and Domestic Dependence: The Dhangadi*
of New South Wales and the Protection of the State', Canberra Anthropology,
1985, Vol. 8, nos 1 & 2.

Morris, B, *Domesticating Resistance: The Dhan Gadi Aborigines*
and the Australian State, St Martins Press, NSW, 1989.

Morris, D, *The Soccer* Tribe, Jonathon Cape, London, 1981.

Mosley, P, Cashman, R, O'Hara, J & Weatherburn, H, *Sporting Immigrants,*
Walla Walla Press, Sydney, 1997.

Munro, K and Tyhuis, M, *Fresh Footprints,* Department of Family
and Community Services, Canberra, 2003.

Murray, B, *The World Game,* University of Illinois Press,
Urbana and Chicago, 1998.

O'Hara, J (ed), *Ethnicity and Soccer in Australia,* Australian Society
for Sports History, No.10, Campbelltown, 1994.

Parbury, N, *Survival: A History of Aboriginal Life in NSW,* David Ell Press,
Sydney, 1998.

Pericles Trifonas, P, *Umberto Eco and Football,* Icon Books,
United Kingdom, 2001.

Perkins, C, *A Bastard Like Me,* Ure Smith, Sydney, 1975.

Oliver-Scerri, GE, *Encyclopedia of Australian Soccer 1922–88,* Showcase Publications, St Leonards, 1988.

Radnedge, K, *SES Encyclopedia of Soccer,* Hardie Grant Publishing, Victoria, 2001.

Read, P, *Charles Perkins,* Allen & Unwin, Sydney, 2001.

Reiner, A, *Kempsey: A Study of Conflict,* Department of Aboriginal Affairs, Canberra, 1985.

Rowley, CD, *Outcasts in White Australia,* Penguin Books, Melbourne, 1973.

Schwab, L, *The Socceroos and Their Opponents*, Newspress Pty Ltd, Melbourne, 1980.

Slater, P & Hall, M, *Robbie Slater - The Hard Way*, Harper Sports, Australia, 1999.

Signy, D, *A Pictorial History of Soccer,* Paul Hamlyn, London, 1969.

Smith, L, *The Aboriginal Population of Australia*, ANU Press, Canberra, 1980.

Solly, R, *Shoot Out - The Passion and the Politics of Soccer's Fight for Survival in Australia,* John Wiley & Sons Australia, Queensland, 2004.

Tatz, C, *Aborigines in Sport,* The Australian Society for Sports History, South Australia, 1987.

Tatz, C, *Black Diamonds,* Allen & Unwin, Sydney, 1996.

Tatz, C, *Obstacle Race - Aborigines in Sport,* Aboriginal Studies Press, Canberra, 1995.

Tatz, C & Tatz, P, *Black Pearls – The Aboriginal and Islander Sports Hall of Fame,* Aboriginal Studies Press, Canberra, 2018

Thompson, A *Archie Thompson – What Doesn't Kill you Makes you Stronger,* Victory Books, Melbourne, 2010

Wallace, N, *Our Socceroos,* Random House, Sydney, 2004.

Warren, J, *Sheilas, Wags and Poofters,* Random House, Sydney, 2002.

Warren, J & Schwab, L, *John Warren's World of Australian Soccer,* Book Print International, Hong Kong, 1980.

Warren, J & Dettre, A, *Soccer in Australia,* Paul Hamlyn, Sydney, 1974.

Whimpress, B, *Johnny Mullagh: Western District Hero or the Black Grace?',* Aboriginal History, 1994, vol. 1.

About the Author

Professor John Maynard is a Worimi Aboriginal man from the Port Stephens region of New South Wales. He is currently Chair of Aboriginal History at the University of Newcastle and Director of the Purai Global Indigenous History Centre. He has held several major positions and served on numerous prominent organizations and committees including, Deputy Chairperson of the Australian Institute of Aboriginal and Torres Strait Islander Studies, Executive Committee of the Australian Historical Association, History Council, Indigenous Higher Education Advisory Council, Australian Research Council College of Experts – Deputy Chair Humanities, National Indigenous Research and Knowledge Network and a Fulbright Ambassador. He was the recipient of the Aboriginal History (Australian National University) Stanner Fellowship 1996, the Indigenous History Fellow 2003, Australian Research Council Postdoctoral Fellow 2004, University of Newcastle Researcher of the Year 2008 and 2012 and Australian National University Allan Martin History Lecturer 2010. In 2014 he was elected a member of the prestigious Australian Social Sciences Academy. He gained his PhD in 2003, examining the rise of early Aboriginal political activism. He has worked with and within many Aboriginal communities, urban, rural and remote. Professor Maynard's publications have concentrated on the intersections of Aboriginal political and social history, and the history of Australian race relations. He is the author of several books, including *Aboriginal Stars of the Turf, Fight for Liberty and Freedom, Aborigines and the Sport of Kings, True Light and Shade: An Aboriginal Perspective of Joseph Lycett's Art and Living with the Locals – Early Indigenous Experience of Indigenous Life*.

Socceroos Luke Wilkshire
and Tim Cahill with John Maynard

Index

Postecoglou, Ange, 110, 228
  media attack on, 146
  as Socceroos coach, 143
  Socceroos departure, 146
Poulter, Jim, 18
Premiers Plates, 96, 100, 129, 131
President's Cup 1987, 119–20
Preston North End, 57, 82
Protection Boards, 27–8, 48, 71,
  219–20
Protector of Aborigines (SA), 48
PSV Eindhoven, 129
Puttikan, 21

Q
Queens Park Rangers, 136
Queensland, early players, 24–6,
  175
Queensland Academy of Sports, 80,
  105, 150, 158, 159, 164, 165
  scholarships, 187
Queensland junior soccer clubs,
  105
Queensland National Premier
  League, 82, 166
Queensland Premier League, 151
Queensland Reds, 105
Queensland Roar, 82, 87–8, 106,
  150 *See also* Brisbane Roar
  W-League, 199
Queensland State League, 117, 165
Queensland Sting, 188, 189
Queensland Times, 25
Quilp, 24–6

R
racism
  on field, 51, 131–2, 201, 210,
    218–19
  institutionalised, 23
  Perkins on, 41, 54, 59–60
  towards migrants, 42–3
Rasic, Rale, 74–5, 76, 133
Redland City Devils, 165
Redlands United, 151, 166
Redskins *See* International United
  'Redskins'
Risdon, Josh, 168, 169
Robbins, Fred, 118
Rochedale Rovers, 84
Rockdale City Suns, 152, 210
Roda JC, 120
AS Roma, 13
Roma, Tashina, 199
Roper River Mission, 40
Rose, Lionel, 67
Rose, Normie, 13

Royal Commission into Aboriginal
  Deaths in Custody, 72
Royal Racing Montegnée, 166
Rudan, Mark, 112
Rudd, Kevin, 3, 79, 205
  apology to Stolen Generations,
    88
rural and remote communities
  absence of soccer in, 34
  commitment of individuals in,
    225
  difficulty of access to services,
    220
  government funding programs,
    215–16, 233
  Indigenous training and
    coaching programs, 214–17
  soccer clinics, 221
Russell, Ian, 168
Russell, Tate, 168–9

S
Saltwater Fella (Moriarty, 2000),
  5, 44
Santrac, Adrian, 189
Sarota, Adam, 111, 112–15
Schaefer, Frank, 166
Schip, John van't, 160–1
Schwarzer, Mark, 122, 139,
  205
Schweinsteiger, Bastian, 141
segregation policy, 23–4
separation of children from families
  See Stolen Generations
Sermanni, Tom, 149, 191–2, 196,
  201, 228
Shanghai Shenhua, 145
Sheffied Shield Cricket,
  168
Sheffield Wednesday, 122
Sheilas, Wogs and Poofters (2002),
  5, 43
Shoulder, Jimmy, 77, 117
Simon, Gema, 192, 199–200, 203,
  235
Simon, Kyah, 174, 185, 190–5,
  197, 203, 223
  ambassadorships, 104, 193
  injuries, 194–5
  Player of the Year 2011, 193
  USA National Women's Soccer
    League, 193, 194
Simon, Pastor Bill, 219–20
Smith, Billy, 74
Smith, Ron, 118
Smith, Shirley (Mum Shirl),
  58

soccer *See also* A-League; women's
  soccer; world game
  Aboriginal involvement in, 11,
    35–8
  Aboriginal underrepresentation,
    3–4
  athletes lost to other codes, 219
  competition from AFL, 213
  derogatory terms for, 6, 44
  encouraging Indigenous flair
    and talent, 228
  first organised match, 6
  first televised recordings, 15
  government funding for
    Indigenous development,
    233, 235
  grassroots programs, 166–7
  Indigenous development
    programs, 206–11, 232–3
  lack of funding impact, 230
  lack of opportunities for
    Aboriginals, 217–18
  longevity of goalkeepers, 30
  outback development programs,
    125, 157, 159, 207
  pathway programs, 94
  proposed all-Aboriginal team to
    England (1886), 35–6
  racial divide, 6–7
  recommendations for
    Indigenous development, 234
  revival post-WWI, 8–9
  as stability and focus for young
    people, 214–16
  trends and training models,
    227–8
  urban connection and, 34
  as working-class migrant sport,
    7–8
soccer clinics, 206, 221
soccer clubs established by
  migrants, 42–4
Soccer in the Outback program, 189
Soccer International, 212
Soccer World, 34, 63–4
Socceroos *See also individual*
  *World Cup*s
  Cahill, 90, 137–47
  Dodd, 95–105
  Farina, 116–25
  Farina as coach, 84–5, 123–5,
    137–8
  first Aboriginal captain, 83
  'Golden Generation,' 123–4,
    130, 138, 143, 228
  Hiddink as coach, 87, 129, 130,
    139, 204

Warren, Johnny, 14, 41, 44, 66, 72, 73, 207
  on ASF's failure to embrace Perkins' vision, 68–9
  death, 69
  Sheilas, Wogs and Poofters (2002), 5, 43
Weekend Australian, 76, 91, 223
Wehrman, Kasey
  joins Norway clubs, 81–2
  player coach at Western Pride, 82
  Socceroos, 8–3, 125
Weifang Cup 2007, 150
Wellington Phoenix, 91, 104, 112, 160
West Wallsend 'Westy,' 15–16
Western Australia, 47–8
Western City Wanderers, 151
Western Melbourne, 169
Western Pride, 82
Western Suburbs Indigenous Gathering Place, 216
Western Sydney Wanderers, 92, 168
  W-League, 190, 193, 200
Westfield W-League, 190, 192, 197
Westfield W-League Grand Final, 193, 197
Weston Bears, 15, 16, 185
Weston Club, 30
Whitmore, Ken, 14, 133
Whyman, Jada, 200–1
Wilkshire, Luke, 231
Williams, David, 149
  accolades, 111
  European trials, 105–6
  joins European clubs, 106–8, 111–12
  joins Melbourne Heart, 111
  joins Socceroos, 105–12
  joins Sydney FC, 110–11
  joins North Queensland Fury, 108–10, 157
  joins Wellington Phoenix, 112
Williams, Harry, 3, 5, 154, 223, 225
  on acceptance by migrants, 74
  joins Canberra City, 78
  on development of Indigenous talent, 207–8, 209
  first international Aboriginal player, 75–6
  as Football NSW ambassador, 208
  joins Socceroos, 72–80
  Socceroos World Tours, 74–7
  St George Budapest, 16
  work in Aboriginal affairs, 78

Williams, Lydia, 174, 185, 191, 195–9, 203, 235
  awards/achievements, 196, 198
  USA National Women's Soccer League, 197
  Young Matildas captaincy, 196
Williams, Mark, 215
W-League, 1
  NSW, 190, 192, 193
  QLD, 197, 201, 202
  SA, 201
  VIC, 190, 194, 197, 200
  WA, 199
wogball, 6, 44
Wollongong Argus, 31
Wollongong Olympic Junior Soccer Club, 169
Wollongong Wolves Football Club, 94, 128, 231
Women's National Soccer League, 185, 188–9, 199
Women's Premier Soccer League, 190
women's soccer, 173–203 *See also* W-League
  Aboriginal involvement in, xiv, 173–5
  assistant coaches, 183, 199
  early, 173
Women's World Cup, 187, 193, 197
World Cup 1962, 21
World Cup 1970, 14–15, 133, 227
  squad, 74
World Cup 1974, 73, 76–7, 80, 173, 227–8
World Cup 1978, 77
World Cup 1986, 119
World Cup 1990, 121
World Cup 1995, 185
World Cup 1999, 186
World Cup 2002, 123, 128
World Cup 2006, 1, 79, 97, 123, 130, 139–41, 204
World Cup 2010, 1, 90, 108, 113, 141–2
  squad, 91, 121–2
World Cup 2014, 1, 142–4
World Cup 2018, 1, 146–7
  Australian bid for, 2, 79, 205
World Cup 2022, 2, 79, 205
world game, 6, 11
The World Game (SBS), 89, 127
World Stars team, 186
World War I, 33
World Youth Championships 1997, 80
World Youth Cup, 117, 118, 196

Wright, Lachlan, 223
Wyatt, Ken, 233
Wynnum Wolves, 165

Y
Young, Leonie, 175–6
Young, Neil, 163
Young Matildas, 191, 192, 196, 200, 202
Young Socceroos, 150, 169
Youth Olympics 2007, 150
Youth World Cup 2001, 188
Yow Yeh, Kevin, 175
Yow Yeh, Leonie *See* Young, Leonie

Z
Zelic, Ned, 87
Zhejiang Greentown, 145
Zullo, Michael, 113

Other really good football books
from Fair Play Publishing

Surfing for England
Our Lost Socceroos
by Jason Goldsmith

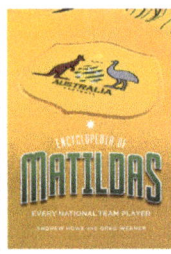

Encyclopedia of Matildas
by Andrew Howe
and Greg Werner

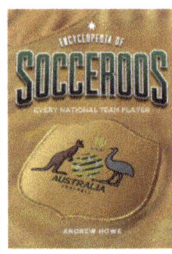

Encyclopedia of Socceroos
by Andrew Howe

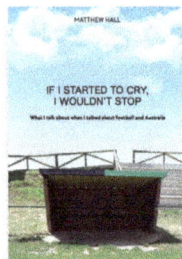

'If I Started to Cry,
I Wouldn't Stop'
by Matthew Hall

Playing for Australia
The First Socceroos,
Asia and the World Game
by Trevor Thompson

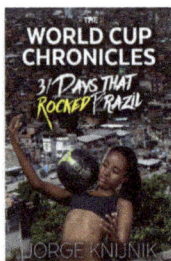

The World Cup Chronicles
31 Days that Rocked Brazil
by Jorge Knijnik

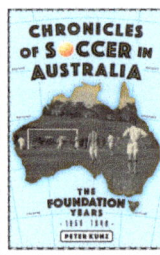

Chronicles of Soccer
in Australia - The
Foundation Years 1859 to
1949 by Peter Kunz

Support Your Local League,
A South-East Asian
Football Odyssey by
Antony Sutton

FAIRPLAY
PUBLISHING

www.fairplaypublishing.com.au

Whatever It Takes - The
Inside Story of the FIFA
Way by Bonita Mersiades
(Powderhouse Press)

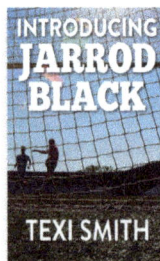

Introducing
Jarrod Black
(Popcorn Press)

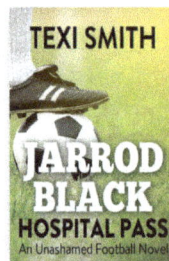

Jarrod Black
Hospital Pass
by Texi Smith
(Popcorn Press)

www.ingramcontent.com/pod-product-compliance
Lightning Source LLC
Chambersburg PA
CBHW051256020426
42333CB00026B/3233